# The Politics
# of AIDS
# in Africa

# CHALLENGE AND CHANGE IN AFRICAN POLITICS

# THE POLITICS

## OF AIDS

## IN AFRICA

AMY S. PATTERSON

LYNNE
RIENNER
PUBLISHERS

BOULDER
LONDON

Published in the United States of America in 2006 by
Lynne Rienner Publishers, Inc.
1800 30th Street, Boulder, Colorado 80301
www.rienner.com

and in the United Kingdom by
Lynne Rienner Publishers, Inc.
3 Henrietta Street, Covent Garden, London WC2E 8LU

**Library of Congress Cataloging-in-Publication Data**
Patterson, Amy S. (Amy Stephenson)
The politics of AIDS in Africa / Amy S. Patterson.
    (Challenge and change in African politics)
    Includes bibliographical references and index.
    ISBN-13: 978-1-58826-452-7 (hardcover: alk. paper)
    ISBN-10: 1-58826-452-1 (hardcover: alk. paper)
    ISBN-13: 978-1-58826-477-0 (pbk.: alk. paper)
    ISBN 10: 1-58826-477-7 (pbk.: alk. paper)
    1. AIDS (Disease)—Africa. 2. AIDS (Disease)—Social aspects—Africa.
3. AIDS (Disease)—Government policy—Africa. I. Title. II. Series.
    RA643.86.A35P378 2007 2006
    362.196'97920096—dc22

                                                          2006011923

**British Cataloguing in Publication Data**
A Cataloguing in Publication record for this book
is available from the British Library.


Printed and bound in the United States of America

        The paper used in this publication meets the requirements
  ∞     of the American National Standard for Permanence of
        Paper for Printed Library Materials Z39.48-1992.

        5   4   3   2   1

*To my children, Sophia Margaret and Isabel Rose,*

*. . . higher than the mountains,*

*. . . longer than the Great Wall*

# Contents

# Tables

# Acknowledgments

MY STUDENTS INSPIRE me. During January 2003, I taught a course on the politics of AIDS in Africa. I pieced together readings, films, and book chapters, hoping to provide students with a political slant on the pandemic. I wanted them to understand that health is not an issue divorced from questions of power, representation, and inequality. The students' comments and eagerness to learn encouraged me to write this book. But to be honest, their final projects made me, a professor with a reputation of being demanding and always having something to say, speechless, in awe at their imagination, desire to learn, and frankly, their hope for a continent facing the huge challenges AIDS brings. Many of those students went on to do research with me, enroll in my other classes, and/or travel with me to conferences and on off-campus learning experiences.

Specific students deserve mention: David Cieminis asked hard questions during a summer of research. As my assistant in 2003, Bernard Haven argued with me, cleverly found sources of information, and graciously shared his independent research on AIDS groups in Ghana. Since his graduation from Calvin, he has continued to keep me on my toes. In 2005, Catie Schierbeek tracked down data I needed in record speed and diligently proofread drafts. It was hard to keep up with her energy! All three never complained and all three made this project possible. Such students reaffirm my love for teaching.

Other individuals gave willingly of their time to read chapters, look over data, and provide kind words as I wrote and rewrote. Patrick Furlong, Simona Goi, Ben Haven, Roland Hoksbergen, Tracy Kuperus, Neil Patterson, and Corwin Smidt read chapters; Jim Penning and Corwin Smidt provided methodological assistance. The manuscript benefited greatly from the suggestions of two anonymous readers. Lynne Rienner and Lisa Tulchin enthusiastically supported this project from its inception. Joyce Steigenga cheerfully answered all my computer questions. Nana Poku and Robert Ostergard encouraged my initial research endeavors on AIDS in Africa and took a leap of faith with my previous edited volume. Calvin College provided summer stipends and research money through the Center for Social Research, the Calvin Research Fellowship, and the McGregor Fellowship program. More importantly, I could not ask for a more supportive environment in which to work than the Department of Political Science. The department has provided me the chance for family leave after the adoption of a daughter from China and the opportunity to spend a semester in Washington, DC.

Several individuals willingly discussed AIDS policies with me either in person or via phone: Adotei Akwei, Richard Cizik, Serge Duss, Paul Farmer, Alan Goodman, Tom Hart, Jodi Jacobson, Stephen Morrison, Jacqui Patterson, Anne Peterson, Josh Ruxin, Peter Salama, Anil Soni, and Bruce Wilkinson. Ann-Louise Colgan, Allen Hertzke, and Robert Groelsema provided helpful information for contacts in Washington, DC.

Finally, I am convinced that no one completes a project like this without some strong behind-the-scenes support. My parents provided hours of child care, many meals, and some help in home (re)construction projects. My husband, Neil, never complained, though I know, despite his passion for Africa, he eagerly awaited this project's end. My daughters, Isabel and Sophia, laughed, babbled, danced, sang, rhymed, painted, and gave me endless hugs. May all the world's parents know such joy! Thank you all.

# The Politics
## of AIDS
## in Africa

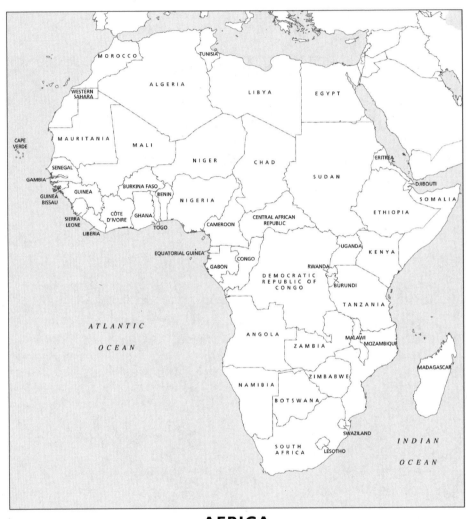

**AFRICA**

# 1

## Why Study the Politics of AIDS?

"MY PEOPLE ARE dying. They are dying before their time, leaving behind their children as orphans, and a nation in a continuous state of mourning," said King Mswati III of Swaziland as he began his speech to the 2001 United Nations General Assembly Special Session on HIV/AIDS. King Mswati's powerful words, and the tragedy of HIV/AIDS in his country, highlight three crucial themes about the politics of AIDS: the magnitude of the disease, the inequalities that surround the pandemic, and the role of formal and informal institutions in shaping AIDS policies.[1] These themes run throughout this book. Despite recent works on the effect of AIDS on state security or the political economy of the pandemic (Ostergard 2002; Price-Smith 2002; Poku and Whiteside 2004), AIDS has been viewed as "too private, too biological, too micro-level and sociological, too behavioral and too cultural to attract the attention of many political scientists in the West" (Boone and Batsell 2001). This book addresses this omission. It provides a systematic analysis of how four aspects of African politics—the state, democratic transitions, civil society, and donors—influence AIDS policymaking. In doing so, it argues that variation in state development, the unevenness of democracy, the tenuous power of civil society, and the uncertain outcomes of donor programs cause the AIDS fight to be insufficiently institutionalized into African politics.

"Institutionalizing" AIDS into Africa's political sphere means state, civil society, and bilateral and multilateral donor officials have a long-term interest and a political stake in the pandemic. In such a situation, political actors talk about the disease regularly, and they are held accountable for their efforts to address the epidemic. AIDS organizations in civil society have the resources, human capacity, and power to shape state AIDS programs. Politicians in Africa and the West devote funds to AIDS, and bureaucratic agencies in Africa and the West jockey for those resources. An institutionalized response means that the multiple actors involved in AIDS work—bilateral and multilateral donors, civil society groups, African state officials, people living with the disease—are partners in decisionmaking. And institutionalizing the AIDS fight is evident when bilateral and multilateral donors have a long-run interest in the disease, not a short-term humanitarian perspective that aims to quickly solve the AIDS emergency.

HIV/AIDS is a public policy problem. Yet, unlike Africa's problems of economic development or internal security, the pandemic has received sporadic attention from African political leaders and multilateral and bilateral donors. This fact reflects several aspects of the disease. HIV/AIDS is spread through intimate, personal behavior. It is closely linked to cultural issues such as women's status, the dominant role of African men in relationships, and the importance of motherhood (Walker et al. 2004; Hunter 2003). No politician wants to speak frankly about sex or challenge cultural patterns. The lag time between HIV infection and the development of AIDS, an average of eight years in Africa, also has made mobilizing interest in the disease more difficult. AIDS seems a distant threat in the face of the immediate concerns of hunger, poverty, and war.

When the first AIDS cases appeared in Africa in the mid-1980s, state reactions varied widely. The apartheid state assured white South Africans the disease was confined to "deviant homosexuals" or poor black migrants from neighboring countries. In an effort to blame outsiders, and in a move that provided false comfort to the population, between 1988 and 1992 the government repatriated about 13,000 Malawian miners, because roughly two hundred of them had tested positive for HIV in 1987 (Chirwa 1998). When the Kenyan press reported "Killer disease in Kenya," medical officers claimed four AIDS deaths were due to skin cancer, not AIDS (Fortin 1987). On the other hand, President Abdou Diouf of Senegal openly acknowledged AIDS in his country and began national AIDS prevention and control programs in 1987 (Green 2003a). President Yoweri Museveni of Uganda started public discussions about the disease in 1986. Not only has attention to AIDS been uneven between countries, it also has varied within countries over time. Thailand, heralded for bringing down HIV infections from 143,000 in 1991 to 20,000 in 2003, has cut its AIDS prevention budget by nearly two-thirds since 1997. In 2004, prevention services reached only 5 percent of teens and condom use among sexually active people was declining. Once a model for best practices for fighting the disease, Thailand may soon exemplify "how to lose the battle with AIDS" (*International Herald Tribune*, November 27, 2005; *New York Times*, July 9, 2004, p. A6).

International commitment to AIDS also has ebbed and flowed. In 1986, the World Health Organization (WHO), one of the United Nations (UN) agencies developed in 1948, formed the Global Program on AIDS (GPA). The GPA developed biomedical standards for diagnosing cases and established a global framework on HIV/AIDS. Funding for the GPA grew astronomically; bilateral donors, particularly the United States, provided over $160.5 million to the GPA in 1988. Yet by the early 1990s, bureaucratic infighting, a decline in American commitment, and the rise of global issues such as the fall of communism and environmental protection led to the decay of the program (Will 1991).

In 1996, renewed interest in AIDS facilitated the formation of the Joint United Nations Program on HIV/AIDS (UNAIDS). UNAIDS advocated greater coordination across UN agencies and between bilateral and multilateral donors. As a result of its efforts, in 2000 the UN Security Council debated AIDS, the first time a health issue was discussed as a security threat. The next year the United Nations held its first-ever special session on a health issue, the aforementioned UN General Assembly Special Session on HIV/AIDS. There, member states signed the Declaration of Commitment on HIV/AIDS, which outlined goals for reducing HIV infections and treating people living with HIV/AIDS (PLWHAs). A crucial aspect of the declaration was its emphasis on political commitment to fight the disease: "Leadership by Governments in combating HIV/AIDS is essential" (United Nations 2001, par. 37). Greater commitment is evident in the growth in spending on AIDS by bilateral and multilateral donors and by national governments to total roughly $6.1 billion in 2004, a twenty-fold increase since 1996 (United Nations 2005, 17). Another example of commitment is the formation of the Global Fund to Fight AIDS, Tuberculosis and Malaria (GFATM), and the fund's approval of over $4 billion in grants between 2002 and 2005 (GFATM 2006a).

Yet, other events counter these examples of commitment. A leadership summit at the 2004 International AIDS Conference in Bangkok was canceled because only one of the thirteen invited political officials accepted the invitation to attend. This low interest caused UNAIDS Director Peter Piot to comment that although political leadership in the fight against the pandemic has improved in recent years, it remains "too weak in many parts of the world" (*New York Times*, July 12, 2004). The

US Department of Health and Human Services cut the number of experts it sent to the 2004 conference to fifty, from the 236 who attended the 2002 conference in Barcelona (*Washington Post*, July 9, 2004). This uneven attention to the pandemic from political scientists, policymakers, and multilateral and bilateral donors necessitates a political analysis of AIDS decisionmaking. This book provides that analysis. I begin by highlighting the themes of magnitude, inequality, and institutions that shape AIDS policies in Africa.

## The Magnitude of the AIDS Pandemic

King Mswati's words, and his country's situation, frame the pandemic. People *are* dying, particularly in Swaziland. The United Nations (2005, 4) reported that HIV infections had risen in Swaziland from what was already the world's highest prevalence rate of 38.8 percent in 2003, to 42.6 percent in 2004. The king reacted: "We do not wish to be the highest country in the world when it comes to the issue of HIV infection" (*UN Integrated Regional Information Networks*, March 19, 2004). Swaziland is one of several southern African countries with HIV prevalence rates over 20 percent; Botswana (37%), Lesotho (28%), Namibia (21%), and South Africa (21%) are others. There are over twenty-five million people who are HIV positive in sub-Saharan Africa. Although the continent has just over 10 percent of the world's population, it has roughly two-thirds of all people living with HIV. In 2004, over three million Africans became infected with HIV, and 2.3 million died (UNAIDS 2004a, 78–79). Table 1.1 provides HIV prevalence rates from 2003 for most sub-Saharan African countries.

Because this book utilizes HIV data on prevalence extensively, it is important to explain more about this data. The prevalence rate is the percentage of the population with the HIV virus at a given time. Prevalence rates are usually given as a percentage of a particular population group: for example, sexually active fifteen to forty-nine-year olds, pregnant women attending antenatal clinics, or sex workers. We must rely on prevalence data instead of AIDS case data because in many African countries, medical personnel are not required to report AIDS cases and not all citizens use formal medical services. Also, medical personnel without training in HIV/AIDS may not recognize the disease as the cause of death. Because it is impossible to test an entire population for HIV, most prevalence data relies on samples of particular population subgroups, such as women attending antenatal clinics. These percentages are then extrapolated to the larger population. The method is not foolproof, because not all pregnant women attend clinics, survey

**Table 1.1    HIV Prevalence Rates in Sub-Saharan Africa, 2003**

| Country | Percentage of Adults, 15–49 Years Old |
| --- | --- |
| Angola | 3.9 |
| Benin | 1.9 |
| Botswana | 37.3 |
| Burkina Faso | 4.2 |
| Burundi | 6.0 |
| Cameroon | 6.9 |
| Central African Republic | 13.5 |
| Chad | 4.8 |
| Congo | 4.9 |
| Côte d'Ivoire | 7.0 |
| Democratic Republic of Congo | 4.2 |
| Djibouti | 2.9 |
| Eritrea | 2.7 |
| Ethiopia | 4.4 |
| Gabon | 8.1 |
| Gambia | 1.2 |
| Ghana | 3.1 |
| Guinea | 3.2 |
| Kenya | 6.7 |
| Lesotho | 28.9 |
| Liberia | 5.9 |
| Madagascar | 1.7 |
| Malawi | 14.2 |
| Mali | 1.9 |
| Mauritania | 0.6 |
| Mozambique | 12.2 |
| Namibia | 21.3 |
| Niger | 1.2 |
| Nigeria | 5.4 |
| Rwanda | 5.1 |
| Senegal | 0.8 |
| South Africa | 21.5 |
| Sudan | 2.3 |
| Swaziland | 38.8 |
| Tanzania | 8.8 |
| Togo | 4.1 |
| Uganda | 4.1 |
| Zambia | 16.5 |
| Zimbabwe | 24.6 |

*Source:* Compiled by author from UNAIDS (2004b).

*Note:* No data provided for prevalence rates for Cape Verde, Comoros, Equatorial Guinea, Guinea-Bissau, Mauritius, Sao Tome and Principe, Seychelles, Sierra Leone, and Somalia.

sites tend to be in urban not rural areas, and HIV decreases fertility so fewer HIV-positive women may become pregnant (Barnett and Whiteside 2002, 51–57). The problem of acquiring an accurate picture of the pandemic's magnitude is a recurring theme among policymakers,

AIDS researchers, and multilateral and bilateral donor officials. On June 20, 2004, the *Boston Globe* reported that HIV prevalence rates had been overestimated in several African countries, a fact with implications for national and international AIDS programs. In the same year, UNAIDS began providing a "plausibility range" for the best-case and worst-case scenario of HIV infection in a country. As more countries begin to complement antenatal data with household surveys, a clearer picture of the pandemic will emerge.

Data accuracy is important, but politics is rarely about hard and fast numbers. Politics is about perceptions. Numbers can shape perceptions, but they usually are not sufficient to place an issue on the policymaking agenda. If citizens, politicians, and international actors believe AIDS is a crucial problem for the continent, they are more likely to act on the problem, regardless of the numbers. The testimonies of individuals living with the disease, the impassioned pleas of AIDS activists, and the pictures of those affected by the disease are as crucial for shaping perceptions about AIDS as are marginal changes in prevalence rates. Chapters 3 and 5 highlight how the pandemic is perceived, both by Africans and citizens in industrialized countries.

The continent's experience with the disease is diverse. As Table 1.1 reveals, in six countries, HIV prevalence is below 2 percent, while in six others, it is over 20 percent. In many countries, HIV rates in urban areas are higher than in rural areas. Urban migration often drives people to communities where they lack social connections and face economic uncertainty; they may engage in sexual relations to stave off loneliness, or for women, out of a need to survive. Yet, there are exceptions to this pattern: rural and urban areas in Swaziland have similar HIV prevalence rates because migrants have carried the virus back to villages. HIV prevalence also is uneven across age cohorts. Because they are the most sexually active age group, people fifteen to twenty-four years old account for nearly half of all new infections worldwide (UNAIDS 2004b, 191–192).

The diversity within the pandemic does not decrease its impact on economics, politics, and society. A few statistics illustrate:

- The disease has already created an estimated twelve million orphans in sub-Saharan Africa. Because many families and communities cannot cope with the demands of caring for these children, a growing number of orphans now live without adult supervision. These children are less likely to attend school and more likely to engage in antisocial behavior such as crime and drug use (Hunter and Williamson 2000; Daly 2003; Guest 2001).[2]

- In Botswana, Central African Republic, Lesotho, Malawi, Mozambique, Swaziland, Malawi, Zambia, and Zimbabwe, life expectancy is now below forty years, because of AIDS (UNAIDS 2004a, 25).

- Swaziland will need to train 13,000 new teachers to replace those who die from AIDS between 2003 and 2011 (Whiteside 2005, 120).

- By 2020, at least 20 percent of agricultural workers in southern African will have died from AIDS (UNAIDS 2004b, 9).

- In 2004, 66 percent of African businesses reported that HIV/AIDS will "affect their bottom line" over the next five years (*Kaiser Daily HIV/AIDS Report*, June 4, 2004).

- By 2020, the labor force in some African countries could be 35 percent smaller because of workers lost to AIDS (Kaiser Family Foundation 2004a).

The large number of people with HIV/AIDS also will affect governance. The loss of civil servants, with their training, expertise, and networks of personal contacts, will hamper the state's ability to provide services, including AIDS prevention and treatment programs (de Waal 2003b). One-fourth of health care workers in Malawi will die of AIDS by 2009, a fact that will make caring for others with HIV/AIDS more difficult (*New York Times*, July 12, 2004, p. A1). The inability of governments to respond to societal problems has the potential to increase citizen discontent and divisions within government. On a continent where many countries have underdeveloped state institutions and experiences with authoritarianism, these demands may contribute to political instability (International Crisis Group 2001). Although the impact of AIDS on politics has yet to be empirically verified, Alex de Waal (2003b, 12) writes, "It is possible that the Weberian model of modernity, progressing from traditional or charismatic authority to rational bureaucratic power, may be halted or reversed." That is, as AIDS decreases state capacity to provide health care, education, security, and basic services, high levels of corruption and repression by state officials may become essential for political survival.

It is important to acknowledge that while the size of the pandemic and its potential effect on Africa make AIDS a monumental issue, political leaders do not always respond to large problems. Issues must get on the policymaking agenda, a process that depends partly on political events (Kingdon 1984, 19). In the United States, the pandemic became a concern of top policymakers after September 11, 2001, although the US government had been aware of the potentially destabilizing effect of AIDS since 1987 (CIA 1987). In the post–September 11 world, leaders of industrial nations have linked disease, poverty, and destitution to terrorism and political instability (*New York Times*, July 7, 2003). UNAIDS Director Peter Piot (2001) said, "The global AIDS epidemic is one of the central security issues of the twenty-first century." As AIDS threatens Africa's gains in socioeconomic development, conquering the disease is crucial for aid organizations that must justify budgets to private donors, taxpayers, and legislators. Some African states have responded to the disease's magnitude. Yet, as the chapters point out, while magnitude is important, it is unclear that it has led to institutionalized efforts against AIDS. Some African states still lack comprehensive AIDS strategies; others have insufficient resources for the pandemic. It was only in the last few years that AIDS became a campaign issue in some of Africa's democracies. And the world's major multilateral AIDS effort, the GFATM, periodically lacks funds to support AIDS projects.

## Inequality and the AIDS Pandemic

A slight clarification of King Mswati's statement illustrates a second theme about the politics of AIDS. It is true that the king's people are dying. But they aren't all dying, and they aren't all dying at the same rate. The impact of AIDS on African individuals "depends on who the individuals are, their place in society and the resources they, their households, communities and societies have available" (Barnett and Whiteside 2002, 182). Globally, AIDS increasingly affects those without economic resources and political power. For example, 50 percent of new HIV infections in the United States are among African Americans, who make up only 12 percent of the US population and who are more likely to be politically and economically disenfranchised than white Americans (UNAIDS 2004b, 7). In Africa, women, children, migrants, and the poor are more likely to be victims of the disease. While AIDS has killed African political leaders, economic elites, and cultural idols,[3] the disease reflects inequality on a continent where the richest 20 percent of the population holds over 50 percent of the wealth and the poorest 20 percent has only 5 percent (World Bank 2002).

In Africa, women bear the burden of HIV/AIDS, both in terms of infection and labor required to care for the sick; 57 percent of those who are HIV positive in Africa are women (UNAIDS 2004b, 3). The numbers have caused UN Envoy on AIDS to Africa Stephen Lewis to remark that in Africa twenty years from now, "you are going to sense and see the loss of women. There will be portions of Africa that will be depopulated of women" (*New York Times*, July 20, 2004, p. A1). HIV-negative women and girls are expected to care for the ill, do additional farm labor, and work more to pay for food, housing, and school fees (Nnoko et al. 2000). Maternal grandmothers usually care for children whose parents die of the disease, even though they often lack economic resources and may be in poor health themselves.

Biology contributes to the gender discrepancy in HIV infection, since the virus easily passes through vaginal membranes, especially the immature membranes of young women. Women are seven times more likely to become infected during sexual intercourse with an infected partner than men (Karim 2004). Yet women's vulnerability to HIV, and the disproportionate impact of the pandemic on women, is also rooted in women's lack of economic power. On average, women in sub-Saharan Africa work longer hours and for lower pay than men. In Uganda, for example, women account for 80 percent of the agricultural labor and 90 percent of the food production; much of this labor is unpaid (Wanyeki 2003, 19). Many women lack the economic opportunities that men have. Female literacy lags behind male literacy, with an estimated 60 percent of African women literate compared to almost 80 percent of African men (CIA 2004). Women's limited economic power shapes the life choices they make—marriage, formal or informal employment, commercial sex work, or relationships with male sponsors. A woman's economic dependence on her husband or boyfriend often makes it impossible to refuse sex or negotiate for condom use even if she knows her partner has had other sexual relationships (Siplon 2005, 24; Irwin et al. 2003, 32). Sexual violence exacerbates these problems because it increases the risk of HIV passing through torn cervical membranes. In South Africa, gang rape and coercion often accompany a woman's first sexual experience, and an estimated one in six women is in an abusive relationship (Walker et al. 2004, 17, 28–30). Because motherhood is crucial to a woman's identity, she may be less likely to request her husband use condoms, since this protection prevents pregnancy. For these reasons, marriage has become a risk factor for contracting HIV in countries with high HIV prevalence levels (Baylies 2002).

Popular portrayals of AIDS in Africa often directly or indirectly blame female prostitutes for the pandemic. This picture, though, ignores the complex reasons women engage in sexual activities (Booth 2004,

49). Women may use transactional sex to pave the way for economic survival: customs agents may require sex from traders; bosses may insist on sexual favors in return for a job. A study of eighteen HIV-positive housemaids in Kenya revealed that most of their employers had sexually abused them (Siplon 2005, 24–25). Young women may find "sugar daddies" to pay for consumption goods or education costs. These older men have more sexual experiences and are more likely to have been exposed to HIV. A study of female university students in Nigeria found that many feel pressure to have sex with both their professors, who will assign passing grades, and a sugar daddy, who will pay education costs (Edet 1997). Sexual relationships between younger women and older men, as well as young women's greater biological vulnerability to HIV, have led to more HIV-positive young women in Africa than HIV-positive young men. Among fifteen to twenty-four-year olds in South Africa, there are twenty women living with HIV for every ten men with HIV; in Kenya these numbers are forty-five women to ten men (UNAIDS 2004b, 3–6; Karim 2004).

Women's lack of political power exacerbates their vulnerability to HIV and the negative impact the pandemic has on them. Women are underrepresented in African governments, making up 15 percent of national legislatures. They hold few positions in powerful ministries, and they have limited political resources at their disposal (Beck 2003, 164). While female officials do not always represent the interests of women, they are more likely than their male counterparts to be concerned with issues related to women and children's well-being (Patterson 2002). Low political representation also means governments are less likely to pass and implement laws to improve the environments that make women vulnerable to HIV. As of 2004, only South Africa, Senegal, and Zimbabwe had laws against domestic violence (Human Rights Watch 2003b, 80). In Lesotho, customary law treats married women as minors who cannot open a bank account or own property (*New York Times*, July 20, 2004, p. A1). While Senegal passed progressive legislation on polygamy in 1972, the country has not done much to enforce it. While the law requires that a couple agree whether the marriage will be monogamous or polygamous when they register the marriage with civil authorities, rural marriages are rarely registered and local officials do not want to enforce the law (Creevey 1991).

King Mswati's country provides an extreme example of how weak political institutions and patriarchal attitudes affect women's vulnerability to HIV/AIDS. Women hold few political positions and, until 2006, were considered to be legal minors. Boys are pressured to have sexual intercourse at an early age to prove their masculinity, while girls are expected to be compliant (Whiteside 2005, 109). The UN Development Program (2002, 1) explains: "The Swazi society expects women to be subordinate and submissive; allows men to have multiple sexual partners; and polygamy, which exposes women to HIV infection, is legal in the country." The result is that approximately 53 percent of people living with HIV/AIDS in Swaziland are women (UNAIDS 2004b, 191). Women's situation reflects the low institutionalization of the AIDS fight into African politics. As Chapter 2 shows, while the centralized, neopatrimonial state in Swaziland has developed an AIDS policymaking structure, it has been unwilling to deal with the gender inequalities that contribute to the spread of HIV. Swazi leaders' narrow view of AIDS as an apolitical issue was apparent when lawmakers advocated a return to male circumcision to limit the spread of AIDS after a South African study found that circumcised men were less likely than uncircumcised men to be HIV positive (*Washington Post*, December 26, 2005, p. A26). Instead of addressing the political and economic structures that contribute to HIV vulnerability—something that would require injecting the AIDS issue into discussions of culture, society, and politics—the lawmakers focused on a technical solution.

Women are not the only ones with heightened vulnerability to HIV infection; an estimated two million children in sub-Saharan Africa were HIV positive in 2003. The primary means of infection is through mother-to-child transmission: the virus passes to the child during pregnancy or delivery, or postnatally through breastfeeding. The probability of a child being infected from an HIV-positive mother ranges from 130 to 480 infections per 1,000 exposures, depending on the mother's viral load. (The risk of transmission increases with higher viral loads.) Transmission through sexual abuse and contaminated needles is less common (Barnett and Whiteside 2002, 38–39; *BBC News*, May 6, 2003). Like women, African children lack political and economic power. Poverty among Africa's children is prevalent, a factor that causes sub-Saharan Africa to have the highest proportion of children working in the world. The more impoverished a country and the larger its rural population, the higher its percentage of children who work. Children also have been caught up in Africa's conflicts, with 40 percent of the world's child soldiers fighting in African wars. Young people in the Democratic Republic of Congo, Rwanda, Uganda, Liberia, and Sierra Leone have been abducted, manipulated, and forced to fight, particularly if families have been separated (Bass 2004, 44–46, 163–165). And children are increasingly exposed to sex at a younger age. In 1995, 30 percent of

South African girls reported they dropped out of school because of an unplanned pregnancy (Walker et al. 2004, 53).

Because AIDS contributes to household poverty and social dislocation, the pandemic directly shapes children's well-being. AIDS-affected households often remove children, particularly girls, from school to save education costs and to provide needed household labor. AIDS has helped push a large percentage of Kenya's estimated 3.5 million working children into the labor market (Human Rights Watch 2001, 14). All African countries except Somalia have signed and ratified the Convention on the Rights of the Child, an action which commits national governments to ensuring children's rights to education, security, and survival (UNICEF 2004). However, most African countries cannot enforce these rights because of underdeveloped judiciaries, children's lack of legal standing, few lawyers willing to represent children, and societal misperceptions about children's rights. For example, AIDS-affected children in Kenya cannot easily protect their inheritance. One child's guardian said: "I asked the local authorities to let the children inherit the land . . . but they just told me, 'Take the children and let us deal with the land'" (Human Rights Watch 2001, 18). Even Africa's democratic states tend to have weak judiciaries, a fact that makes institutionalizing the AIDS fight through legal precedents more difficult. Bilateral and multilateral donors also may discount children's rights, excluding their participation in project design or evaluation (Patterson 2003a; Lentfer 2002; *Toronto Star*, December 14, 2005). Because children are relatively invisible in the policy process, national and global institutions are not forced to garner the political will to address children's problems.

Women and children are not the only groups in Africa with heightened vulnerability to HIV/AIDS. Several studies detail the high levels of HIV prevalence among migrants (Hunter 2003, 26; Walker et al. 2004, 62–66; Barnett and Whiteside 2002, 151). Before the appearance of HIV/AIDS, migrant miners in southern Africa experienced health problems such as tuberculosis and pneumonia. Anxiety about money and long periods away from rural family members made migrants more likely to engage in sex with local sex workers; women in need of money migrated to camps to meet this demand. The lack of social cohesion in migrant communities may also make migrants more likely to engage in risky sexual behavior (Campbell 2003, 34).[4] The fluid nature of migrant communities can shape the political power migrants wield. Transient citizens are less likely to participate in politics, either through grassroots involvement or voting. In such a community, it is more difficult to build social capital, or the networks of trust among people who cooperate to achieve a common goal. With low levels of social capital, it may be more difficult for migrants—people with relatively high vulnerability to HIV—to shape or implement policies to fight the disease. This is not to say that local HIV/AIDS awareness, support, care, and treatment programs cannot and do not exist in migrant communities. They can and do.[5] But, as Chapter 4 asserts, the difficulty of mobilizing AIDS-affected populations can contribute to weak civil society organizations, whose long-term activities in the AIDS fight can be tenuous.

Inequality also shapes the global experience with AIDS. It is telling that an African leader spoke to the United Nations about his people dying, not an official from an industrialized country. Ninety-six percent of people with HIV/AIDS live in what the World Bank terms low- and middle-income countries. One way that inequality between wealthy and poor countries manifests itself is in differences in access to antiretroviral (ARV) drugs for treating PLWHAs and preventing mother-to-child transmission. For many HIV-positive citizens in the West, ARVs have made AIDS a manageable condition. Private health insurance and government programs pay for these drugs. Yet, UNAIDS estimated that by mid-2004 only 12 percent of the people needing ARVs in low- and middle-income countries had access to them (United Nations 2005, 5). Because of well-developed health care systems, widespread use of prenatal health care and HIV testing, and the use of ARVs during pregnancy and labor, roughly 300 HIV-positive babies are born annually in the United States. In contrast, approximately 700,000 babies are born with HIV in the developing world (*Grand Rapids Press*, July 14, 2002, p. A4).

Global inequalities mean African states have to rely on bilateral and multilateral donors for resources to fight AIDS. Chapter 5 analyzes two donor programs: the GFATM and the US President's Emergency Plan for AIDS Relief (PEPFAR). It compares the potential of each to foster political commitment among both donors and African political leaders. The chapter defines political commitment as funding for AIDS and accountability to those individuals the disease affects. It argues that while both PEPFAR and the GFATM have made important contributions, each faces limitations in building the long-term commitment needed to institutionalize the AIDS fight. PEPFAR may get US government agencies and nongovernmental organizations (NGOs) entrenched in AIDS efforts, but its short-term emergency focus makes addressing AIDS as a long-term problem complicated. On the other hand, while the GFATM may build accountability among African state leaders to those

AIDS affects, its tenuous financial situation presents other challenges for institutionalizing the AIDS fight. As the conclusion asserts, neither program forces the world's citizens who are not directly affected by AIDS to develop a long-term interest in the pandemic.

The continent's response to AIDS is also shaped by its relative weakness in global negotiations over debt and trade. By the early 1980s, most African states had borrowed heavily from the International Monetary Fund (IMF) and the World Bank; these levels of debt were unsustainable, particularly as African states faced declining demands for export commodities. As part of renegotiating loans, international financial institutions required that African states implement structural adjustment programs (SAPs), including privatization, trade liberalization, reductions in government spending, and currency devaluation. Although scholars have debated the impact of these reforms on economic development (e.g., Lurie et al. 2004; van de Walle 2001; Boafo-Arthur 1999), it is clear that SAPs have shaped the continent's ability to fight AIDS, particularly through their effect on health care budgets. Between 1980 and 1985, spending on health, education, and welfare in sub-Saharan Africa declined 26 percent (UNDP 1990). State cutbacks have negatively affected public health infrastructure. The *New York Times* (July 12, 2004, p. A1) reported that over 60 percent of all nursing positions at public hospitals in Malawi are vacant; the low salaries, long hours, and terrible working conditions have caused hundreds of nurses to emigrate. The lack of state capacity means Africa must rely more on donors for AIDS resources, further exacerbating global inequalities. Moreover, because of dependence on donors, African states may have less incentive to entrench AIDS into all government sectors, election campaigns, and bureaucratic budgets.

Africa's relative weakness on the global stage is also evident in global trade negotiations that determine the price of ARVs. In 2000, the cost of a combination ARV regimen for one patient was between $10,000 and $12,000 annually, a prohibitive amount for most people in poor countries. Because producers hold the patent for these drugs, they can set prices; they argue that high ARV prices are necessary to recoup their investments in research for drug development.[6] At the 1995 negotiations to establish the World Trade Organization (WTO), the United States and the European Union demanded protection for the intellectual property rights of drug producers. This negotiating position reflects Western countries' comparative advantage in high-technology goods such as pharmaceuticals and computer software. Their success in the WTO negotiations resulted partially from the large size of their trade negotiating teams and the relative disorganization of developing countries (Halbert and May 2005, 198).

The outcome was the Trade-Related Aspects of Intellectual Property Rights (TRIPS) Agreement, which limits compulsory licensing and parallel importing. Compulsory licensing allows a country to require a patent owner to provide a license to manufacture a product at a negotiated price; parallel importing allows a country to import from the producer with the lowest price. Since the 2001 Doha Declaration on TRIPS and Public Health, which asserted the right of poor countries to use these two practices in health emergencies, prices for ARVs have dropped to roughly $300 per person per year for some generic combinations. These price declines reflect activist pressure on pharmaceutical companies, particularly in South Africa; negotiated price reductions between African states and drug companies; and the belief among donors, politicians, and the public that treatment and prevention efforts must go together (Patterson and Cieminis 2005, 173). However, while supporting multilateral drug price negotiations or drug giveaway programs, several industrialized countries continue to use bilateral trade agreements to pressure developing countries not to import or produce generics (*Wall Street Journal*, July 6, 2004). In a written statement to the 2004 International AIDS conference that evoked strong US reaction, French President Jacques Chirac said this tactic was "tantamount to blackmail" (*Agence France Presse*, July 14, 2004). More broadly, the lack of a systematic approach to ARVs among donors hampers institutionalizing widespread treatment programs in Africa.

To be clear, African states are not powerless. Nicolas van de Walle (2001) illustrates that most African states have only partially implemented SAPs and they have been able to portray the World Bank and IMF as callous institutions in order to move global public opinion against loan conditions. Debora Halbert and Christopher May (2005) demonstrate how African states have begun to resist international trade agreements by importing more generic drugs. Despite these examples, resource differences and inequalities in policymaking continue to shape the politics of AIDS, both within African countries and between wealthy and poor countries. The pandemic does not affect all people equally. Not all people are dying.

## Political Institutions and the AIDS Pandemic

An analysis of the politics of AIDS in Africa cannot be divorced from an examination of the institutions in which policy decisions are made.

Institutions provide formal and informal norms, patterns, conventions, and procedures that shape economic, political, and social life (March and Olsen 1989, 1; North 1990, 3). I focus on what I term political institutions, or the rules, processes, and structures that shape decisions about resource allocation, leadership positions, and policy implementation. Both formal and informal political institutions shape AIDS policy outcomes. Formal institutions include elections, legislatures, constitutions, or bilateral and multilateral donors' rules for allocating AIDS resources. The patron-client networks apparent in neopatrimonial rule or the unwritten powers of traditional leaders exemplify informal political institutions. While not codified, these informal structures affect policy outcomes (Berry 1993; Patterson 2003b). Institutions also exist in civil society organizations and they can influence the participation and legitimacy of such groups.

Institutions result from formal or informal bargaining among goal-oriented actors who need to meet common objectives. Institutional negotiations imply a process of give and take, although all actors usually do not have the same power advantages or similar interests in the bargaining process. Individuals who participate in and adhere to institutions do so because they believe themselves to be better off with them than without them (Hechter 1987, 41; Ostrom 1990, 29–57). Institutions that emerge from unequal bargaining may lead to inequalities in policy outcomes (Knight 1992, 19–21; Moe 1990).

The Swazi king illustrates the role of political institutions in the AIDS fight. The king's authority and legitimacy derive not from constitutional powers and popular election, but from family lineage and traditional rule. The weakness of Swaziland's formal political institutions such as the legislature and judiciary heightens the importance of the informal institution of the monarch for the AIDS fight. Yet, as Alan Whiteside (2005, 120) argues, the king's record on HIV/AIDS is mixed. While Swaziland has formal AIDS institutions, centralization of decisionmaking power within the monarchy hampers government efforts to fight AIDS. AIDS organizations in the country also tend to be weak, lacking internal resources and legitimate structures. Moreover, women's lack of legal equality until 2006 and the informal institution of patriarchy harm state AIDS endeavors.

This book demonstrates that formal and informal institutions in Africa matter for the AIDS fight, but that they have mixed effects on AIDS efforts. Chapter 2 asserts that four patterns within African state institutions—centralization of power, neopatrimonial networks that promote patronage and corruption, low state capacity, and state instability—

lead to different AIDS policy outcomes depending on the country. Institutions that centralize decisionmaking and resource allocation in the executive have harmed AIDS efforts in Zimbabwe, but not in Uganda. Democratic institutions such as elections and legislatures have no clear positive impact on state efforts to address the disease. While Africa's democracies tend to spend more money on public health than non-democracies, this pattern is not well established. Because institutions may foster unequal outcomes in representation, parliaments, elections, judiciaries, and AIDS decisionmaking bodies may underrepresent society's least powerful, but most HIV-vulnerable, members such as children and women. Structures and processes also may influence the strength of civil society organizations: associations with internal rules to promote communication and participation may be more likely to mobilize for AIDS advocacy than organizations without such structures. Bilateral and multilateral donors also have rules that shape their AIDS programs. Donor procedures determine who gets funds and to whom those funding recipients are accountable. These structures influence how such donor programs can respond to the AIDS crisis. In the following chapters, I am less concerned about the type of institution (e.g., democratic legislature, traditional ruler, national AIDS commission, multilateral donor, civil society organization) than the ways the rules and procedures of these institutions influence AIDS efforts.

## The Argument

The themes of magnitude, inequality, and institutions are woven through the analysis in the chapters to follow to support my argument that AIDS has not been fully entrenched in African politics. Four distinct elements of the African state—centralization, neopatrimonialism, capacity, and stability—are examined in South Africa, Swaziland, Uganda, and Zimbabwe, revealing that these aspects have inconsistent effects on state commitment to the AIDS fight. The case studies examine some of the reasons why state centralization in Swaziland, for example, has been so detrimental to AIDS efforts, while it has not had the same impact in Uganda. Chapters 3 and 4 focus on the relationship between the democratic transitions that some African states have experienced and AIDS policies. Chapter 3 argues that the development of multiparty elections, legislatures, judiciaries, and subnational governments has had an uneven impact on state actions on AIDS. The underdevelopment of these institutions has facilitated inconsistent representation and accountability in AIDS policymaking in Africa's new democracies. And while there is a pattern that African democracies are more likely than nondemocracies to devote resources to health, the pattern is tenuous and suggests that the AIDS fight has not been fully institutionalized into budgetary decisions.

Chapter 4 specifically highlights the role of civil society in decisionmaking on AIDS. Five associations are used to examine two interrelated questions: (1) What makes a strong AIDS organization? (2) What makes an effective AIDS organization? To answer the first question, I focus on resources, human capacity, and internal structures. To answer the second, I examine democracy, political culture, coalitions, and state-civil society relations. Civil society organizations differ in their ability to advocate for AIDS policies, a fact that may lead to haphazard AIDS efforts across the continent.

Chapter 5 investigates the role of bilateral and multilateral donors in shaping Africa's AIDS efforts through a comparison of PEPFAR and the GFATM. Donors play a crucial role in the development of AIDS policies, but these donor programs may not always promote representation, accountability, or political commitment to the disease among African political leaders or the donors themselves. The conclusion argues that more must be done to institutionalize the AIDS fight into politics, by addressing questions of unequal power and representation in AIDS decisionmaking, by empowering civil society associations, by giving all global citizens a stake in the pandemic, and by fighting the disease itself.

## Notes

1. I use both *pandemic* and *epidemic*. An epidemic is when the incidence of a disease exceeds the expected rate in a particular area. A pandemic is an epidemic affecting multiple countries. I use the word pandemic when discussing AIDS across the continent, but epidemic when describing the disease in a particular country.

2. However, a 2004 monograph questioned the assumptions scholars make about orphan vulnerability. It challenged scholars to see the diversity of experiences and family support systems that orphans have and it asserted that the negative experiences of some orphans do not necessarily result in negative psychosocial outcomes (Pharoah 2004, xii-xiii).

3. For example, the son of Chief Mangosuthu Buthelezi, leader of South Africa's Inkatha Freedom Party, died in 2004 of AIDS. Congolese musician Luambo Makiadi and novelist Sony Labou Tansi died of the disease, as did family members of the late Mobutu Sese Seko and former Zambian president Kenneth Kaunda (Eaton 2004; TAC 2004c).

4. In support of theories linking social cohesion and HIV vulnerability, Kristin Velyvis (2002) finds that young female migrants to Dakar from southern Senegal are less likely to engage in sex because of high social cohesion. They

live with women from their villages whom they know and trust and they are afraid that any sexual indiscretions will be reported back to their families.

5. The AIDS education programs found in Summertown, South Africa, a gold mining town of 170,000 residents, of whom 70,000 are migrant miners, illustrate that migrant communities can support AIDS projects (Campbell 2003, 12).

6. For example, in May 2004, Abbott Laboratories announced it would increase the price of Norvir (generic name ritonavir) by 400 percent, from $54 per month to $265 per month for the per-patient wholesale price. The company said it had spent more than $300 million on clinical trials and other expenses to bring the drug to the market (*Wall Street Journal*, May 24, 2004).

# 2

## The African State
## and the AIDS Pandemic

"HIV/AIDS is promoted by an individual in the manner he or she goes about with his or her life. Otherwise, polygamy is not a factor."
—King Mswati III of Swaziland, Swazi television interview
cited by United Press International, April 2, 2003

"Whether I would take an HIV test or not, I think is irrelevant to the matter."
—South African President Thabo Mbeki,
interview cited in *Prospect,* February 21, 2002

"Here in Uganda . . . we gave HIV/AIDS a face because a faceless enemy is a very dangerous enemy. Denial and concealment, we realized, would not get rid of the disease, but only make it worse."
—Ugandan President Yoweri Museveni,
national speech on World AIDS Day, December 1, 2003

THESE QUOTES HIGHLIGHT different approaches to AIDS among African leaders, from Mswati's defense of tradition in the face of AIDS, to Mbeki's distancing himself from HIV, to Museveni's desire to tackle the AIDS stigma. But the quotes also point to one of the most touched-on topics in the AIDS fight: the role of African state leaders (United Nations 2001). This chapter places this leadership in the larger context of the African state. Although there are numerous aspects of the African state, I limit my analysis to how four elements—centralization of power, neopatrimonialism, state capacity, and security concerns—affect state efforts to fight AIDS. By using the case studies of Zimbabwe, Uganda, Swaziland, and South Africa, I argue there is no clear pattern of state institutions that leads to AIDS policies. Further, it is unlikely that one state characteristic provides full explanation for a country's AIDS efforts, since many of these state aspects are interrelated in their effect on AIDS policies and because civil society and donors affect AIDS policies too. While the case studies provide some reference to civil society and donors, Chapters 4 and 5 concentrate on their role in AIDS policymaking.

A state is the set of continuous administrative, legal, bureaucratic, and coercive systems that structure relationships between civil society and the public authority. According to the realist theory of international relations, states emerge in order to protect territory from other states or to promote internal security (Ostergard and Barcelo 2005). The Weberian model of statehood assumes legal-rational norms that guide state behavior and state institutions that are autonomous from societal pressures (Englebert 2002, 4; Skocpol 1985, 9). In the Weberian state, officials advance through meritocracy; the public and private realms are functionally distinct; there are institutionalized means for gaining and allocating resources; and citizens relate to the state through the ideal of citizenship, not ethnic, regional, or religious ties (Chabal and Daloz 1999, 6–7). To ensure transparency and to check the power of authorities, power is often diffused among various state institutions and shared with nonstate actors. In reality, few African states exhibit all these qualities.

First, although it is simplistic to assert that Africa's "big men" shape all political outcomes (Bauer and Taylor 2005, 10), the African state tends to centralize power in the executive, with the president using the bureaucracy and party apparatus to extend power and control over society. In such systems, the actions and rhetoric of individual leaders have heightened importance in policymaking, and formal political processes may have limited power to check these leaders' actions (Rosberg and Jackson 1982a). State centralization varies across the continent. Further, because the state is a combination of formal and informal institutions, both traditional rulers and elected officials play a role in many African states.

Table 2.1 provides the measures for the four state characteristics—centralization, neopatrimonialism, capacity, and security. To assess state centralization, I use two scores from the World Bank (2005b) governance indicators: "rule of law" and "voice and accountability." The World Bank gives a percentile rank from one to one hundred. The rank indicates the percentage of countries worldwide that rate above and below the country listed. For example, 9.2 percent of the world's countries rank below Zimbabwe in voice and accountability, and a little over 90 percent rank above it. The voice-and-accountability indicator com-

**Table 2.1    State Centralization, Neopatrimonialism, Capacity, Security, and AIDS Program Effort Index (API) Scores**

| Country | Centralization | | Neo-patrimonialism | Capacity | Security | API Score |
|---|---|---|---|---|---|---|
| | Rule of Law[a] (Percentile) (2004) | Voice & Accountability[a] (Percentile) (2004) | Corruption[a] (Percentile) (2004) | GNI/ Capita ($US) (2004) | Political[a] Stability (Percentile) (2004) | (2003) |
| South Africa | 60.9 | 72.3 | 70.9 | $3,630 | 38.3 | 75 |
| Swaziland | 19.3 | 10.2 | 13.8 | $1,660 | 53.9 | 60 |
| Uganda | 25.6 | 30.6 | 30 | $270 | 10.7 | 76 |
| Zimbabwe | 3.9 | 9.2 | 11.8 | $440[b] | 4.4 | 61 |

*Source:* Compiled by author from World Bank (2005b, 2005c) and USAID et al. (2003, 21).

a. The numbers given are a percentile rank from 1–100. The number indicates the percentage of countries worldwide that are above or below the country listed. For example, 3.9 percent of the world's countries rank below Zimbabwe in rule of law, and 95.6 percent rank above it in political stability.

b. Data from 2000.

bines various measures that examine civil liberties, political and human rights, and opportunities for citizen participation in government. It highlights the ability of citizens, the press, and civil society to constrain the actions of an arbitrary executive. The rule-of-law indicator tells how accountable a leader is to other institutions and the country's constitution; it also elucidates how willing leaders are to transparently follow constitutional processes and rules limiting their power, instead of acting capriciously. I classify a state as highly centralized if it has a ranking below fifty for each measure. I realize that there is great variation between countries within the fifty-point span. However, because my goal is not to compare countries in terms of centralization, but to discern patterns between state structures and AIDS efforts, this simple classification will suffice.

Second, African states have been described as neopatrimonial, because state elites use state resources to build alliances, control civil society organizations, and buy off potential challengers (van de Walle 2001, 118–128). Patron-client relations between the state and societal supporters mean that the state is not autonomous from societal pressures; state elites must respond to the demands of ethnic, regional, religious, and/or political factions (Migdal 1988, 210; Chabal and Daloz 1999, 4–5). Because public resources are used for the private advancement of state elites and their allies, resources are distributed unequally, often excluding those citizens who most need them (Fatton 1988). State control over resources hinders transparency and accountability, with the outcome often being corruption. In Table 2.1 I use the World Bank (2005b) "corruption" score as a proxy for neopatrimonialism. This measure is imperfect, since it does not take into account the nature of patron-client networks, but it is hard to envision any indicator that could operationalize such fluid ties well. As I did with the centralization measures, I use fifty as a dividing line for classifying states: those with a ranking below fifty have high neopatrimonialism, while those above fifty have low neopatrimonialism.

A third general element of African states is their lack of capacity. I define capacity as the ability of a state to design policies to promote economic growth and/or social development. There are many ways to operationalize capacity, from level of infrastructure development, to available economic resources, to spending on health and education (see Engelbert 2002, 27–37; Bratton 2005; Price-Smith et al. 2004). My aim is not to outline an exhaustive measure of state capacity, but to provide an indicator with which to classify the country case studies. Because resources are essential for social and economic development, I utilize gross national income (GNI) per capita, as indicated in Table 2.1. To classify cases as high or low capacity, I label countries with a GNI per capita of above $826 as high capacity. The World Bank (2005c) considers countries below this level to be low income. Since only one-fourth of sub-Saharan African states have a GNI per capita above $826, my classification provides a contextually appropriate distinction.[1]

Fourth, as territorial entities with internationally recognized sovereignty, African states are the creation of colonialism, not the reflection of societal demands for nationhood. African states are unlike European states that emerged to provide security for a nation and a territory (Rosberg and Jackson 1982b). In many African countries, societal divisions have contributed to social conflict, civil war, and in extreme cases, ethnic genocide. Mere survival remains a concern for many state leaders, who fear future internal rebellions. The concern for survival may cause state leaders to adopt particular policies, from spending more on the military to providing more state resources to potential challengers. In order to assess a state's security concerns and stability, in Table 2.1 I use the World Bank (2005b) "political stability" indicator. Countries with scores above fifty are considered to have high stability.

I examine how these four state characteristics shape state efforts to fight AIDS. To operationalize state AIDS efforts, I use the AIDS program effort index (API) score. Compiled by USAID, UNAIDS, WHO, and the POLICY Project (2003), the API score measures state effort in ten different areas related to AIDS. Table 2.2, which includes the four case studies plus Botswana and Rwanda, shows each country's overall API score, computed from scores in ten categories, and its scores in five of the ten categories that relate to politics. The rankings are based on surveys (combining quantitative and qualitative elements) with officials from NGOs, government, civil society, donors, and the private sector in fifty-four countries worldwide. While the scores do not provide a precise measure to compare state effort (respondents can differ in their standards for judgment), they are the most comprehensive data available for general comparisons. Countries are given a score of one to one hundred, with one hundred being the highest. In 2003, the latest year for the index, the highest ranking in Africa was eighty-two (Burkina Faso); the lowest was thirty-nine (Lesotho). The political categories for which countries received scores were: (1) political support; (2) policy and planning; (3) organizational structure; (4) legal and regulatory environment; and (5) human rights. *Political support* is defined as political leaders speaking publicly and regularly about AIDS. *Policy and planning* is defined as the country having a national strategy for AIDS. *Organizational structure* examines whether or not a country has incorporated AIDS into the work of all its governmental sectors. The *legal and regulatory* measure examines legislation and policies to limit HIV transmission, to prevent discrimination of PLWHAs, to protect consumers, to guarantee confidentiality in HIV testing, and to ensure access to safe medication. The *human rights* category measures country mechanisms to monitor and enforce human rights violations related to AIDS. Of the five areas, policy and planning and political support received the highest API scores among the fifty-four countries. The lowest scores

**Table 2.2    AIDS Program Effort Index (API) Scores, Political Measures**

| Country | Political Support | Policy and Planning | Organizational Structure | Legal and Regulatory | Human Rights | Overall API Score |
|---------|-------------------|---------------------|--------------------------|----------------------|--------------|-------------------|
| Botswana[a] | 95 | 100 | 77 | 73 | 55 | 80 |
| Rwanda[a] | 89 | 93 | 90 | 70 | 58 | 81 |
| South Africa | 79 | 69 | 90 | 70 | 58 | 75 |
| Swaziland | 78 | 81 | 50 | 67 | 15 | 60 |
| Uganda | 94 | 83 | 95 | 69 | 74 | 76 |
| Zimbabwe | 80 | 79 | 39 | 70 | 37 | 61 |

*Source:* Selected measures from USAID et al. (2003, 21).
a. I include Botswana and Rwanda for comparisons used in the chapter. I do not analyze them in depth.

were in organizational structure and human rights (USAID et al. 2003, 9–11). The components were not highly correlated. To be clear, the index only measures state efforts to address AIDS, not the effect of those efforts on HIV prevalence rates. In terms of a country's total API score, I classify high scores as above sixty-four, the average for the twenty-nine sub-Saharan countries in the study.

I hypothesize about several relationships between the four state characteristics (state centralization, neopatrimonialism, state capacity, and state security) and a country's API score. First, high state centralization will correlate with a low API. (Or the converse: low state centralization will correlate with a high API.) Because personal rulers have few checks on their authority and allow little, if any, civil society input, their policies may be ill informed and lack legitimacy. In the West, legislatures, judiciaries, subnational governments, and civil society organizations were all crucial in developing AIDS policies (Siplon 2002). Power decentralization should lead to more robust AIDS efforts.

Second, states with low neopatrimonialism (measured by corruption) will have a high API score. (Or, states with high neopatrimonialism will have a low API score.) In states with little neopatrimonialism, government officials will be less concerned about providing state resources to patronage for cronies and more concerned about spending on public goods such as health. AIDS efforts will benefit.

Third, states with high capacity will have a high API score. (Or, states with low capacity will have a low API score.) Capacity enables a state to hire doctors, purchase ARVs, provide health clinics to treat opportunistic infections, and implement AIDS education programs. It also gives a state the needed personnel and infrastructure to protect the rights of PLWHAs and implement national AIDS strategies. Because of the importance of state capacity, I speculate that even if a country has high centralization and high neopatrimonialism, it will have a high API score if it has high capacity. My speculation is rooted in a 2004 study that discovered while "capacity alone does not sufficiently explain AIDS adaptation," capacity plays "an important role" (Price-Smith et al. 2004, 7).

Fourth, states with low stability will have a low API score. (Or, stable states will have a high API score.) States that face security concerns such as an invasion or internal conflict will focus less attention on AIDS, since the disease is a long-term threat, not an immediate concern.

To be clear, the state characteristics examined here—centralization, neopatrimonialism, capacity, and stability—are interrelated. For example, neopatrimonial states may not have resources to build state capacity; low state capacity (e.g., dilapidated state infrastructure or no police protection) may contribute to instability. My goal is not to examine the relationships among the four state aspects, but to analyze how each of these elements affects AIDS policies in the case studies.

## The Case Studies

The cases of Zimbabwe, Uganda, Swaziland, and South Africa illustrate that the impact of these state elements differs widely with the country. These cases were chosen based on three criteria: first, their geographic location in the epicenter of the pandemic. HIV/AIDS has greatly affected southern and eastern Africa; the first cases emerged there in the early 1980s and, by the early 1990s, HIV prevalence rates had escalated. The twenty-year history of the disease—and its high mortality and morbidity rates in those countries—provides a long time period during which states could have developed AIDS policies. Also, theoretically the magnitude of the disease in the region makes it more likely state officials will have acted. In contrast, countries in West Africa have felt less of the pandemic's impact, a fact that may make their leaders less likely to act. Because I am interested in the effect of state characteristics on AIDS policies, not the point during the pandemic's cycle when states act, I chose countries that have experienced AIDS for roughly the same length of time. Second, I selected these countries because they provide some variation in HIV prevalence within this geographic region. According to UNAIDS (2004b, 191), Uganda has a 4.1 percent prevalence rate; South Africa, 21.5 percent; Zimbabwe, 24.6 percent; and Swaziland, 38.8 percent. My goal is not to assert that particular aspects of the state *cause* a higher or lower HIV prevalence rate, but that elements of the state shape policies to fight AIDS. Over time, these policies may lead to declines in prevalence, though decreases in HIV prevalence can reflect factors beyond government policies, such as individual behavior change, the activities of civil society, migration, and death (UNAIDS 2005b).

Third, the countries provide variation in the four state elements under discussion. Because it is impossible to find more than two countries in east and southern Africa that are similar in all of the four elements, I chose cases that differ in size, GNI, type of rule, and stability on the assumption that this variation provides important lessons about state AIDS efforts. For each country, Table 2.1 gives measures for the state characteristics, as well as the country's total API score. The table shows that South Africa is the least centralized and neopatrimonial, and it has the most state capacity. Swaziland has high state centralization, high neopatrimonialism, relatively high capacity, and high stability. Zimbabwe has high centralization, high neopatrimonialism, low capacity, and low stability. Uganda has low state capacity and low stability. While I classify Uganda as high in neopatrimonialism and centralization, it is not as high in those measures as Zimbabwe or Swaziland.

In terms of the hypotheses, I would expect South Africa to have the best API score, because of its relatively low state centralization and neopatrimonialism and its relatively high capacity. For the opposite reasons, Zimbabwe should have the worst score. Because of Swaziland's high capacity and stability, I predict it should have a high API despite its high centralization and neopatrimonialism. In contrast, Uganda's low capacity, low stability, high neopatrimonialism, and high centralization should depress its score even though it is not as neopatrimonial or centralized as Zimbabwe or Swaziland. The expected relationships among the state aspects and the API scores are provided in Table 2.3.

As Table 2.1 points out, Uganda has the highest score with seventy-six, followed by South Africa with seventy-five. Swaziland's ranking is roughly equal to Zimbabwe's (sixty and sixty-one, respectively). What explains these differences? Also, given its high state capacity, relative stability, low neopatrimonialism, and low centralization, why has South Africa not performed better than Uganda? Or, in another example, why does South Africa not have a score higher than Rwanda, which gets an eighty-one? Rwanda is more centralized, more neopatrimonial, less stable, and less well endowed with state capacity than South Africa.[2] My question is not what makes Rwanda unique, but why South Africa, which is exceptional on the continent in its wealth and democracy, does

**Table 2.3    Expected Relationships Between State Aspects and AIDS Program Effort Index (API) Scores**

|  | Level of State Centralization | Level of Neopatrimonialism | Level of State Capacity | Level of Stability | Predicted API Score |
|---|---|---|---|---|---|
| South Africa | low | low | high | low | high (>64) |
| Swaziland | high | high | high | high | high (>64) |
| Uganda | high | high | low | low | low (<64) |
| Zimbabwe | high | high | low | low | low (<64) |

*Source:* Derived from author's hypotheses based on data from World Bank (2005b, 2005c) and USAID et al. (2003, 31).

*Note:* High centralization = rule-of-law and voice-and-accountability scores under 50; high neopatrimonialism = corruption score under 50; high state capacity = GNI per capita over $826; high stability = security score over 50.

not have a higher API score. I turn to the case studies to answer these questions.

### Uganda: High AIDS Effort Despite Low Stability and Low Capacity

Bilateral and multilateral donors herald Uganda for its success in tackling AIDS. In 1991, its HIV prevalence rate was around 20 percent; by 2003, it was 4.1 percent (Green 2003b, 141; UNAIDS 2004b, 191). Chapter 5 examines the debates about Uganda's HIV decline, and my goal is not to argue that state policies were the direct cause of this decline. Uganda differs from South Africa in that it was a de jure one-party state from 1986 until 2005, although it has more civil liberties than Swaziland or Zimbabwe. Also, Uganda has experienced a nineteen-year rebellion in the north by the Lord's Resistance Army (LRA). According to Human Rights Watch (2005b), the LRA has abducted over 30,000 children and the war has contributed to the displacement of 1.3 million people. Because the LRA has received support from the government of Sudan, the rebellion threatens stability not only in Uganda, but also in the region. Yet, Uganda has successfully combated AIDS, as evidenced by its high API score.

Table 2.2 gives the total API scores and the API scores in the five political categories, for the four case study countries, plus Botswana and Rwanda. The high numbers in the political support and organizational structure categories reflect President Yoweri Museveni's public and unambiguous speeches about AIDS. When he came to power in 1986, Museveni spoke clearly about the need for Ugandans to limit their number of sexual partners—what he termed "zero grazing." He used metaphors that the largely rural population could understand: He likened AIDS to a lion at a village's edge and said it was everyone's responsibility to protect the community from the lion's destructive power (Green 2003b, 168). The president's frank discussion destigmatized the disease: if the president could talk about it, others could too. By saying that everyone was at risk, the president made AIDS not a disease of "others," but something with the potential to affect everyone. The high API scores also reflect the fact that Uganda was one of the first African states to work with the GPA to develop a multisectoral response to AIDS that incorporated civil society (Mameli 1998).

Museveni and his National Resistance Army (NRA) came to power after the tyrannical reign of Idi Amin (1971–1979) and a five-year guerrilla war (1980–1985) that pitted the NRA against Milton Obote's Ugandan National Liberation Army (UNLA). Roughly fifteen years of dictatorship and conflict had decimated the economy, left 400,000 dead, created large numbers of refugees, and fueled the spread of HIV. The war, and the Amin regime that preceded it, had divided the North against the South, Muslims against Christians, and the Nubian, Langi, and Acholi ethnic groups against each other during various periods. Museveni set about rebuilding the state, transforming the NRA into a national military organization, consolidating power, and fostering nationwide support for the National Resistance Movement (NRM, or simply "Movement").

To achieve these objectives, the NRM centralized power in some institutions, while allowing for some local control and civil society activities. Hence, the measures of state centralization in Uganda are not as strong as they are for Zimbabwe or Swaziland. As evidence of centralized power, the NRM installed "movement democracy" out of fear that explicit party competition would foment ethnic and regional divisions. Parties were not forcibly disbanded, but they could not hold meetings, recruit members, campaign openly in elections, or officially support candidates. Although citizens voted overwhelmingly in 2000 to continue movement democracy, by 2005 they supported multipartyism. During the 2005 campaign, the opposition advocated an election boycott and the president supported multipartyism. Many speculated the president's changed position reflected his confidence that he would maintain power in the 2006 election, since parliament had ended presidential term limits in 2005 (*BBC News*, July 29, 2005). The 2006 election campaign began when Museveni's opponent Dr. Kissa Besigye returned to the country and was arrested on charges of treason and rape; protests and police crackdowns ensued (*BBC News*, November 30, 2005). Many argue the president's focus on maintaining power demonstrates that he is less of a "new breed" African leader than many scholars and donors initially had hoped (Oloka-Onyango 2004; Bratton and Lambright 2001; Mugisha 2004).

On the other hand, the NRM has allowed some decentralization through its "resistance councils," governing entities composed of locally elected officials without party backgrounds. Linked hierarchically from the village to the district level, councils have given citizens some control over local affairs and have increased political participation (Ottaway 1999, 36–37). This decentralization reflected Museveni's rural experiences from 1980 to 1985, his belief that Uganda is pre-industrial and needs a peasant-based system, and his desire to decrease the power of unelected chiefs (Oloka-Onyango 2004, 36; Russell 2000, 282–283). It should be acknowledged, though, that as the councils mobilized local populations to rebuild the country's economy, they helped foster support for the NRM and distribute patronage.

The NRM also has allowed the formation of civil society organizations, some of which have been able to influence policy. For example, relatively autonomous women's rights organizations have helped to advance women's situation. Women have been appointed to high-level cabinet posts and the vice presidency, and the legislature has passed laws setting quotas for women's representation at the national and local levels. As of 2005, women were 24 percent of national parliamentarians, and although women tend to support the NRM, they have challenged government policies such as the 1988 land bill and the 2004 domestic violence bill (Inter-parliamentary Union 2005; Tripp 2001, 100–103). Women's participation in the economy also has increased greatly since 1986, with 73 percent of women reporting employment in 2002. Women's relatively high levels of political and economic participation may be one reason they feel more able to negotiate safer sex than women in Malawi, Rwanda, Tanzania, or Zimbabwe do (Green 2003b, 171).[3]

The resistance councils and civil society activities have been positive for the AIDS fight. Ugandan AIDS education efforts emphasized interpersonal communication over mass media messages. The ministry of health targeted a variety of local officials for AIDS education, from traditional healers and birth attendants, to religious leaders, teachers, and leaders of youth groups. The country's poor economy in 1986 and its lack of rural health care infrastructure necessitated using low-tech AIDS education efforts and focusing on behavioral change through sexual abstinence and faithfulness (Green 2003b, 153, 174). Some of the activities at the local level were sometimes heavy handed. For example, security officers associated with some resistance councils sought to control and constrain young people's social interactions and their opportunities for sexual intercourse (de Waal 2003a, 260). Because of this grassroots approach, the main source of AIDS information for Ugandans is family members and friends, unlike many other African countries where radio and print media are crucial education tools.

The state's willingness to give civil society space also helped with the AIDS fight, as AIDS service organizations formed and influenced policy. For example, in 1987, Dr. Noerine Kaleeba and fifteen of her peers, who were either infected with or affected by HIV, formed one of the country's first AIDS groups, The AIDS Support Organisation (TASO). Today TASO is the largest indigenous NGO providing HIV/AIDS services in Uganda, with roughly 83,000 PLWHAs as members, and 22,000 PLWHAs directly receiving TASO care and support. The organization's leaders have articulated a message of "living positively with HIV/AIDS" in policy development and implementation (TASO 2005). While Uganda has high centralization in the NRM, it has a good track record on AIDS because of the efforts of local governments, civil society, and a vocal president.

A state without competitive elections may be neopatrimonial because of the limited checks on government officials. While not as neopatrimonial as Zimbabwe or Swaziland, I rank Uganda as high for this state element. Journalists and donors have begun to echo this point: A 2005 World Bank report recommended cutting aid to Uganda because donor-funded budget support had been diverted to patronage (*allAfrica.com*, May 17, 2005; *Washington Times*, July 5, 2005; *Economist Newspapers*, July 2, 2005). While Ugandan journalists and scholars have criticized Museveni's use of state resources to reward his family and cronies, there have not been reports of diverting AIDS resources to patronage (Tangri and Mwenda 2001; Mwenda and Tangri 2005). The only hint of this possibility came from the GFATM, which briefly suspended its grants to the country in 2005 after auditors found some reporting irregularities. After the government assured the GFATM that it had corrected the problem, the grants resumed (Human Rights Watch 2005b).

One reason that Uganda's high neopatrimonialism may have little discernible effect on AIDS policies relates to state capacity. As Table 2.1 illustrates, Uganda has low state capacity. However, President Museveni has been able to meet some of his immediate resource needs through high levels of donor assistance. After the country's civil war, the president astutely realized that he needed outside resources to rebuild Uganda, and, for the most part, he has been willing to follow the neoliberal policies of the IMF and World Bank to get aid. Bilateral aid roughly doubled from $179 million in 1989 to $342 million in 1994, and foreign investment increased from nothing in 1990 to 3.1 percent of gross domestic product (GDP) in 2003 (Hauser 1999, 626; World Bank 2005d, 272). In 2005, approximately 50 percent of the country's budget came from donor support (*Monitor*, July 20, 2005). The country's GDP grew roughly 6.7 percent each year between 1986 and 1999; poverty declined from 56 percent of the population below the national poverty level in the early 1990s to 38 percent in 2002. Despite these gains, Uganda remains a poor country, with a GNI per capita of $270 in 2004. As the economy grew and inflation remained low, donors rewarded Uganda with more loans. In 1997, when Uganda was spending three times as much on debt servicing as it did on health care, donors approved the country as the first participant in the Heavily Indebted Poor Country initiative. Uganda then got roughly $2 billion in debt relief, resources it has used on poverty-reduction efforts like education and primary health care (*Financial Times*, February 16, 2005; *Washington Times*, July 5, 2005; UNDP 2004, 186). The 2005 debt relief package passed at the Group of Eight meeting will further benefit Uganda. These donor resources have not necessarily been used to build state capacity, though some may have that long-term impact.

There has been little donor pressure to encourage democracy or curtail neopatrimonialism. For example, after the parliament voted to remove presidential term limits, the United Kingdom, Norway, and Ireland suspended roughly $12 million in aid (*Agence France Presse*, May 18, 2005; *Agence France Presse,* July 19, 2005). Yet, because the country receives approximately $980 million annually, including $76 million from the United Kingdom, this action meant little (*Worldpress.org*, July 25, 2005). Ellen Hauser (1999, 633) explains why: "Uganda's overall success was important because of donor governments' need to have success stories, especially in Africa." President Museveni is viewed as a Western ally, because of his stand against the Sudanese Islamic government and his support for the Iraq war (Oloka-Onyango 2004, 47). As Chapter 5 shows, the country receives more foreign money per HIV-positive person than any other country in sub-Saharan Africa. Contrary to my hypothesis, because of donor funding, Uganda's low state capacity has not hampered its AIDS efforts.

Political instability has been a constant theme in Uganda, from before Museveni came to power until the present. In contrast to my expectation that high insecurity would thwart AIDS efforts, instability pushed Museveni's early AIDS policies. When Museveni came to power he faced security threats from UNLA supporters in the north, particularly since the NRA's political wing, the NRM, was viewed as a southern organization (Ottaway 1999, 30). When several military officers who had been sent to Cuba for training tested HIV positive, the president realized that AIDS was a potential obstacle in achieving his security objectives (Garbus and Marseille 2003, 11–12). It would be difficult to maintain power with a military that was sick, demoralized, or dying. Joseph Oloka-Onyango (2004, 37) writes, "Central to Museveni's worldview is the primacy of security over virtually any other public good." This focus urged Museveni to quickly begin a national AIDS response and it has continued to fuel the president's concern about the disease in the face of the LRA rebellion.

In summary, the unique nature of state centralization in Uganda has had an unexpected effect on AIDS efforts. Despite high state centralization, the development of resistance councils and the relatively open political space for civil society have facilitated local AIDS education programs and AIDS support groups. Also, while power is centralized in the NRM, the president has used his bully pulpit position to discuss AIDS. As the next section shows, Uganda contrasts with South Africa, because Uganda capitalized on its political transition, and the new institutions it developed, to fight AIDS. Neopatrimonialism has not had an apparent impact on AIDS policies, though some donors have begun to more openly question providing financial resources to the Ugandan government. While state capacity is low, unlike in Zimbabwe, donors have provided resources to address AIDS. Finally, contrary to my hypothesis, state instability has been crucial for mobilizing action against AIDS: The president first realized the seriousness of AIDS because of its link to the military. Uganda refutes my expectations about the nature of the state and AIDS efforts.

### Why Has South Africa Not Done Better?

In 2003, roughly five million South Africans, or 21.5 percent of the population, were HIV-positive, an increase from 2.2 percent in 1992 (UNAIDS 2004b, 191; South Africa Government 2002, 6). In 2005, UNAIDS reported that South Africa shows no decline in HIV infection rates, with 2004 data putting prevalence among pregnant women at 29.5 percent. The epidemic has evolved at "astonishing speed" within the last ten years; mortality among people fifteen years or older increased 62 percent between 1997 and 2002 (UNAIDS 2005e, 21–22). Several economic and social factors have contributed to the spread of HIV. Economically, the unemployment rate among blacks is 28 percent, though only 4 percent for whites. While 56 percent of blacks lived below the national poverty line in 2002, only 7 percent of whites did. The country's Gini coefficient rose from .596 in 1995 to .635 in 2001 (Nation Master 2005; Adelzadeh 2003, 5–6).[4] Limited economic opportunities, economic inequalities, and low social cohesion have increased the likelihood that people will engage in behavior such as crime, migration, and survival sex that heightens their risk of contracting HIV.

When Nelson Mandela came to power in 1994, the government faced pressing demands to create jobs, encourage foreign investment, and provide services to millions of poor South Africans. AIDS was just one of the government's twenty-two priorities, and the government tended to view AIDS solely as a health issue. The government did, though, increase spending on HIV/AIDS education, condom distribution, and primary care health centers (Furlong and Ball 2005, 135–136). After 1999, when Thabo Mbeki was elected president, government efforts became more obvious. Funding for AIDS in the national budget increased from R343 million in 2001/02 to R2.3 billion for 2006/07 (Hickey et al. 2004, 36). In 2000, the government developed the South African National AIDS Council (SANAC) to oversee a multisectoral approach to AIDS (Furlong and Ball 2005, 128). As Table 2.2 reveals, while South Africa's overall API score is high, it is roughly equal to Uganda's. Moreover, its API scores for political support, policy and planning, and human rights seem low given its low centralization, low neopatrimonialism, and high state capacity.

Of the four countries, South Africa is by far the least politically centralized (see Table 2.1). Freedom House (2005b) classifies the country as "free" in political and civil liberties. As Chapters 3 and 4 illustrate, South Africa has an independent judiciary that has required the executive to change AIDS policies. The media and civil society, including AIDS organizations, have been active in AIDS policymaking and implementation. In its constitutional structures and its protection of civil liberties, South Africa is a democracy. Yet, over the last decade, power has become more centralized in the ruling party, national government, and presidency. Gretchen Bauer and Ian Taylor (2005, 258) write: "South Africa has acquired all the trappings of the dominant-party state observed elsewhere on the continent." The ruling African National Congress (ANC) dominates the system and, after the 2004 election, it holds two-thirds of the national legislative seats and controls premierships in all nine provinces. The system rests on strong party loyalty, and dissenters within the ANC at times have been vilified as antipatriotic enemies of black achievement (Matshiqi 2005, 52–53). Some regional and cabinet leaders who have challenged President Mbeki or his policies have been redeployed to less powerful positions or replaced by his supporters. And while the 1996 constitution gives provincial governments some jurisdiction over health issues, since 98 percent of the provincial budgets comes from the national government, the center retains much control (Hickey et al. 2004).

Much of the increased centralization in the ANC and in high-level policy institutions has occurred during Mbeki's presidency and has been particularly evident in AIDS policy. While SANAC is theoretically supposed to work with the cabinet to oversee AIDS policymaking (hence the country's high API score for organizational structure), the president has shifted policymaking from this structure to the presidency. Mbeki created policy-planning clusters, each coordinated by the presidency, "thus usurping the cabinet's ability to mobilize knowledge across government" (Butler 2005, 600). This had the effect of removing cabinet responsibility to parliament (and the people) for AIDS. Furthermore, the appointment of unelected officials who are loyal to Mbeki but lack political weight and constituencies has reduced internal debate over AIDS policies. Because of this centralization in the presidency, the nature of Mbeki's leadership is crucial for understanding why South Africa's total API score is not higher. It also partially explains why South Africa receives a score of sixty-nine in policy and planning, in comparison to the higher ratings for Swaziland, Uganda, and Zimbabwe (see Table 2.2). It is not centralization of state institutions *per se* that provides an explanation, but Mbeki's crucial role in the specific policy arena of AIDS.

One aspect of Mbeki's ideology and experiences that has affected his actions on AIDS is his history in the wing of the ANC that was in exile during apartheid. He contrasts with leaders of unions and civil society organizations who stayed in South Africa and engaged in resistance. Although the distinction between the exiles and domestic resisters can be overdrawn, it does provide some insights into Mbeki's political approach. Because government agents routinely penetrated the exile movement, exiles learned to suspect outsiders. For exiles, compromise was neither possible nor necessary; the hierarchical military discipline needed for the exile guerrilla movement meant decisionmaking was concentrated among a few trusted individuals. In contrast, civic activists had to compromise with local government leaders, and they had to engage in participatory consensus building to mobilize constituents for mass action (Friedman 2004, 234–236; Deegan 2001, 57–59). Additionally, many exiles were trained in Leninist thought in socialist states or the Soviet Union, making them more receptive to ideas about conspiracies of international capital.[5]

The exile experience and Leninist views on capitalism partly explain Mbeki's suspicion of Western drug companies and ARVs. As early as 1998, Mbeki defended the health minister's decision to cease providing zidovudine (AZT; brand name Retrovir) to HIV-positive pregnant women for prevention of mother-to-child transmission (PMTCT). He said the drug was "toxic" and between 1998 and 2000, he repeatedly questioned the motives of its producer, Glaxo Wellcome.[6] When criticized, he responded: "I am taken aback by the determination of many people in our country to sacrifice all intellectual integrity to act as salespersons of the product of one pharmaceutical company" (*Agence France Presse*, March 26, 2000). Rather than address his critics' concerns, Mbeki attacked his opponents as "sellouts" to Western drug companies. Mbeki's administration proposed that drug companies were financing the Treatment Action Campaign (TAC), a civil society group that demanded ARV access, in order to stir up demand for the companies' products (*Star*, January 31, 2000). The perceived conspiracy expanded when Mbeki accused the US Central Intelligence Agency (CIA) of promoting the view that HIV causes AIDS, so that African countries would buy American-produced ARVs, drugs that stop the spread of HIV in the body (*Agence France Presse*, October 6, 2000).

Along this line, Mbeki wrote a five-page letter to world leaders in April 2000 in which he defended serious discussion of minority scientific views on AIDS. He accused the West of "intellectual intimidation" akin "to the racist apartheid tyranny we opposed." He wrote that he was being asked to discredit ideas, just as the white racist apartheid regime did, "because, it is said, there exists a scientific view that is supported by the majority, against which dissent is prohibited" (Mbeki 2000). Through the letter, Mbeki may have hoped to "secure a place for those previously lacking representation and to demand some evenhandedness in the treatment of different points of view" (Eboko 2005, 42). On the other hand, by attacking the West for dangerous ARVs, profiteering drug companies, and intellectual censorship, the president may have sought to deflect criticism about the ANC's poor record on the epidemic (Scheckels 2004).

The exile experience created a vanguard approach to politics evident in Mbeki's AIDS actions. Because of their Leninist training, some ANC leaders seem to believe that the party must guide and protect the transition. Such an ideology assigns the state "the role of knowledge producer, able to develop policy and set the agenda for social transformation" (Johnson 2004, 121). While Mbeki's desire to control knowledge is consistent with a Leninist notion of the vanguard state, his support of neoliberal economic policies is not. At times, his neoliberalism has put him at odds with the more Marxist elements of the ANC and its governing partner, the South African Communist Party (SACP). My point is not that Mbeki accepts socialism, but that his view of the state as knowledge producer stems from Leninist thought. This approach is apparent in Mbeki's most infamous AIDS incident: his questioning the link between HIV and AIDS.

In May 2000, Mbeki appointed a presidential panel to investigate why HIV tends to be transmitted heterosexually in Africa, but homosexually and intravenously in the West. Mbeki framed the panel as a way to learn more about the unique nature of AIDS in Africa. In one sense, Mbeki acted as a world leader who wanted to increase his knowledge and as someone who was "just asking questions" (Scheckels 2004, 72). Yet, half of the panelists were scientists who doubted the link between the HIV virus and AIDS, and one argued that the HIV test causes AIDS. Additionally, in what seemed inconsistent with Mbeki's suspicions of the West and his desire to highlight African perspectives, several of the panel members were white Americans and Afrikaner scholars. In September 2000, Mbeki further explained his views:

> A whole variety of things can cause the immune system to collapse.
> . . . But the notion that immune deficiency is only acquired from a sin-
> gle virus cannot be sustained. Once you say immune deficiency is
> acquired from that virus your response will be antiretroviral drugs. But
> if you accept that there can be a variety of reasons, including poverty
> and the many diseases that afflict Africans, then you have a more com-
> prehensive treatment response. (*Time Magazine Europe*, September
> 11, 2000)

In his speeches in 2000, Mbeki clearly struggles with the complexity of AIDS and its relationship to poverty. However, in a larger sense, his desire to examine the science of AIDS demonstrates the vanguard philosophy that governing elites must understand and define problems. Before the AIDS panel met, he said, "The problem [of AIDS] was so big that I personally felt that I wanted to understand this matter better." South African scholar Tom Lodge responded: "[The AIDS panel is] an admirable indication of an extremely conscientious and intelligent chief executive. But I think he's also a compulsive interferer" (*New York Times*, May 7, 2000).

The vanguard approach was evident in 2001, when the government insisted it had to conduct a two-year study of nevirapine for PMTCT before the drug could be widely distributed in public hospitals.[7] The pilot research in eighteen hospitals would barely reach 10 percent of HIV-positive pregnant women needing the drug (Steytler 2003, 63). As the next two chapters detail, pressure from civil society, the courts, and provincial governments eventually caused the administration to change this policy. Similarly, Mbeki's administration insisted it had to study widespread ARV distribution before developing a national treatment program. As a result, the government did not announce universal ARV access until 2003, and then only after advocacy from civil society. The need to study issues, control the agenda, and dictate policy outcomes reflects the view that only government elites can understand problems and develop solutions.

Some of President Mbeki's closest allies are former exiles. Steven Friedman (2004, 239) argues that the exiles' rise to power in 1999 has coincided with the "diminution of democratic practice within the ANC." As of 2005, seventeen of the thirty cabinet members were exiles, including the close presidential advisor Minister without Portfolio Essop Pahad and Minister of Health Manto Tshabalala-Msimang. Mbeki's loyal supporter since they both left South Africa in 1962, Tshabalala-Msimang has defended the president's questioning of the link between HIV and AIDS, has challenged donors who questioned South Africa's ARV policies, has echoed Mbeki's assertion that ARVs are poisons, and has tussled with civil society organizations on numerous occasions (Lodge 2003, 263; *Newsday*, July 8, 2002; *Financial Times*, December 12, 2003; *InterPress Service*, July 19, 2002; *BBC News*, July 16, 2002). Many argue that her unwavering support for the president was the reason she was reappointed to her position in 2004, despite her unpopularity.[8]

However, the exile experience, with its suspicion of outsiders and Leninist vanguard training, does not fully explain the president's AIDS actions. For example, two ANC leaders who quietly worked to get the president to accept universal ARV access before the 2004 election had been exiles: education minister Kader Asmal and ex-Department of Health director general Olive Shisana.[9] And some of the president's biggest critics are not those who worked in community organizations during apartheid, but angry youth who think the president has "sold out" to big business with his conservative economic policies. They are suspicious of some former ANC leaders such as Cyril Ramaphosa and Manne Dipico who have financially benefited from the president's Black Economic Empowerment Program (*Guardian*, November 9, 2005). Further explanation for Mbeki's perspectives comes from South Africa's larger historical context. During apartheid, the medical sciences often denigrated blacks and population policy focused on controlling black reproduction. Black suspicion of medicine, coupled with Leninist conspiracy theories, shape the AIDS debate. Furthermore, Mbeki and his supporters remember that Western governments did not side with the ANC to oppose apartheid. The United States only enacted sanctions against the country in 1986, despite strong opposition from President Ronald Reagan. No doubt, these relatively recent events influence Mbeki's ideas about Western pharmaceutical companies.

Another element of Mbeki's philosophy that relates to AIDS is his call for an African renaissance. In a parliamentary address on June 10, 1997, then Deputy President Mbeki spoke of "the obligation to contribute to the common African continental effort, at last, to achieve an African Renaissance" (Mbeki 1997). The renaissance encompasses the use of African heritage to humanize the impersonal forces of bureaucracy, international markets, and technology. Implicit in Mbeki's words is that South Africa is the only country on the continent with the ability and moral legitimacy to lead the renaissance (Lodge 2003, 228–229). The 2001 formation of the New Partnership for Africa's Development (NEPAD) and South Africa's efforts to gain a permanent seat on the UN Security Council reflect these ideas.

Celebration of African identity is not new: Senegal's first president Léopold Sédar Senghor spoke of *negritude* to highlight Africa's uniqueness. But Mbeki's concept of African identity is often couched in racial terms (Lodge 2003, 237). The president has capitalized on this race-based imagery when opposed on his AIDS policies. For example, when Democratic Alliance leader Tony Leon criticized Mbeki for questioning the link between HIV and AIDS, the president denounced Leon for "entrenched white racism that is a millennium old" (*Times London*, August 14, 2000). In 2004, when the white journalist Charlene Smith, a former Mbeki friend and ally in the antiapartheid struggle, wrote that the slight drop in reported rapes ignored the horrifying consequences for rape survivors who became HIV positive, the president attacked her for playing to stereotypes of blacks as animalistic, savage rapists (*New York Times*, November 24, 2004, p. A3). The president's words led several politicians and religious leaders to demand Mbeki quit using race as a "red herring" in response to AIDS. While the president asserts that discussing the sexual behavior that contributes to HIV transmission degrades Africans, his rhetoric has helped to infuse the AIDS stigma with racist imagery. Mbeki himself has not been above stigmatizing AIDS. When the president denied in 2003 that he knew anyone with AIDS, he distanced himself from "those people," the very same people the president claims his critics have portrayed using racist stereotypes. Many South Africans doubted his statement, given the country's high HIV prevalence and the widely believed rumor that Mbeki's spokesman Parks Mankahlana had died of AIDS in 2000 (*Panafrican News Agency*, September 26, 2003; Cameron 2005, 114).

The president also has defined the renaissance as finding African solutions to African problems. For example, in 1997, Mbeki supported the experimental AIDS drug Virodene that was developed in South Africa, even after the country's Medical Research Council questioned its toxicity. The health minister's support of alleged AIDS remedies such as garlic and lemon juice can also be viewed as a search for an African AIDS response (*International Herald Tribune*, November 17, 2004; *New York Times*, February 10, 2004, p. A8). However, what these actions do not emphasize from the African renaissance philosophy is the idea that people realize their humanity through interaction with others (Lodge 2003, 230). The government's refusal to seriously consider ARV medicines until 2003 did not recognize HIV-positive Africans as crucial community members whose deaths impact everyone. Instead, the government ignored the death and suffering that affects predominantly the black majority. The regime's actions on AIDS also reflect a growing distance between the ruling elite and the poor, since government officials and South Africa's wealthy citizens can access private hospitals and ARVs, but the poor majority cannot (Friedman and Chipkin 2001; Steytler 2003; Cameron 2005; Vavi 2005).

Although South Africa has a high API score, the implications of Mbeki's actions may have prevented it from being higher. South African AIDS organizations have reported that the president's embrace of dissident science has increased public resistance to AIDS education messages (Lodge 2003, 263). A 2002 survey found that over 20 percent of South Africans lacked the specific knowledge that HIV causes AIDS, and 5 percent affirmed the statement that HIV does *not* cause AIDS (Human Sciences Research Council 2002, 82–86). While the president's actions did not cause one-fifth of South Africans to know little about AIDS, his statements did not *help* to increase AIDS knowledge. They also may have led the 5 percent of respondents to think HIV does not cause AIDS. Additionally, by debating the science of HIV/AIDS, Mbeki has distracted citizens, policymakers, and activists from discussion of important AIDS issues such as sex, responsibility, and gender equality (Power 2003a, 63). Mbeki's rhetoric, and civil society's response to it, have curtailed debate over how to allocate resources for AIDS or what to prioritize when addressing the epidemic.

Mbeki's rhetoric has burned proverbial bridges that are essential for fighting HIV. South Africa needs assistance from civil society, donors, and citizens to combat AIDS. Chapter 4 illustrates the distrust that has emerged between the government and AIDS organizations, particularly TAC. Rather than consulting with civil society, the regime has struck out alone on AIDS policies (Johnson 2004, 121). Even civil servants who do not agree with the president's statements have been lambasted by citizens, further eroding the trust needed for a comprehensive AIDS approach (Walker et al. 2004, 108). According to one bilateral donor official who has worked in South Africa, Mbeki's suspicion of the West and drug companies has tainted the relationship between the government and donors, with donors suspicious of Mbeki's motives and South African officials viewing requirements for grants as yet another imperialist obstacle preventing them from helping their people. While this suspicion is not enough to make donors end programs in the country, it does strain relations.[10]

In terms of neopatrimonialism, South Africa's lower corruption score indicates that it has not experienced as much neopatrimonial behavior as the other three countries, though it has not been completely immune. In June 2005, President Mbeki fired Deputy President Jacob Zuma for his ties to a convicted financial advisor who allegedly paid Zuma bribes. The action cleared the way for Zuma's indictment (*New York Times*, June 15, 2005, p. A8). In terms of AIDS, one of the Mandela government's first AIDS efforts, the educational play *Sarafina II*, came under scrutiny for funding mismanagement in 1996. Although President Mandela supported the endeavor, the public prosecutor determined that the contract submission process for the play was fraudulent (Lodge 2003, 256; Furlong and Ball 2005, 140). While damaging, the *Sarafina II* fiasco was only one known incident of corruption in the arena of AIDS, and because South Africa has independent courts and a free media, it was dealt with relatively quickly. This incident alone does not suggest that a pattern of neopatrimonialism has contributed to South Africa's API score.

South Africa also has high state capacity, with a GNI per capita over twice that of Swaziland and over thirteen times that of Uganda. This relative wealth has contributed to more doctors, health care facilities, and universities than other sub-Saharan African states (UNDP 2005). Of course, this does not mean that South Africa has sufficient capacity to address AIDS. Between 1989 and 1997, 80,000 health workers emigrated; in 2003, there were roughly 30,000 unfilled positions in the public health sector (Butler 2005, 599). While I do not deny that these are crucial problems, in comparison to Uganda and Zimbabwe, South Africa has high state capacity.

However, the Mbeki government has adamantly argued that it does *not* have the capacity to provide ARVs for PMTCT and universal treatment. Because Mbeki's government has focused on showing the world that it can govern using financial accountability and technical and managerial efficiency (Friedman 2004, 241), it has repeatedly focused on the technical issue of cost as a reason for not providing AIDS drugs. The government has relied heavily on a narrow cost-benefit analysis, rather than considering the long-term costs to the country's economic, social, and political stability if it does not provide ARVs. The government also has refused to begin any ARV programs, whether PMTCT, prophylactics for rape survivors, or universal treatment, if it does not think they are sustainable. Even after its 2003 announcement on universal access, the government has used cost and sustainability arguments to delay the treatment program. Nicoli Nattrass (2004, 17) comments, "By locating the AIDS policy discussion in a seemingly technical discourse of affordability and sustainability, the space for public deliberation over the appropriate size of a national treatment programme has been sharply curtailed."

Yet, the government's "lack of capacity" argument is also rooted in political calculations. Because the country *has* more resources, citizen expectations for government AIDS programs are high. Anthony Butler (2005, 610) points to the political challenges the situation presents:

> The public promise to scale up [ARV treatment] from a few thousand to more than a million ARV recipients poses an evident political hazard. *De facto* rationing of treatment will be inequitable, and will bring political risks that the government must be concerned to minimize. A discriminatory and rationed antiretroviral programme might arouse public discontent and generate further "new social movement" protests.

Therefore, while South Africa's high state capacity contributes to a relatively high API score, the government's desire to temper citizen expectations with cost and sustainability arguments has prevented the government from doing more for AIDS.

In terms of state stability, Mbeki has tried to deflect attention from the epidemic's magnitude by claiming crime, not AIDS, is the country's biggest killer (*Financial Times*, August 7, 2001). However, it is unclear that crime has negatively affected the government's AIDS efforts. The country is politically stable: the ANC continues to have high levels of support, as evidenced by the 2004 election. South Africa does not face threats from its neighbors. Since 1990, the country has cut military spending from 3.8 percent of GDP in 1990 to 1.6 percent in 2003 (UNDP 2005, 286). Although Mbeki increased arms spending in 2004, this spending was not in response to a specific threat and, as evidenced by the higher AIDS financing cited above, it does not seem that funds have been diverted from fighting the epidemic to the military.

Although South Africa has a high API score, many AIDS activists, donors, and scholars think that it could do much more. It has high capacity, low neopatrimonialism, and low centralization. The somewhat disappointing nature of South Africa's AIDS efforts reflects presidential action on the issue. It is not the centralization of the state itself, but the centralization of AIDS policymaking in the presidency and more particularly, the presidency of Thabo Mbeki, that is crucial for understanding why South Africa has not done better.

### Swaziland: Limited AIDS Effort Despite High State Capacity and Stability

With a prevalence rate in 2004 of 42.6 percent (up from 38.8 percent in 2003), Swaziland has the highest HIV rate in the world (United Nations 2005, 4). Approximately 10 percent of Swazi households are now headed by children and 60 percent of the country's population lives below the poverty line (UNICEF 2005a). It is estimated that this country of roughly 1.2 million people will have 120,000 orphans by 2010, to total 10 percent to 15 percent of the *entire* population (Lewis 2004). The probability of a young Swazi who is fifteen years old today reaching the age of fifty is 28 percent for males and 22 percent for females, compared to 94 percent for males and 97 percent for females without AIDS. These horrendous numbers reflect factors common throughout southern Africa that have contributed to the pandemic: male migration; a culture of male dominance that gives women little power to demand their partners use condoms; and social expectations that encourage men to have multiple partners (*allAfrica.com*, May 11, 2005).

Table 2.2 shows how state actions to address AIDS have varied in the country. The Swazi government has a relatively high API ranking for political support and policy and planning. It proactively developed the National AIDS Prevention and Control Program in the late 1980s. Swaziland also was one of the first African countries to mention HIV in its national development plan. In 2001, the government created the National Emergency Response Committee on HIV/AIDS (NERCHA) to coordinate the actions of implementing agencies, approve funding allocations, and advise the prime minister and cabinet on AIDS issues (NERCHA 2004). NERCHA has conducted research and worked with multilateral donors to develop AIDS policies (Whiteside 2005, 98). Despite the creation of NERCHA, the country only has an API score of fifty for organizational structure and fifteen for human rights. The low human rights number partly reflects the fact that Swazi women—who are most likely to be HIV-positive—did not have legal equality under the country's constitution until January 2006. Of the four countries studied here, Swaziland has the worst total API score. While the Swazi state has high stability and relatively high capacity, its high centralization and neopatrimonialism have detracted from the country's AIDS efforts.

As the continent's last remaining absolute monarchy, Swaziland presents an extreme example of state centralization. As a traditional leader, King Mswati III derives his power and legitimacy from family lineage, history, and symbolism, not constitutional rules or elections. Decisions about resources and leadership positions are based on the king's personal prerogatives. For example, in March 2004, the king forced the speaker of parliament Marwick Khumalo out of office after Khumalo criticized the monarch (*Sunday Times*, March 28, 2004). The king's father suspended the constitution in 1973, after opposition parties won enough legislative seats to challenge the monarch. In 1996, the current king called for a constitutional review commission to draft a new constitution, which was finally unveiled in May 2003. Two of the king's brothers headed the constitutional process, and his brothers-in-law, uncles, and family friends comprised the commission (*Agence France Presse*, June 27, 2004). The new constitution, which went into effect in 2006, maintained the king's power to appoint the prime minister, cabinet ministers, judges, and some legislators and continued the ban on political parties. While it included a detailed bill of rights, the monarch can abrogate those rights if he considers them in conflict with the public interest. When pro-democracy groups criticized the constitution in 2005, the High Court prohibited them from submitting suggestions, saying that in terms of the law, "[these groups] are nonexistent" (*Agence France Presse*, March 24, 2005; *Mail & Guardian*, July 5, 2005; Staley 2005; *allAfrica.com*, January 11, 2006).

Despite the new constitution's bill of rights, laws curtailing the media and civil society remain. Freedom House (2005b) ranks the country as "not free" for both political rights and civil liberties. In 2001, the king decreed that he had the power to ban any book, magazine, or newspaper and that anyone who impersonated or ridiculed the king or his decisions was subject to punishment. After strong outcry, the king repealed the formal decree, although freedom of expression on political issues or those related to the royal family remains restricted. The state controls all radio and TV stations, and the only private daily newspaper is devoted to news trivia, entertainment, and sports (Freedom House 2005b; *BBC News*, June 25, 2001; *BBC News*, May 18, 2005; *Afrol News*, May 2, 2005). While there are community organizations working on AIDS in Swaziland (Dowden 2002), the larger political environment has prevented their having much influence on AIDS policies.

As the country's major AIDS policymaking body, NERCHA was an important first step in fighting the pandemic. However, NERCHA has made some decisions that, in the opinion of many AIDS activists and donors, have led to unwise use of resources (*allAfrica.com,* April 22, 2005). For example, critics wondered why NERCHA spent millions on new community centers for orphans, when community-based programs already existed (*Baltimore Sun,* September 12, 2004). AIDS activists and multilateral donors have criticized NERCHA for resisting ARVs until 2004, for its foot-dragging in negotiations with the GFATM, and for not educating traditional leaders about ARV treatment (Lewis 2004; *UN Integrated Regional Information Networks,* July 1, 2004; *allAfrica.com,* March 5, 2004). NERCHA decisions may reflect a larger political environment in which civil society organizations have not been brought into the policymaking process because of state centralization.

Because the monarch plays a central role in the political system, and because there is little political space for other actors, the king's activities are crucial for AIDS policy outcomes. His position blurs formal and informal institutions and conflates public and private actions. Despite the king's support of NERCHA, his leadership, particularly on the factors making women vulnerable to HIV, is lacking. The king has twelve wives, some of whom he has chosen from videos of the annual Reed Dance where up to 50,000 young virgins dance bare breasted before him, hoping to be selected as his future wife. He married his eleventh wife in May 2005; she was already pregnant with his twenty-fifth child. When chosen at age eighteen, she was forced to leave high school. Less than one month later, the king married his twelfth wife, an eighteen-year-old woman he selected in the 2004 Reed Dance (*BBC News,* May 30, 2005; *Daily Telegraph,* June 13, 2005).

Local AIDS activists, international journalists, and donor officials have criticized the king's blatant disregard for the factors that contribute to the HIV/AIDS epidemic in his country: women's lack of power, polygamy, male promiscuity, and women's limited educational and economic opportunities. They point out that the king advocated traditional chastity rules, such as girls wearing tassels as a symbol of virginity and virgins abstaining from sex for five years, but then lost an opportunity to lead when he chose a young virgin, a school girl, for his eleventh wife: "People respect the king. They would have followed his lead." Other activists point out that while the palace screens future brides for HIV so the king will not become infected, the same is not true of most Swazis who do not know their serostatus (*InterPress Service,* August 29, 2003). The king's "playboy lifestyle," including global travel with singer Michael Jackson and extensive parties at discos, has created doubt about his genuine desire to lead on HIV/AIDS (*Business Day*, July 20, 2004; *Sunday Times*, March 28, 2004). Perhaps in response to this criticism, or because he realized that the country needed more than a return to tradition to conquer AIDS, the king abandoned his chastity rules in August 2005 (*Independent*, August 20, 2005).

Customs and traditions can promote social cohesion and strengthen communities, and those are important elements for the fight against AIDS. However, the king's actions seem to have perverted customs and ignored how traditions rooted in gender inequality can contribute to the spread of HIV. Swazi state actions on HIV/AIDS mix traditional and modern, formal and informal structures, and these sometimes are at odds. Citizens receive mixed messages from the state (i.e., the king) about AIDS. Alan Whiteside (2005, 121) writes, "There is a tendency for political, economic, and cultural leaders to say, 'Do as I say, not as I do.' Typically, older men advocate abstinence and fidelity, but their behavior contradicts this." In a country where power is centralized in the monarch, his advisors, and the legislators, judges, and ministers that he selects, there are few opportunities for other institutions to counter these mixed messages. Power centralization has had a detrimental impact on AIDS policy outcomes.

Neopatrimonialism stems from this centralization of power and has had additional negative effects on AIDS policies. In 2004, the king spent $600,000 on his thirty-sixth birthday party, a sum that reportedly covered the cost of new cars, guests' accommodations, and food (*Financial Times*, April 17, 2004). A year later, he increased his birthday spending to $1.7 million, including $500,000 for a Daimler-Chrysler Maybach 62 for himself (*Mail & Guardian*, June 13, 2005). This lack of state accountability fuels corruption. In a rare candid moment, the Finance Minister Majozi Sithole said that the government loses $5 million each month to corruption: "The twin evils of bribery and corruption have become the order of the day in the country" (*allAfrica.com*, March 9, 2005; *Daily Mail London*, June 2, 2005).

King Mswati's spending illustrates Patrick Chabal and Jean-Pascal Daloz's point that neopatrimonial state leaders engage in consumption not production: "Ostentation remains, and is likely to remain, one of the chief political virtues in Africa." But they also caution that ostentation must include redistributing resources to clients (1999, 160), a fact the king seems to have forgotten. There are signs that Swazis are becoming unhappy with the way the king runs this country where 200,000 people survive on food from aid organizations. For example, in January 2005, the Swazi Federation of Trade Unions organized a two-day strike over the king's spending habits (*Sunday Telegraph*, February 20, 2005).

I hypothesized that high neopatrimonialism will have a negative impact on AIDS efforts because state leaders will divert resources from AIDS programs to patronage. Another possible impact is that neopatrimonialism will drive donors from providing needed funding to fight AIDS. Both of these outcomes are somewhat evident in Swaziland. First, a contrast between spending on the royal family and spending on health (AIDS spending amounts are not available) illustrates the negative effect of neopatrimonialism for citizens' general welfare. In 2004, the king spent $14 million to construct new palaces for each of his wives, $2.8 million for luxury homes for relatives, $11 million for palace building programs, and $45 million for a private jet. In contrast, the government allocated $30.8 million for all national health services (*UN Integrated Regional Information Networks*, January 19, 2004; March 19, 2004). While it is impossible to say that corruption *per se* led to low health spending, it does seem clear that the government has not prioritized health.

Neopatrimonialism, as well as the king's personal behavior, has made some donors relatively unenthusiastic about fighting AIDS in the country. As of 2005, the country had received $15 million of a $50 million grant from the GFATM. Although the United States has doubled funding to Swaziland in recent years, most of this AIDS money goes through USAID's Southern Africa Regional AIDS Program (US Embassy 2005). On the other hand, Swaziland is not one of the focus countries for PEPFAR, despite its high HIV prevalence rate. The UK Department for International Development (DFID) decreased its overall assistance to the country from £3.1 million in 1999 to £907,000 in 2003 (DFID 2004), and aid from the Canadian International Development Agency (CIDA) also declined between 1999 and 2003 (CIDA 2005). When the king spent roughly the same amount on his 2005 birthday bash as the United Kingdom gives the country, DFID officials were not pleased (*Sunday Telegraph*, February 20, 2005). One multilateral donor official conceded: "There is no question that unfavourable reports about the country are making Swaziland a harder sell" (*InterPress Service*, April 6, 2004). Neopatrimonialism appears to have had a negative impact on the country's AIDS efforts.

In comparison to Uganda and Zimbabwe, Swaziland has high state capacity (see Table 2.1). I hypothesized that states with high capacity would have high API scores, but this is not true of Swaziland. It seems that despite the country's relative economic resources, at least one-third of the graduating nursing students left the country in 2003 for more lucrative jobs abroad (*UN Integrated Regional Information Networks*, April 2, 2004; CIA 2004). This lack of health care personnel further harms the AIDS fight. And, as previously asserted, because of corruption and the monarch's rule, Swaziland has not been as successful as Uganda in attracting donor funds to meet some of its resource gaps.

I acknowledge that in terms of its political system, geographical size, and high HIV prevalence rate, Swaziland is relatively unique. However, Botswana is also small in population (1.6 million people) and has a 37 percent prevalence rate, yet, as Table 2.2 reveals, it has an API total score of eighty, twenty points above Swaziland's (USAID et al. 2003, 21). In Botswana, government officials have prioritized AIDS, have gained the trust of donors, and have sought to send coherent messages about the disease. While Botswana has low centralization (with voice-and-accountability and rule-of-law scores near seventy), highly centralized Uganda also has made huge efforts to fight AIDS. Although Uganda's attention to AIDS reflects donor resources and the president's framing AIDS as a security issue, it also demonstrates that political leaders in centralized, neopatrimonial states like Swaziland can shape AIDS policies *if they so choose*. Despite Swaziland's capacity and secure environment, its neopatrimonialism and power centralization in a traditional leader whose private actions the public interprets as downplaying the AIDS risk have constrained its response to the epidemic.

### Zimbabwe: Confirming the Hypotheses

Although not as dire as Botswana's or Swaziland's, Zimbabwe's AIDS situation is a crisis. In 2003, Zimbabwe's HIV rate was estimated to be 24.6 percent (UNAIDS 2004b, 191). One in five Zimbabwean children is now an orphan and one hundred HIV-positive infants are born each day (UNICEF 2005b). However, in late 2005, UNAIDS announced that Zimbabwe's HIV rate declined to 21 percent between 2000 and 2004 (UNAIDS 2005b, 43–44). The decline was attributed to several factors: a rising adult mortality rate from the mid-1990s, a substantial increase in condom use with non-regular partners, and a reduction in the rate of sexual partner change (i.e., an increase in faithfulness). Zimbabwe raises an important point: in the short run, state efforts (as measured by the API score) may have little relation to HIV prevalence. While the hope is that state policies will lead to a decline in prevalence over time, my goal is not to analyze that potential relationship.

Zimbabwe's initial reaction to AIDS was similar to that of many other African states. Throughout the 1990s, the government ignored the disease, with funding actually declining for AIDS prevention. The president did not speak publicly about AIDS until 1999, when he acknowledged that the disease was a national epidemic (Batsell 2005, 63–69). Table 2.2 shows Zimbabwe's API scores. The seventy-nine in policy and planning reflects the country's national strategy and its development of a revenue source for AIDS programs. In 1999, the government established the National AIDS Trust Fund, which comes from a 3 percent levy on all individual and corporate taxable income. By 2002, the "AIDS levy" had raised $42 million (UNDP 2003b, 130). In terms of organizational structure, Zimbabwe set up the Zimbabwe National AIDS Council (ZNAC) in 2000 to oversee subnational AIDS committees and allocate funding (Hatendi et al. 2005, 10–13). Although the AIDS policymaking and implementation structure for HIV/AIDS is decentralized, the central government tends to control these institutions. Centralized control and an overall environment of repression contribute to low API scores in organizational structure and human rights. Zimbabwe confirms my four hypotheses: high state centralization, high neopatrimonialism, low capacity, and low stability correlate with a low API score.

Although both Zimbabwe and Swaziland are highly centralized, the World Bank (2005b) and Freedom House (2005b) indicate that Zimbabwe is even more centralized and repressive than Swaziland. When President Robert Mugabe's Zimbabwe African National Union-Patriotic Front (ZANU-PF) came to power in 1980 after a protracted guerrilla campaign and negotiations with Ian Smith's white government, citizens, scholars, and international observers were optimistic about the country's future. Mugabe appeared willing to build a multiracial democracy, to invest in education, and to foster "growth with equity" (Maclean 2002). Yet over the past twenty-five years, Mugabe has come to epitomize the stereotype of an African personal ruler: arbitrary, repressive, and solely concerned about his political survival. Scholars describe Mugabe as quick to detect enemies (a skill that has enabled him to survive), introverted, studious, petulant, ambitious, spiteful, uncompromising, and unconcerned about the victims of his repression (Norman 2004, 165; Power 2003b; Legum 2001; Kriger 2003). Mugabe is "deeply ideological, convinced of his own call to lead the nation" in what he sees as Zimbabwe's ongoing revolution. Because the current revolution casts aside liberation through democratic processes, his regime has turned on citizens, particularly urban and educated individuals (Ranger 2002).

Since Mugabe distrusts others, power is concentrated in the president and his close advisors. Although elements of power centralization have existed since independence, they increased dramatically after the 2000 constitutional referendum, when voters defeated Mugabe's proposals to formally increase presidential power and to seize white-owned land if Britain did not compensate white farmers. The regime's narrow defeat emboldened the opposition Movement for Democratic Change (MDC), formed in 1999 and headed by former Zimbabwe Congress of Trade Unions President Morgan Tsvangirai (Russell 2000, 311–312). In the 2000 legislative elections, the MDC won nearly half of the seats, despite widespread gerrymandering, campaign violence, and numerous polling irregularities.

In response to what Mugabe terms the MDC "traitors of the revolution," the regime increased control over the media, civil society, white-owned land, and the legislature. In 2000, parliament passed the Posts and Telecommunications Act, which permits the government to monitor and intercept the email correspondence of private citizens. The president authorized the expulsion of foreign journalists and he condoned the destruction of Zimbabwe's independent *Daily News* in 2001 (Media Monitoring Project Zimbabwe 2003). In 2002, the ZANU-PF–dominated legislature passed the Access to Information and Protection of Privacy Act and the Broadcasting Services Act, both of which heighten government control of media through registration requirements. It then supported the Public Order and Security Act of 2002 that restricts freedom of assembly, movement, and expression. The Presidential Powers Act of 2002 increased the president's legislative powers and denied the courts jurisdiction in several cases (Privacy International 2003; Freedom House 2004; *BBC News*, July 16, 2002). To ensure that future elections would not be competitive, parliament passed the Electoral Act of 2002, effectively disenfranchising hundreds of thousands of Zimbabweans living abroad and banning foreign funding for voter education (TroCaire 2004). The police arrested Tsvangirai several times before the 2002 presidential election, and in February 2003, he was sent to jail on charges of plotting to kill the president. He was acquitted in October 2004 (*Herald*, October 19, 2004). In the same year, the parliament passed a bill to prohibit local NGOs from receiving foreign funding for governance or human rights activities. Although Mugabe eventually did not sign the legislation, rural district councils began implementing the law to the detriment of local NGOs (Bureau of Democracy 2004; *Mail & Guardian*, June 28, 2005).

In an action with long-term economic consequences, the regime unilaterally changed the constitution to allow the takeover of white-owned land after this provision had failed in the 2000 referendum. The change enabled the government to redistribute white-owned land to black citizens. ZANU-PF paid war veterans, and the youth they mobilized, to invade farms, and the police and army provided support for these efforts. The land grabs turned violent, with most of the victims being poor, rural black Zimbabweans. Those targeted often were affiliated with the MDC, while those gaining land tended to be ZANU-PF party leaders. Court orders to end the land invasions and the forcible removal of owners were ignored. The program contributed to a decline in food production and an increase in hunger (Human Rights Watch 2002, 20; Kriger 2003, 309).

The 2005 legislative elections provide further evidence of state centralization. MDC officials were barely allowed in rural areas, the stronghold of ZANU-PF; intimidation, a lack of independent media coverage, and ZANU-PF threats to withhold food from communities that supported the MDC characterized the election (*News VOA.com*, April 11, 2005; *Mail & Guardian*, April 7, 2005; *Mail & Guardian*, April 12, 2005). After the elections, the government punished MDC supporters by detaining, arresting, and evicting urban residents; over one million people were forced from their homes and entire neighborhoods were razed (*New York Times*, June 2, 2005, p. A4). This number adds to the estimated 100,000 Zimbabweans who were internally displaced in 2003 (US Committee for Refugees 2004). In the November 2005 elections for a newly formed senate, the MDC divided over participation in the election. The division, which some argue ZANU-PF infiltrators helped to foment, greatly weakened the MDC (*New York Times*, December 29, 2005; *BBC News*, November 28, 2005).

State centralization has had three effects on the AIDS fight. The first, and most immediate, has been that HIV-positive people displaced by the urban demolitions after the May 2005 elections have been cut off from ARV treatment. Many have been forced to return to rural areas, where ZANU-PF dominates and where there are few treatment centers. In late 2005, human rights workers estimated that hundreds of Zimbabweans receiving ARVs in Harare would die (*Kaiser Daily HIV/AIDS Report*, September 13, 2005; *Chicago Tribune*, November 7, 2005). Second, state centralization has curtailed the political space in which AIDS groups can participate in policymaking and implementation. Laws against freedom of assembly and state control of the media make it more difficult to mobilize citizens for AIDS protests or to educate citizens about AIDS policies. Broadly interpreted, such laws also can hinder meetings and communication between group leaders and members. Sarah Michael (2004, 63) quotes one Zimbabwe NGO official to explain how these limits, as well as state repression, create a culture of fear: "We are constantly followed. . . . We are dealing with a very powerful system . . . And they have tried to infiltrate [our NGO]." As the case of the Zimbabwe National Network for Positive People (ZNNP+) in Chapter 4 illustrates, the state has co-opted organizations that may threaten it or charged their leaders with corruption.

Third, centralization of power in the presidency means that citizens wanting to advance AIDS policies through institutions beyond the executive have few opportunities to do so. The president and his supporters control executive agencies including ZNAC, which has low civil society participation (Batsell 2005, 63–64). (As Chapter 3 demonstrates, this low civil society representation is also evident on Zimbabwe's GFATM-mandated country coordinating mechanism.) In 2004, stakeholders reported that ZNAC was too reliant on the views of senior government officials and did not act independently. Because the president chairs ZNAC and appoints its members, the council is viewed as an extension of the presidency. At the provincial, district, and village levels, AIDS council members have been perceived as aligned with the ruling party (Hatendi et al. 2005, 32–33). These problems are reflected in the country's low organizational structure API score.

Zimbabwe's high neopatrimonialism appears to have affected the state's AIDS efforts. Many AIDS activists assert that the state has diverted resources from health to patronage in order to maintain the support of key societal groups. For example, before the 2002 presidential election, the government allegedly diverted funds from the district AIDS committees to the ZANU-PF–dominated district councils for patronage. Some journalists also report that ARVs have been used as patronage: government purchases of ARVs immediately after the 2002 election allowed ZANU-PF to reward its supporters (Batsell 2005, 65). These allegations have caused people to question ARV treatment programs, which have tended to be situated in Harare and Bulawayo, two MDC strongholds. Patients in Bulawayo were promised free treatment, only to start the government program and then be told they must pay Z$50,000 per month (*ZimOnline*, September 25, 2004; *New York Times*, March 28, 2005).[11] In early 2005, the government started its first rural treatment program, causing some to speculate about the motivation for the program (*Boston Globe,* May 3, 2005). While it is impossible to prove that the government is using, or is planning to use, ARV access as a political tool, Randy Cheek (2001, 24) argues that such manipulation of health benefits is not out of the question. Although HIV prevalence is highest among the minority Ndebele people in Zimbabwe's south, government health spending is highest in the north (UNAIDS 2004c, 5). If the Zimbabwean regime allegedly used food as a political tool in the May 2005 election, it seems possible that it could use access to ARVs for the same purpose. Rationing of ARVs is already occurring throughout Africa, by NGO officials who decide about treatment program participants or by government officials who allocate resources for drugs or clinics (de Waal 2003b, 19). What makes rationing dangerous in Zimbabwe is that such decisions are more likely to be made by a ruler who has centralized power and crushed his opponents than by accountable politicians and civil society.

Zimbabwe's low state capacity also shapes its low API score. In 2005, the country faced annual inflation rates over 600 percent, 70 percent of the population lived below the poverty line, over seven million people needed humanitarian assistance, and life expectancy had dropped from sixty-one years in 1990 to thirty-four years in 2002 (USAID 2005c). The country's human development index (HDI), a broad measure of state investment in education and health, dropped from .640 in 1985 to .505 in 2003 (UNDP 2005, 225).[12] Because the country's economy is in shambles, resources for HIV/AIDS are practically nonexistent (Hatendi et al. 2005, 53). For example, only 6,500 individuals received ARV treatment in 2004 (UNAIDS 2005f). While this increased to 16,000 in December 2005, the number was still only 5 percent of Zimbabweans needing the drugs. The country's lack of foreign exchange has prevented a local producer from importing drug components, and doctors are leery of starting patients on ARVs if the supply is inconsistent (*Los Angeles Times*, December 25, 2005).

Unlike Uganda, which has turned to donors to fill its resource gaps, Zimbabwe's high centralization and high neopatrimonialism have caused bilateral and multilateral donors to decrease official development assistance from a high of $792 million in 1992 to $186 million in 2003 (World Bank 2005d, 352). While money from DFID has increased, those resources, like USAID funding, have been entirely channeled to NGOs. UNICEF (2005b) noted that in 2004–2005 the country received little to no HIV/AIDS funding from the three main donor initiatives: the World Bank Multi-Country AIDS Program (MAP), the GFATM, and PEPFAR. In southern Africa, the average annual donor spending per HIV-infected person among the three initiatives is $74; in Zimbabwe, it is $4.[13] The most striking example of this global ostracism was the GFATM's 2005 decision to deny Zimbabwe's $218 million grant application for an ARV program. In 2002, the country received a $10 million grant, although negotiations over its dispersal meant the money was not released until the spring of 2005 (*Boston Globe*, May 3, 2005). GFATM Executive Director Richard Feacham explained the 2005 decision: "The politics of a nation plays a role when we determine the country's application. . . . It does not help the people of Zimbabwe to pass money through channels which are not well worked out." In response, President Mugabe said donors are "heartless" oppressors, intent on destroying his country (*Newzimbabwe.com*, June 14, 2005).

Finally, although in 2006 the state did not face an internal rebellion like Uganda, Table 2.1 shows that it is extremely volatile. This instability is partly a reflection of state centralization and repression, as seen with the 2005 slum-razing activities. But, it also reflects the long-term outcomes of Zimbabwe's involvement in the war of the Democratic Republic of Congo (DRC) from 1998 to 2001. Explanations for this involvement vary. Sandra Maclean (2002) maintains that the war provided opportunities to win over potential opponents, ZANU-PF advisors, and military officers with lucrative mineral contracts in the DRC. Martin Rupiya (2002) asserts that Zimbabwe intervened for security reasons: Uganda and Rwanda had explicit designs on the DRC, which would disrupt the region's power balance. Whatever the reason, Zimbabwe spent over $500 million to deploy 16,000 troops, necessitating that health and education budgets be cut. Because the war was deeply unpopular, it helped to fuel the emergence of the MDC and its success in the 2000 election (Rupiya 2002). As we have seen, Mugabe reacted to the MDC's formation with increased repression, which has further contributed to political instability and diverted state resources from AIDS. While impossible to prove, concern for state survival probably has made AIDS less of a priority than it might be in a more stable country. And, unlike Museveni, Mugabe appears to not view AIDS as a security issue that requires resources to adequately address. As such, Zimbabwe affirms the hypothesis that unstable countries will have low API scores.

The nature of the state in Zimbabwe directly shapes the country's response to HIV/AIDS. State centralization has created a precarious environment for AIDS NGOs and has limited the independence of government AIDS structures. Neopatrimonialism has allegedly fostered corruption in the AIDS levy and driven away donors. Low state capacity (and limited donor assistance) means the state cannot address AIDS. The country's lack of stability appears to have caused the government to downplay AIDS over concerns about immediate political survival.

## Is the Role of Personal Leadership Key?

The four case studies highlighted here demonstrate the inconsistent effect of each state characteristic for AIDS efforts. High state centralization and neopatrimonialism harm AIDS policymaking in Zimbabwe and Swaziland, but not in Uganda. High state capacity helps South Africa, but low state capacity does not seem to matter for efforts in Uganda. Low state stability facilitated the initial Ugandan AIDS efforts, but it has curtailed them in Zimbabwe. And, despite South Africa's low centralization, low neopatrimonialism, high state capacity, and (relative) stability, the country has basically the same API score as Uganda, which does not have those state characteristics.

Clearly the four aspects of the state examined in this chapter are interrelated. Because of this, it is impossible to say that one element—state centralization or stability, for example—is the most important driver of AIDS efforts in a particular country. Similarly, state aspects shape the impact of donors and civil society on AIDS efforts. It also seems probable that the importance of factors changes with time. For example, while security concerns pushed Uganda to address AIDS in 1986, they may be less important today. While neopatrimonialism may not have hindered Zimbabwe's AIDS efforts in the late 1990s—as recently as 1998, the World Bank (2005b) gave Zimbabwe a score near sixty for corruption—by 2002, cronyism and patronage politics harmed AIDS efforts.

In one sense, it appears that the deciding factor for AIDS efforts in these four countries is personal leadership. President Museveni's public, forthright statements on AIDS contributed to Uganda's efforts. In South Africa, the personal views of President Mbeki have meant that AIDS policies have been confusing. King Mswati contradicts the efforts of the country's AIDS institutions with his personal behavior. President Mugabe's repression, neopatrimonialism, and concern for political survival have detracted from its AIDS programs.

However, to base all the explanation for a country's AIDS score on its "big man" is somewhat reductionist. In Uganda, the resistance councils and civil society also played a role. While President Mbeki has tried to control AIDS policymaking, the country's high API score reflects how South Africa's low state centralization has enabled subnational institutions and the judiciary to challenge national AIDS policies. Even in highly centralized countries such as Zimbabwe and Swaziland, rulers alone have not caused the low AIDS response. Leaders can get away with poor responses to AIDS because of a lack of institutions to check their power, a culture of neopatrimonialism, and, in Zimbabwe, an overall environment of instability. State officials shape political context, but they also can be constrained by it. For example, Mugabe works within the context of ZANU-PF, and actions such as the land reform fiasco illustrate his need to appease party members through patronage resources.

These four countries have felt the brunt of the pandemic's magnitude. But the large scale of the problem has led to different levels of institutionalization of the AIDS fight. While Uganda acted in 1986, Zimbabwe and Swaziland did not develop national AIDS coordinating bodies until over ten years after their first AIDS cases appeared. Similarly, the inequality that runs throughout these cases has made it harder to entrench the AIDS fight in politics and to give all political actors a stake in AIDS policies. In Swaziland, there are limited voices in the AIDS debate; in Zimbabwe, AIDS groups, like other civil society organizations, have been driven from the policy realm through repression. The alleged corruption in the AIDS levy and the unequal distribution of ARVs in Zimbabwe raise questions about how that government distributes the public goods of AIDS programs. In contrast, because Ugandan women have been essential for the NRM's power, they have participated in decisionmaking and they have been a large focus of the country's AIDS programs. President Mbeki's rhetoric on racial inequality has had the inadvertent effect of tainting the AIDS stigma with racist imagery. Rather than foster participation, though, this imagery may weaken those with the disease and drive them from public participation. As such, this ostracism limits their stake in what the state does to address AIDS.

Finally, this chapter illustrates that political institutions affect AIDS policies, though not always in the ways one would expect. High state centralization has prevented AIDS efforts in Zimbabwe and Swaziland, but not in Uganda. Low capacity has harmed Zimbabwe's efforts, but not Uganda's. South Africa's high capacity and low centralization cause AIDS activists and scholars to think it should do better. As the next chapter illustrates, democratic institutions provide some avenues for shaping state AIDS policies, though, as Uganda shows, democracy is not a necessary and sufficient condition for state efforts to fight AIDS. Because state institutions have uneven effects, it is unclear that they have helped to entrench the AIDS issue into political life.

## Notes

1. I realize that my classification places Swaziland and South Africa in the same "high capacity" category, which may overestimate Swaziland's ability

to fight AIDS. However, because Swaziland is closer to South Africa than it is to Zimbabwe and Uganda in other measures of capacity such as number of phones, number of doctors, and public spending on education, and because I want to maintain parsimony in my classifications, I place Swaziland in the "high capacity" category (UNDP 2005).

2. In terms of the four state characteristics, Rwanda's scores are centralization (18.9 voice and accountability; 21.3 rule of law); neopatrimonialism (corruption 44.3); security (political stability 18.9); and state capacity ($220 GNI per capita) (World Bank 2005b, 2005c).

3. Women's involvement in the economy and politics may be a necessary, but not sufficient, condition for their ability to negotiate safer sex. In South Africa, for example, women have achieved much politically and economically (e.g., they are over one-third of the national ministers), but many women have been unable to protect themselves from HIV infection.

4. The Gini coefficient measures a country's income distribution on a scale of zero to one, with zero being the most equal and one being the most unequal.

5. As of early 2006, roughly one-third of the cabinet ministers had studied in a socialist country or the Soviet Union during the exile period. For example, Health Minister Tshabalala-Msimang studied medicine in the Soviet Union from 1962 to 1969. The biographies for government officials are available at http://www.gcis.gov.za/gcis/directory.jsp?dir=4&heading=Profiles.

6. In 2000 Glaxo Wellcome merged with SmithKline Beecham to become GlaxoSmithKline.

7. One dose of nevirapine is given to the mother during labor and one dose is given to the infant after birth to prevent the transmission of HIV from mother to child.

8. Anonymous representative of bilateral donor organization, interview with author, Washington, DC, April 1, 2005.

9. It is notable that Kader Asmal was not given a cabinet position after the 2004 election, and although there was speculation that Manne Dipico, former premier of Northern Cape and ANC elections chief who pushed for the ARV rollout would be given a cabinet position, he was not (*Sunday Times*, February 1, 2004).

10. Anonymous representative of bilateral donor organization, April 1, 2005.

11. Because of inflation, the exchange rate between the US dollar and Zimbabwean dollar fluctuates widely. In September 2004, this amount was $8.90; by February 2006, it was $.51. See http://www.oanda.com/convert/classic.

12. The Human Development Index measures the average achievements in a country in three areas: health (life expectancy at birth), education (adult literacy rate and school enrollment ratio), and standard of living (GDP per capita). The measure is on a scale of zero to one, with one indicating the highest level of human development.

13. Table 5.1 shows that Zimbabwe receives $18 per HIV-positive person. The reason for the higher number is that USAID money is included in the calculations for Chapter 5.

# 3

## Democratic Transitions: A New Opportunity to Fight AIDS?

OVER THE PAST thirty years, there has been a general trend toward freedom and democracy in sub-Saharan Africa. In 1972, Freedom House (2005b) classified two countries as free, nine as partly free, and twenty-eight as not free. By 2004, there were eleven free countries, twenty-two partly free countries, and fifteen not free.[1] Competitive electoral arenas have replaced one-party states; opposition parties have gained control of governments in Ghana, Senegal, Zambia, and Kenya. Although there is great variation in the continent's democratic experiences, many societies have become more open, with fewer constraints on civil society organizations and the media. Amartya Sen (2001, 8) asserts that one of democracy's greatest assets is its power to protect the well-being of its citizens. Democratically elected leaders are more likely than dictators to invest in public goods to benefit a wide range of supporters. They are less likely than authoritarian regimes to use state resources for the benefit of small groups. The sanction of the ballot box encourages democratically elected leaders to address major societal problems. Open, democratic societies also have checks on government, through free media, opposition parties, and civil society organizations. Thomas Zweifel and Patricio Navia (2000) confirm the theoretical link between democracy and citizens' overall health: democracies tend to have infant mortality rates 10 percent lower than nondemocracies. Life expectancy is roughly five years higher in democracies than it is in comparable nondemocracies (Przeworski et al. 2000). These health benefits derive primarily from higher government spending on health in democratic political systems (Ghobarah et al. 2004).

This chapter does not dispute these aggregate, cross-national findings. Instead, I investigate how these trends apply *particularly* to

Africa's new democracies and *specifically* to AIDS. I define Africa's new democracies as those countries that Freedom House (2005a) ranked as free in 2004.[2] The eleven countries were Cape Verde, Mauritius, South Africa, Benin, Botswana, Ghana, Mali, Sao Tome and Principe, Lesotho, Namibia, and Senegal. Of these eleven, Cape Verde, Botswana, Mauritius, and Namibia were classified as free in 1990. I also pay some attention to countries such as Kenya and Malawi, which moved from Freedom House's not free category to its partly free category between 1990 and 2004. This chapter places government actions on AIDS in the context of the continent's democratic changes. I argue that despite the emergence of democratic institutions, the influence of democracy on AIDS policymaking across the continent is tentative at best. In many countries, public opinion has yet to prioritize AIDS. Elections have not served to hold governments accountable for AIDS policies, though in a few democratic countries with recent elections, politicians have begun to discuss AIDS in their campaigns. Because new democratic institutions are underdeveloped, they provide limited avenues for representation and accountability. Even for institutions formed specifically to make AIDS policies, the impact of democracy on the nature of representation on those institutions is uneven. And although spending on health is generally higher in African democracies than nondemocracies, this relationship is not statistically significant. Emmanuel Gyimah-Boadi (2004a, 19) sums up this inconclusive relationship between African democracy and AIDS:

> At the very least, the HIV/AIDS pandemic highlights the weak quality of governance in Africa, including in its democratizing nations: the persistence of a culture of nontransparency, weak political responsiveness and accountability, and misplaced priorities. The AIDS crisis underscores the fact that democratic politics has not sufficiently translated into enhanced transparency in certain areas of African life such as death.

This chapter examines five assumptions embedded in the idea that democracies promote health, and it applies these assumptions to AIDS: (1) citizens want government to prioritize AIDS; (2) citizens, primarily through civil society, mobilize to affect government policies on AIDS; (3) government responds to public concerns about AIDS because it fears electoral repercussions; (4) democratic institutions provide avenues for participating in AIDS policy development; (5) governments respond to public concern about AIDS and political pressures by providing financial resources to combat the disease through increasing state spending on health. Several of these assumptions are interrelated. For example, public concern about AIDS may encourage the formation of AIDS advocacy groups; citizen demands may cause government to prioritize AIDS spending. To simplify the analysis, I have disaggregated the assumptions and I have left the examination of civil society till the next chapter.

To be clear, the relationship between AIDS and democracy is not unidirectional. Though this chapter focuses on how democracy shapes Africa's ability to address AIDS, it is important to acknowledge that AIDS can affect democracy too. Voters with AIDS may be too sick to participate in elections or, as the next chapter illustrates, to join civil society organizations that advocate for AIDS policies. A 2004 study found that voter rolls before the 2004 South African election were bloated with names of individuals who had died of AIDS and that party organizations in some of that country's provinces suffered a loss of campaign personnel from AIDS (Chirambo and Caesar 2004). As the next section asserts, the AIDS stigma, and the time lag between HIV infection and the onset of AIDS, also may prevent citizens from viewing the disease as a political issue.

## Citizen Demands for State Actions on AIDS

In a democracy, the relationship between public opinion and government policy is often indirect. Most often, public opinion provides a broad constraint on government actions, rather than a means of forcing government to address specific policy issues (Weissberg 1976, 242; Page and Shapiro 1983). For public opinion to play this role, citizens must have opinions on a topic. Yet, unique aspects of HIV/AIDS complicate the emergence of the disease as a salient public issue. Because the period between HIV infection and the development of AIDS is between six and eight years in sub-Saharan Africa, citizens perceive the disease as a distant or hypothetical threat (Barnett and Whiteside 2002, 33). This fact has been particularly true in West Africa where the epidemic is in its beginning stages and HIV prevalence is low. For example, in Ghana, where 3.1 percent of citizens are HIV positive, perception of risk is low. Joseph Oppong and Samuel Agyei-Mensah (2004, 78) write that while over 90 percent of Ghanaians know about HIV/AIDS, over 70 percent do not consider themselves or their families to be at risk of infection: "People seemed to perceive AIDS as a problem that affected 'other people.'"

The perception that "others" get AIDS makes mobilizing public attention to the disease problematic. HIV/AIDS has been associated with behaviors that societies tend to stigmatize. As Karen Booth (2004, 99) illustrates, the perception that most people living with HIV/AIDS are prostitutes, homosexuals, deviants, or promiscuous individuals is a simplistic, but powerful, paradigm that has led international actors to develop "one-size-fits-all" models for AIDS programs. Additionally, the assumption that women who get HIV/AIDS are prostitutes "helps to reinforce the fiction that some people . . . are immune and do not need to change their behaviors, talk about this disease, or join in efforts to improve conditions for people with HIV." This sense of false immunity causes AIDS to be a low priority for many individuals. The result is low public pressure for government to address the disease.

The immediate concerns of poverty, hunger, and employment also push AIDS off the public agenda. Poverty in Africa has worsened, with the number of people living on less than $1 per day increasing from 291 million in 1998 to 314 million in 2001 (World Bank 2001b, 23; Africa: Learning to Survive 2004). In 2001, 32 percent of the population in sub-Saharan Africa was undernourished (UNDP 2003a, 202). Ann Waweru, director of the Voluntary Women's Rehabilitation Center that helps sex workers in Nairobi find alternative employment, says: "The women I work with say they'd rather die of AIDS tomorrow than die of hunger today" (*Village Voice*, December 1–7, 1999). Poverty and AIDS are tied into a vicious cycle. Poverty causes citizens to be most concerned about current needs and to engage in behaviors that may put them at risk for HIV infection. HIV infection, and then AIDS, increases individual and household poverty (Whiteside 2002). Poverty's oppressive and immediate nature makes AIDS a low public priority. A 2004 survey conducted in fifteen sub-Saharan African countries illustrates this point. Respondents were asked to name up to three issues that they thought were the most important problems their country faced. Across all fifteen countries, only 11 percent named AIDS as one of the top three concerns. The highest levels were in Botswana (30%), Namibia (28%), and South Africa (26%); the lowest were in Senegal (1%), Ghana (3%), and Malawi (3%) (Afrobarometer 2004, 4).

While these low numbers in Ghana and Senegal may reflect low HIV prevalence rates in those two countries (3.1% and 0.8%, respectively), indifference in Malawi is more complicated. In 2003, UNAIDS estimated that the country's HIV prevalence rate for people between fifteen and forty-nine years old was 14.2 percent; over 700,000 of the country's eleven million citizens are infected with HIV. Because of AIDS, Malawi has experienced a decline in life expectancy from fifty-nine years to thirty-seven years and a rise in infant mortality rates (Garbus 2003, 7;

UNAIDS 2004b, 191–193). One might expect AIDS to be a low priority in Malawi if the disease had not personally affected people. However, of the fifteen countries surveyed, Malawi has the highest percentage of citizens who report feeling a direct burden from AIDS. Forty-three percent of Malawians say they care for someone with AIDS, 25 percent say they care for an AIDS orphan, and 57 percent report losing a friend or relative to the disease (Afrobarometer 2004, 4).

What is striking about the data from the Afrobarometer survey is that the magnitude of the pandemic has not meant the disease is on the public agenda. Even though people are dying and those left behind have directly felt the effects of the disease, there is limited public demand for government actions. In Uganda, 85 percent of those surveyed say they have lost a friend or relative to AIDS; among those who say they have lost someone, the average Ugandan has lost five close relatives or friends, more than in any other country surveyed. (In Kenya, Zambia, Tanzania, and Namibia, the average was three.) Yet, only 7 percent of Ugandans say that AIDS should be one of the government's top three priorities. A similar situation exists in Zambia, where 74 percent of those surveyed have lost a friend or relative to the disease, but only 3 percent say that AIDS should be a top priority (Afrobarometer 2004, 1, 7). It is striking that in many African countries, the magnitude of the pandemic has been insufficient to push AIDS to the public agenda.

These attitudes about AIDS reflect the impact of poverty on the continent's policy agenda. Across the fifteen countries, individuals living in poverty were less likely to prioritize AIDS. The same was true at the aggregate level: the poorer a country was, the less likely its population was to prioritize AIDS (Afrobarometer 2004, 5). For example, Malawi is one of the poorest countries in the world; 28.8 percent of the population lives in "dire poverty," and 65.3 percent lives below the national poverty line (Malawi 2002, 10). Its GNI per capita was $160 in 2003, well below the $500 average for sub-Saharan Africa (UNDP 2004, 11). It also has one of the highest rates of malaria in the world, with eight million citizens suffering from the disease each year. Malawians face immediate problems that push AIDS out of the public arena. Malawians, like other Africans who do not prioritize AIDS, also may not expect their government to be able to address AIDS given its lack of resources and its past failures to provide socioeconomic development.

Despite these obstacles, issues can get on the public agenda if political leaders or the media call attention to them (Bardes and Oldendick 2000, 94). Senegal's proactive AIDS education programs have had this impact on public perceptions about the disease, although not on citizens' opinions that AIDS should be a major government priority. Despite the country's low HIV prevalence rate of approximately 1 percent, many Senegalese feel personally at risk for contracting HIV. Among all African women, those in Senegal are the most likely to report feeling this risk. The government's effective AIDS education campaign is one large reason for this perception (Green 2003a, 11). Similarly, the relatively high level of public saliency of AIDS in Botswana may reflect not only the country's 37.3 percent HIV prevalence rate, but also the public attention President Festus Mogae has given to the disease. In South Africa, where roughly 21.5 percent of the population is HIV positive, AIDS also has received political attention. As the previous chapter highlighted, in 2000 President Thabo Mbeki questioned the link between HIV and AIDS. The ensuing controversy led to heightened media coverage, and for better or worse, AIDS was on the public agenda. Additionally, former President Nelson Mandela, who had an 82 percent approval rating in 2004, has challenged the AIDS stigma by disclosing AIDS deaths in his family and traveling globally to call attention to the pandemic (*Washington Post* et al. 2004, 3; *Kaiser Daily HIV/AIDS Report*, January 14, 2005). As the next chapter illustrates, the actions of South African organizations such as TAC also made citizens more aware of AIDS.

Unlike in Senegal, Botswana, and South Africa, AIDS has received limited government attention in Malawi, something that also may contribute to the public's low level of concern. Since 1994, Malawi has undergone widespread political transformation. From 1966 to 1994, Dr. Hastings Kamuzu Banda and his Malawi Congress Party ruled the country as an official one-party state. Human rights abuses were common, and the ruling party's paramilitary wing maintained order through harassment and repression. Freedom House classified the country as not free as recently as 1993 (Freedom House 2005b). Even though the first AIDS case appeared in 1985, "very little interest was taken by the Kamuzu Banda regime to call a spade a spade and to address the issue. Despite the fact that the leadership [was] comprised of well qualified medical practitioners, the scope of the pandemic remained a closely guarded secret" (AIDS activist, editorial in *Chronicle*, April 26, 2004). Under the auspices of the GPA, Banda established a National AIDS Control Program within the ministry of health in 1989. It sought to promote AIDS awareness, but did not reach across economic sectors or work with community organizations. It had a limited effect.

Until the 2004 election, government actions on AIDS in Malawi remained within the realm of bureaucratic and technical discussions, rather than high-level, public debates like those in South Africa or Botswana. In 1999, five years after Bakili Muluzi and his United Democratic Front ousted President Banda in elections, Muluzi named AIDS a national emergency. With the help of the World Bank MAP initiative, the government redesigned AIDS policymaking structures and developed a National Strategic Framework for AIDS (Garbus 2003, 8). Despite these activities, AIDS remained on the backburner of the public agenda. This situation has not been unique to Malawi. One representative from a bilateral donor organization in Ghana said that he wanted HIV/AIDS to become "one of the big things that every political organization talks about in their bid to win power in Ghana" (Patterson and Haven 2005, 92–93). Maybe then more than 3 percent of Ghanaians will prioritize the disease.

Government actions and public beliefs about AIDS are intricately linked. Most Africans do not see AIDS as the most pressing problem their countries face. As a result, political actors face little pressure on the issue. In some countries such as Senegal, government has proactively addressed AIDS without public pressure. Yet, if government does not respond to AIDS and public opinion does not encourage it to do so, African citizens may continue to perceive AIDS to be just one of many societal problems, and a distant problem at best. Low public saliency on AIDS may enable governments to do the minimum to fight AIDS; government's inaction may fuel low public concern about the disease.

## Electoral Ramifications for Government Policies on AIDS

The relation between AIDS policymaking and elections in Africa's newly democratic systems is tenuous. We have already seen that citizens in many African countries have yet to prioritize AIDS. This low public salience means that AIDS often has not been discussed as a campaign issue in African elections. Kenya's historic 2002 elections exemplify how parties have paid limited attention to AIDS. The elections overthrew the Kenya African National Union, which had controlled the country for over forty years. During the height of the campaign, officials from the UN Children's Fund (UNICEF) called for candidates to prioritize AIDS: "Kenya's elections provide a timely opportunity for the sensitization and mobilization of the country's future leadership to address the issue" (*East African Standard*, November 29, 2002). Yet, when one of the largest NGOs in the country, the Kenya Coalition on Access to Essential Medicines, organized a televised debate for five presidential candidates on World AIDS Day, no candidate showed up. Although the five had confirmed their participation, they provided no comments about why they did not appear. The *Nation* (December 1, 2002) wrote: "They declined an opportunity to publicly air their views on an issue that touches each and every Kenyan, a condition which directly afflicts probably up to 1.5 million registered voters."

Uganda's 2001 presidential election illustrates the negative use of AIDS on the campaign trail. While President Yoweri Museveni trumpeted his administration's success in fighting the disease, he and his opponent Dr. Kissa Besigye accused each other of being HIV positive. (Besigye also ran against Museveni in the 2006 election.) The accusations were made more powerful because Besigye had been Museveni's personal physician. Although this negative campaigning did not impact the election's outcome, it may have reinforced the stigma associated with the disease (Ostergard 2002).

An examination of the major newspapers for each of the eleven countries Freedom House ranked as free in 2004 reveals that only politicians in Namibia, South Africa, Ghana, and Botswana discussed AIDS extensively during their most recent election campaigns.[3] As the previous section illustrated, three of these countries—Namibia, Botswana, and South Africa—had the highest percentage of citizens who believed that AIDS should be a government priority. It is impossible to determine if public opinion pushed candidates to discuss AIDS or if candidates' discussions shaped public opinion in those three countries. Of the four countries, the debate in the run-up to the 2004 Ghanaian elections was the most limited. In the official launch of his reelection campaign President John Kufour did not mention AIDS (*Accra Mail*, October 27, 2004). The most attention the president gave AIDS was in a speech on World AIDS Day, less than one week before the election (*Panafrican News Agency*, December 1, 2004). The president's opponent, John Evans Atta Mills, never discussed the disease at a major campaign event.

In comparison, during Botswana's 2004 elections, a group of NGOs criticized the ruling Botswana Democratic Party (BDP) for a campaign billboard that featured a prominent AIDS advocate with the words "Free HIV/AIDS drugs. Vote BDP." Critics claimed the ad implied that BDP supporters would be entitled to free ARVs, and they maintained it "politicized a serious national tragedy." BDP officials responded that the HIV/AIDS struggle is already a political issue. In evidence that some voters had considered AIDS programs in their electoral decisions, the *Kaiser Daily HIV/AIDS Report* (November 2, 2004) said that some voters feared a BDP loss might "undermine" the country's AIDS treatment programs. The reelected President Festus Mogae pledged to continue to fight AIDS in his inauguration speech (*Reuters*, November 2, 2004). Similarly, in Namibia, the opposition National Unity Democratic Organization (NUDO) and the ruling South West Africa People's Organization (SWAPO) made AIDS a topic in their party platforms and publicly discussed the disease. Lukas Hifikepunye Pohamba, the SWAPO presidential candidate, termed HIV/AIDS a "very, very big problem in our country." Yet when Pohamba refused to get an HIV test, some NUDO activists questioned his commitment to fighting AIDS (*InterPress Service*, June 17, 2004; *allAfrica.com*, October 13, 2004). South Africa resembled Namibia and Botswana, in that candidates from the ruling ANC and the opposition Democratic Alliance talked about AIDS on the campaign trail before the April 2004 election (*South African Press Association*, April 14, 2004).

On the other hand, in 2004 AIDS became a topic of discussion in Malawi, a country Freedom House classifies as partly free. As mentioned above, the Malawian government has been slow to develop AIDS policies. It took the government from 2000 until 2004 to develop a national HIV/AIDS policy, two years longer than anticipated. Until 2004, Malawi did not have formal policies on AIDS and travel, prisons, confidentiality, workplace discrimination, or surveillance (*UN Development Program News*, February 24, 2004). AIDS became a campaign issue in 2004 when outgoing President Muluzi acknowledged for the first time that AIDS had affected his family: "We should never be ashamed. . . . I am not ashamed to disclose that my beloved brother, Dickson, died of AIDS" (*Independent*, February 11, 2004). Two weeks before the May 2004 election, the president launched the Bakili Muluzi AIDS Foundation, an action that became politically controversial when it was reported that the foundation received a grant from the National AIDS Commission without going through the standard approval process. A commission official commented, "AIDS is now becoming a political ploy—a means to gain political mileage" (*allAfrica.com*, May 10, 2004). On May 12, the government also unveiled a plan for a five-year, $196 million program financed by the GFATM for free ARVs to HIV-positive people. The opposition said the announcement was politically motivated, since the government announced the program months before its launch date (*Kaiser Daily HIV/AIDS Report*, May 13, 2004). Opposition parties also called attention to AIDS during the campaign. The platforms of all parties included AIDS policy statements, most concerning access to ARVs and the need to mandate AIDS education in schools (*allAfrica.com*, April 26, 2004). On the campaign trail, opposition party leader Brown Mpinganjira spoke of losing six siblings to AIDS (*Guardian,* May 20, 2004).

Heightened political interest in AIDS in Malawi reflects several factors. Although the incumbent United Democratic Front easily won the presidential election, the opposition's legislative gains show the campaign's competitiveness (Elections in Malawi 2004). In power since 1994, the ruling party has been increasingly blamed for the country's debt, poverty, and underdevelopment (*South African Press Association,* April 7, 2004); government attention to AIDS may have helped to address these shortfalls. AIDS activists and some international donors believed partisan concern about AIDS was a way to win votes, not a reflection of political commitment to fighting the disease. Yet, this assessment is simplistic, because even if politicians discuss AIDS to gain votes, they *are* discussing a topic that had previously received little public attention. In contrast, the *Guardian* (May 20, 2004) wrote that the election confirmed that people with AIDS were an emerging force in African politics, and it quoted a DFID advisor: "One can deduce that they [the parties] think there are votes to be had [from discussing AIDS]."

It is impossible to know why politicians in some countries like democratic Botswana, South Africa, and Namibia and partly democratic Malawi discussed AIDS in elections, while candidates in the democracies of Benin, Lesotho, Mali, Cape Verde, and Senegal did not. Part of the reason may be prevalence rates: countries with higher rates (e.g., Botswana, Namibia, and South Africa) may be more likely to have politicians discuss AIDS than countries with lower rates (Mali, Senegal, and Benin). However, prevalence does not explain the lack of discussion in Lesotho (28.9% prevalence) or the presence of debate in Ghana (3.1% prevalence) (UNAIDS 2004b, 191). Part of the explanation may also be timing. Countries in which AIDS became a campaign issue—Ghana, Namibia, Botswana, and South Africa—held elections in 2004. With the exception of Mauritius (2005 election), democracies where AIDS was not a campaign issue had presidential elections in 2000 (Senegal), 2001 (Benin, Cape Verde, and Sao Tome and Principe), and 2002 (Lesotho and Mali). As asserted in Chapter 1, it was only after 2000 that bilateral and multilateral donors began to pay more attention to AIDS and to assert the need for political commitment to the disease. While it is impossible to say that heightened donor concern caused African leaders to speak publicly about AIDS, this rhetorical attention is a relatively recent phenomenon in many countries.

For voters to effectively hold governments accountable for AIDS policies, elections have to be somewhat competitive. Michael Bratton (1999, 23–27) shows that competitiveness declined between Africa's founding multiparty elections in the early 1990s and the second elections in the mid- to late-1990s. If ruling parties face limited electoral challenges, and if they face pressure to meet citizens' immediate needs of food, security, and jobs, there are few political reasons to develop AIDS policies. The foot-dragging, which has exemplified the development of AIDS policies in South Africa, illustrates this point. As the previous chapter showed, because AIDS was just one of many post-apartheid challenges, President Nelson Mandela made limited strides against the disease.[4] And despite increased spending on HIV education, voluntary counseling and testing (VCT) centers, and treatment for sexually transmitted infections (STIs), the Mbeki government has procrastinated on highly salient issues such as access to AIDS medicines (Human Sciences Research Council 2002; South Africa Government 2000). For example, it was only in April 2002 that the government announced that it would offer comprehensive treatment to rape survivors, including VCT and prophylactic treatment (South Africa Government 2000; *allAfrica.com*, October 2, 2003). As part of this policy, however, the cabinet stressed that rape victims must be counseled on the "effectiveness and risks" of HIV preventative drugs, a reflection of Mbeki's continued unease with ARVs (Furlong and Ball 2005, 143). Human Rights Watch (2004, 1) criticized this policy: "There is a deadly disconnect between the government's stated intention to provide drugs that can prevent HIV and the reality for rape survivors who can't get them." As Chapters 2 and 4 argue, this procrastination is also evident in policy development and implementation of PMTCT and universal ARV treatment programs.

As the South African government has dragged its feet on ARV access, the country's elections have become increasingly noncompetitive. These two developments are not related, but the lack of competition removes electoral pressure on the ANC for some of its AIDS policy decisions. In 1999, the ANC increased its share of the vote by 7 percent from 1994, winning 66.35 percent of the ballots and 266 of the 400 legislative seats (Reynolds 1999, 175). In 2004, the ANC won 69.7 percent of the votes cast, while the next most competitive party, the Democratic Alliance, only won 12.4 percent. At the same time, voter turnout has decreased from 90 percent in the 1994 election to roughly 50 percent in 2004 (*Washington Post*, April 16, 2004, p. A12). Citizen distrust of government has increased, with AIDS being one of several issues contributing to this distrust. In a 2003 survey, only 37 percent of South Africans reported trusting the president and only 32 percent of citizens (and 38% of blacks) thought government was more trustworthy in 2003 than it was under apartheid (Mattes et al. 2003, 4, 25). Citizens viewed government to be somewhat unresponsive, especially on AIDS (Cheek 2001). In 2002, only 47 percent of respondents believed that government allocated enough money to AIDS, while roughly 95 percent thought that the government should provide ARVs to all individuals with the disease (Human Sciences Research Council 2002, 91).[5]

Because the ANC has not faced competitive elections, it may have been somewhat immune to public opinion on AIDS, even though 26 percent of South Africans in 2004 said the disease should be a government priority, an increase from 13 percent in 1999 (Giliomee 1999; Afrobarometer 2004, 5). Instead, other factors that may challenge the ANC's long-term future have shaped government actions on AIDS. Overall support for the ANC has declined. The number of South Africans who said they would vote for the ANC fell 12 percent between 2000 and 2002; support among blacks decreased 14 percent (Afrobarometer 2003, 1). For the most part, these individuals have joined the ranks of nonvoters. This decline is coupled with increased criticism from ANC alliance members, the SACP, and the Congress of South African Trade Unions (COSATU) (Cheek 2001; *Independent*, January 5, 2005). If a future challenge to ANC dominance were to occur, it probably would come from a split in the ruling alliance (Butler 2002, 9). Internal tension within the ANC was apparent when Education Minister Kader Asmal, former Department of Health Director-General Dr. Olive Shisana, ANC elections chief Manne Dipico, and party chief strategist Joel Netshitenze reportedly defied Mbeki on the issue of universal ARV access (*Mail & Guardian*, August 15–21, 2003). Additionally, Nelson Mandela has publicly supported treatment for all PLWHAs (*Xinhua News*, December 12, 2002; *allAfrica.com*, February 8, 2002). Mbeki cannot ignore Mandela, because of the former president's stature. These internal party dynamics may have contributed to the government's 2003 decision to provide universal access to ARVs.

However, Mbeki's large margin of victory in the 2004 election put no pressure on his administration to develop future AIDS policies or to speed up implementation of the 2003 treatment plan. Two post-election events hint at the president's continued reluctance to tackle AIDS. First, Mbeki did not mention AIDS in his 2004 inauguration address (African National Congress 2004). While only symbolic, this slight provides insight into the president's priorities. Second, the president reappointed

Manto Tshabalala-Msimang as health minister, despite opposition from AIDS activists. She has been criticized for being unnecessarily slow in developing the plan for ARV treatment and for controversial statements about ARVs. Tony Leon, leader of the opposition Democratic Alliance, said her reappointment was a "slap in the face" to those with AIDS (*Washington Post*, April 29, 2004, p. A22). South Africa illustrates that democracies that face little electoral competition may feel limited pressure to develop AIDS policies.

Although they appear relatively ineffective for holding governments accountable, elections can create a political space in which new administrations can develop AIDS policies. For example, after coming to power in 2003, Kenyan President Mwai Kibaki has devoted increasing personal attention to the disease. On September 21, 2003, one AIDS activist wrote in the *Nation*:

> For the first time in Kenya, we are witnessing a serious commitment from "above" to fight the deadly scourge. . . . I recall a few years ago when retired President Moi [whose party lost the 2002 election] dismissed AIDS as a problem only for people who could not control their sexual desires. He, indeed, advised the nation to be like him and live celibate lives. This was the height of trivialising a serious problem that went beyond an individual decision to remain celibate.

A similar situation existed in Ghana after the 2000 election, when John Evans Atta Mills, the handpicked successor of military-leader-turned-president Jerry Rawlings, lost the election to John Kufour by a margin of 57 percent to 43 percent (Gyimah-Boadi 2001).[6] Ghana's actions to address AIDS before the 2000 election were limited. President Rawlings established the Ghana AIDS Commission, although it lacked legal status until President Kufour's inauguration in 2001. Prior to then, the government had viewed AIDS solely as a health concern and had channeled few state resources to the disease (Ghana National AIDS/STDs Control Programme 2000; Ghana Ministry of Health 2001). Since the 2000 election, the Ghana AIDS Commission has set policy directives for national ministries and subnational AIDS committees, it has distributed money from the Ghana AIDS Response Fund, and it has tried to combat stigma and discrimination (Ghana AIDS Commission 2003; *Accra Mail*, September 12, 2003; *Ghanaian Chronicle*, December 2, 2004).[7]

The 2000 election provided Kufour's National Patriotic Party (NPP) with a unique opportunity to increase state efforts against AIDS. The NPP campaigned with the slogan of "Positive Change," which signaled to voters that not only was the NPP a change from the Rawlings era, but also that the party would address new issues. The excitement surrounding the democratic election gave the government initial legitimacy (Gyimah-Boadi 2001). According to a 1999 survey, 55 percent of Ghanaians expressed satisfaction with the country's democratic process (Bratton et al. 2001). By 2003, that number had risen to 72 percent, and 74 percent of Ghanaians reported high levels of confidence in political leaders (Gyimah-Boadi and Mensah 2003). Government benefited from this goodwill, and could use this opportunity to lead on the AIDS issue. It was not that AIDS was a 2000 campaign issue; and as we saw earlier, only 3 percent of the public in 2004 viewed AIDS to be a top government priority. Rather, once the NPP was in power, its youth and urban base did not *prevent* it from developing policies on AIDS (Nugent 2001; Gyimah-Boadi 2001; Ghana AIDS Commission 2003; UNAIDS 2002a). The 2000 alternation of power provided an opportunity for government action on AIDS.

This section has illustrated the difficulties of using the ballot box to hold Africa's democratic governments accountable for their AIDS activities. Parties have rarely felt compelled to campaign with AIDS proposals, though 2004 elections in Namibia, Botswana, and South Africa, where AIDS is more politically salient than in many countries, may signal some changes in this regard. The lack of electoral competition has made it easier for ruling parties to forge their own AIDS policies without pressure from voters or the opposition. In rare cases such as Ghana (2000) and Kenya (2002), elections, and the alternation of power that has accompanied them, have given new leaders the political space to begin to address the disease.

## Democratic Institutions
## Facilitate Participation and Accountability

This section focuses on the formal institutions of the executive, legislature, subnational governments, and the courts. Implicit in the democracies-promote-health thesis is the idea that such institutions provide avenues through which citizens and interest groups can influence government actions. However, because the African state is a hybrid of formal and informal institutions, these institutions, with the possible exception of the executive, are underdeveloped in Africa (van de Walle 2001, 51). This underdevelopment reflects a lack of capacity, professionalism, and formal decisionmaking power. Most judiciaries have limited independence to challenge executive actions; subnational institutions have few resources and power; legislatures are weak and relatively unprofessional. As a result, policymaking has been concentrated in the executive, a situation with advantages and disadvantages. According to Dr. Victor Bampoe, HIV/AIDS advisor for DFID in Ghana, involving the executive calls political attention to AIDS: "I would rather have people like members of the cabinet sitting on the commission because for four years . . . you know that you have people with clout who can move things forward" (Patterson and Haven 2005, 85). On the other hand, these high-level commissions may lack autonomy from the president, and PLWHAs and other people most vulnerable to HIV may be underrepresented.

*Executive Bodies: The Example of the*
*Country Coordinating Mechanisms (CCMs)*

Most countries in sub-Saharan Africa have established a Country Coordinating Mechanism (CCM), a national-level committee that writes grants to the GFATM and manages any received grant money. To apply to the GFATM, a country must establish a CCM and demonstrate that it has worked with various nonstate actors to develop its grant proposal. The GFATM reported that in 2004, 99 percent of CCMs were chaired by government officials, the majority from the ministry of health (Patterson and Cieminis 2005, 175; GFATM 2005a). Because the GFATM gives CCM membership lists on its website, this institution provides an opportunity to investigate: (1) the level of civil society representation on these AIDS policymaking bodies; and (2) the relationship between democracy and civil society representation on the CCM.

First, civil society groups, including PLWHAs, have tended to be underrepresented on the CCMs. The GFATM reported that in 2004 government representatives were 37 percent of CCM members; multilateral and bilateral donors and multinational NGOs were 23 percent; local NGOs, 15 percent; academic institutions, 5 percent; private sector/business, 6 percent; faith-based organizations (FBOs), 5 percent; people living with AIDS, TB, and/or malaria, 4 percent; and other organizations, 5 percent (GFATM 2005a). While these numbers were for all CCMs worldwide, they demonstrate the majority voice of governments and donors, and the minority voice of civil society representatives from NGOs, business, academic institutions, faith-based organizations, and people living with one of the diseases. Table 3.1 provides CCM membership for forty-three countries in sub-Saharan Africa. Countries report their CCM membership to the GFATM, though the GFATM clearly

**Table 3.1   Number of Sectoral Representatives to Country Coordinating Mechanisms in Sub-Saharan Africa**

| Country | Gov't | Donor[a] | Local NGO | FBO | Business Group | Academic Institution | PLWHA Group | % CCM from Civil Society (not govt. & donors) | Freedom House Ranking |
|---|---|---|---|---|---|---|---|---|---|
| Angola | 14 | 13 | 7 | 0 | 2 | 1 | 1 | 29 | 5.5 |
| Benin | 15 | 14 | 1 | 3 | 2 | 1 | 2 | 20 | 2 |
| Botswana | 5 | 4 | 3 | 1 | 2 | 1 | 3 | 53 | 2 |
| Burkina Faso | 11 | 10 | 3 | 3 | 1 | 1 | 1 | 30 | 4.5 |
| Burundi | 11 | 2 | 4 | 3 | 1 | 1 | 1 | 43 | 5 |
| Cameroon | 15 | 9 | 3 | 3 | 1 | 2 | 1 | 29 | 6 |
| Cape Verde[b] | no successful proposal | | | | | | | | 1 |
| Cen. Afr. Rep. | 33 | 6 | 11 | 1 | 3 | 1 | 1 | 30 | 5 |
| Chad | 13 | 12 | 7 | 2 | 2 | 1 | 1 | 34 | 5.5 |
| Comoros | 7 | 6 | 3 | 0 | 1 | 0 | 0 | 23 | 4 |
| Congo[b] | no successful proposal | | | | | | | | 4.5 |
| DR Congo | 9 | 15 | 5 | 5 | 2 | 1 | 1 | 37 | 6 |
| Côte d'Ivoire | 10 | 7 | 9 | 1 | 3 | 1 | 1 | 47 | 6 |
| Djibouti | 13 | 6 | 4 | 0 | 1 | 0 | 1 | 24 | 5 |
| E. Guinea | 8 | 5 | 5 | 2 | 1 | 1 | 0 | 41 | 6.5 |
| Eritrea | 5 | 4 | 2 | 1 | 1 | 0 | 1 | 28 | 6.5 |
| Ethiopia | 6 | 5 | 2 | 0 | 1 | 1 | 1 | 31 | 5 |
| Gabon | 16 | 12 | 6 | 3 | 1 | 1 | 2 | 32 | 4.5 |
| Gambia | 11 | 5 | 4 | 2 | 2 | 2 | 2 | 43 | 4 |
| Ghana | 14 | 11 | 8 | 1 | 3 | 3 | 1 | 39 | 2 |
| Guinea | 14 | 12 | 10 | 2 | 4 | 1 | 2 | 40 | 5.5 |
| G. Bissau | 6 | 4 | 3 | 1 | 1 | 1 | 1 | 41 | 4 |
| Kenya | 9 | 5 | 2 | 3 | 2 | 1 | 2 | 42 | 3 |
| Lesotho | 9 | 8 | 4 | 0 | 2 | 1 | 2 | 35 | 2.5 |

*(continues)*

| | | | | | | | |
|---|---|---|---|---|---|---|---|
| Liberia | 10 | 3 | 2 | 0 | 2 | 0 | 25 | 4.5 |
| Madagascar | 11 | 1 | 1 | 0 | 1 | 0 | 13 | 3 |
| Malawi | 5 | 3 | 2 | 1 | 3 | 1 | 56 | 4 |
| Mali | 12 | 7 | 3 | 0 | 1 | 2 | 38 | 2 |
| Mauritania | 9 | 5 | 1 | 0 | 2 | 1 | 43 | 5.5 |
| Mauritius[b] | no successful proposal | | | | | | | 1 |
| Mozambique | 6 | 2 | 1 | 1 | 0 | 1 | 38 | 3.5 |
| Namibia | 20 | 8 | 2 | 4 | 2 | 4 | 45 | 2.5 |
| Niger | 7 | 2 | 2 | 0 | 1 | 1 | 31 | 3 |
| Nigeria | 10 | 13 | 2 | 7 | 6 | 2 | 55 | 4 |
| Rwanda | 12 | 2 | 1 | 1 | 1 | 1 | 25 | 5.5 |
| Sao Tome | 8 | 3 | 2 | 1 | 0 | 0 | 24 | 2 |
| Senegal | 10 | 4 | 2 | 2 | 2 | 2 | 50 | 2.5 |
| Seychelles[b] | no successful proposal | | | | | | | 3 |
| Sierra Leone | 14 | 7 | 2 | 1 | 2 | 1 | 33 | 3.5 |
| Somalia[c] | no government | | | | | | | 6.5 |
| South Africa | 26 | 8 | 2 | 2 | 2 | 3 | 40 | 1.5 |
| Sudan | 15 | 11 | 3 | 1 | 1 | 2 | 31 | 7 |
| Swaziland | 4 | 4 | 1 | 1 | 1 | 1 | 42 | 6 |
| Tanzania | 10 | 2 | 2 | 6 | 1 | 1 | 44 | 3.5 |
| Togo | 12 | 4 | 1 | 2 | 1 | 3 | 33 | 5.5 |
| Uganda | 14 | 3 | 1 | 3 | 1 | 3 | 37 | 4.5 |
| Zambia | 7 | 4 | 1 | 1 | 1 | 1 | 42 | 4 |
| Zimbabwe | 8 | 3 | 1 | 2 | 0 | 1 | 31 | 6.5 |

*Source:* Compiled by author from Freedom House (2005b) and from CCM member lists and successful GFATM proposals available at GFATM (2005b, 2005c).

a. Donor is defined as a multilateral or bilateral aid organization or a multilateral NGO (such as CARE).

b. As of early 2006, four sub-Saharan African countries either had not submitted a proposal to the GFATM or had not had a proposal approved. The GFATM provides no listing for Cape Verde, Congo, Mauritius, and Seychelles.

c. Because Somalia had no functioning government when it applied to the GFATM in 2004, multilateral donors and NGOs formed its CCM. Because I want to demonstrate the relationship between government and CCM representation, I do not include Somalia in the analysis.

asserts it is not responsible for the accuracy of these reports. Some countries have not provided this data; in those cases, I have determined CCM membership from a country's grant proposals. However, because some of the proposals are from 2002 and 2003, CCM membership may have changed. I have included multinational NGOs in the donor category because they often are accountable to Western governments and citizens for funding, not local populations. Hence, they may bring an outsider's perspective to the CCM that differs from the viewpoint of local NGOs.

Table 3.1 illustrates several points about the CCMs. First, civil society representation varies greatly across the countries. Some countries, such as Nigeria, Malawi, Botswana, and Senegal, have approximately half of the members from civil society, while others, such as Comoros, Liberia, Madagascar, Rwanda, and Benin, have 25 percent or less from civil society. Second, in all countries except Botswana, Malawi, Nigeria, and Senegal, government officials and donors constitute at least 50 percent of members. Third, in the DRC, Liberia, Nigeria, Rwanda, Sao Tome and Principe, Sudan, and Swaziland, there are more international donor representatives than government officials. This situation probably reflects the political instability of the DRC, Congo, Liberia, and Sudan; concerns about corruption for Swaziland and Nigeria; and/or the need for technical expertise in small countries like Rwanda and Sao Tome and Principe.

In terms of democracy and CCM representation, the relationship is somewhat inconclusive. Table 3.1 provides Freedom House rankings for each of the forty-three countries. The mean percentage of civil society representation on the CCMs in free countries (with a 1–2.5 Freedom House score) is 38.2; in partly free countries (3–5 score), it is 35.6; in not free countries (5.5–7 score), it is 35.98. Thus, while free countries have a slightly higher percentage of representatives from civil society, the margin is not large. The correlation between civil society representation on a country's CCM and democracy rank in 2004 was -.116. In general, this correlation indicates that as democracy increased (as measured by a declining Freedom House score), civil society representation increased, though the correlation did not attain statistical significance.

Table 3.2 provides another picture of the relationship between civil society representation on the CCM and democracy. The table divides the forty-three CCMs into three groups: low civil society representation (13–31% of CCM), medium representation (32–42%) and high representation (43–56%). The table demonstrates that free countries are less likely than partly free or not free countries to have low civil society rep-

**Table 3.2   Democracy and Percentage of Civil Society Representatives on Country Coordinating Mechanisms**

| Civil Society Representation on CCM | Democracy Ranking, 2004 | | |
|---|---|---|---|
| | Free | Partly Free | Not Free |
| 13–31 | 22.2 | 40 | 42.9 |
| 32–42 | 44.4 | 35 | 42.9 |
| 43–56 | 33.3 | 25 | 14.3 |
| Total | 100 | 100 | 100 |
| | N=9 | N=20 | N=14 |

*Source:* Calculated from data compiled from Freedom House (2005b) and from CCM member lists and successful GFATM proposals available at GFATM (2005b, 2005c).

resentation, and that free countries are more likely than partly free and not free countries to have high levels of civil society representation. However, free and not free countries are just about as likely to have medium levels of civil society representation. While the general pattern that reveals democracies may be slightly more likely to include civil society representatives on their CCMs confirms the democracies-promote-health thesis, the inconsistencies in the relationship make drawing broad conclusions from these data problematic.

Moreover, there are other issues the data cannot answer. It is impossible to know *why* these civil society groups are represented on the CCMs in Africa's democracies. Is it because AIDS organizations demand representation, because governments value civil society involvement, or because donors insist on civil society members? No doubt the answers to these questions vary with the country. The data also do not tell us how these civil society representatives are chosen and to whom they are accountable. The Global Network of People Living with HIV/AIDS (GNP+) investigated this question in Cameroon, Malawi, and Nigeria, looking specifically at AIDS NGOs or organizations of PLWHAs. GNP+ found that these representatives tended to be appointed by government and, therefore, they were less likely to challenge state policies (GNP+ 2004). The organization also found that because of stigma and discrimination, it was sometimes difficult for only one or two PLWHAs on a CCM of thirty or more members to effectively voice their concerns. Further research on CCMs is needed to better understand how they foster representation and how their composition relates to a country's overall governance.

*Legislatures*

Unlike executives, African legislatures have been relatively absent from debates on AIDS policymaking or have merely rubber-stamped presidential AIDS proposals. For example, after the 2002 Kenyan election, President Kibaki introduced several pieces of AIDS legislation, all of which passed with little discussion (Kenya Government 2003). There are several reasons why AIDS policies have been the prerogative of the executive. Periods of military rule, dictatorship, and one-party dominance have prevented the development of legislative committees or independent leadership positions. Legislatures lack personnel and equipment, and legislators often receive low pay, a fact that encourages neopatrimonial behavior. Additionally, citizens have tended to trust executives more than legislatures, creating a political culture that de facto marginalizes legislatures (Gyimah-Boadi 1999, 42). The propensity of presidents to develop new executive bodies to address issues, and to keep these structures under presidential control, further marginalizes legislatures (van de Walle 2001, 101–106).

There are additional reasons for executive dominance in AIDS decisionmaking. Because of the stigma attached to HIV/AIDS, it is less likely that members of a majoritarian institution will eagerly prioritize the issue. Since legislators often see their job as providing patronage benefits to their districts, the development of long-term AIDS education, care, and support programs may not be as appealing to voters as development projects such as roads or schools (Beck 2003). One representative from an AIDS NGO in Malawi commented that members of parliament in that country do not take HIV/AIDS issues seriously in their constituencies.[8] The underdevelopment of independent media sources in Africa and the tenuous nature of press freedoms throughout the continent further shape legislatures' responsiveness to AIDS. The media in Kenya, Senegal, Malawi, Zambia, Nigeria, and Namibia continue to face intimidation, self-censorship, and government pressure to avoid certain topics (Freedom House 2005b). Reporters may lack training on AIDS, media outlets have limited resources to devote to the issue, and there are few, if any, media representatives on African CCMs or other AIDS policymaking bodies. Media coverage can generate public interest on the topic, encourage legislators to address AIDS, and ensure that AIDS funds are used appropriately. For example, the Media Network on Orphans and Vulnerable Children in Zambia has played this watchdog role over unscrupulous organizations (Representative of Media Network on Orphans and Vulnerable Children, PartnersGF eForum at http://forum.theglobalfund.org/en, June 2, 2004).

Finally, donors have helped to foster executive dominance on AIDS. In 1999, several UN agencies created the International Partnership against HIV/AIDS in Africa to foster collaboration between the international community and African leaders. Carolyn Baylies (1999, 388) writes that the initiative was an attempt "to cajole, to instill a greater sense of political responsibility, and to induce a greater economic contribution from African governments, calling on them to take the initiative." The need to rapidly build this partnership necessitated working with executives, not legislatures. Further, the World Bank MAP initiative that started in 2000 required that, in return for loans, governments set up national AIDS commissions, composed of high-level state, donor, and civil society officials who would oversee national AIDS policies and funding (Haven 2005). While expedient, this structure undermines the legislative institutions that are supposed to represent citizens.

### Subnational Governments

Similarly, subnational institutions have played a minimal role in AIDS policy development. Although some decentralized institutions can foster development because they are responsive to local populations (Clark 1990; Esman and Uphoff 1984), others may not be accountable or may lack needed resources for the development demands the state has assigned them (Ribot 1995, 1999; Patterson 2002; Mamdani 1996, 37). As part of Malawi's decentralization process, for example, the country designed district AIDS coordination committees to develop AIDS awareness, care, and support programs. While this move incorporates many voices into AIDS decisionmaking, these committees have not formalized their coordination with local political institutions. They also lack trained personnel, operating funds, and monitoring and financial management systems. One outcome has been their inability to meet the needs of PLWHAs and those who care for them (Garbus 2003, 80–81).

On the other hand, the actions of South Africa's provinces on use of nevirapine for PMTCT illustrate that subnational institutions are not always impotent. The South African constitution makes health services a concurrent competence of the provinces and national government. However, even though the minister of health and provincial members are supposed to work together to develop policy, the national ministry has tended to dominate this process (Pottie 1999, 23). In 2001, the national government and nine provinces endorsed a policy in which two research sites to test nevirapine would be established in each of the provinces for a two-year period. This meant that doctors at other public hospitals could not prescribe the drug, even though its producer offered to provide it free. Although the Western Cape government, which was controlled by the opposition Democratic Alliance, agreed to the research project, it refused to limit provision of the drug at other sites. By 2002, over 70 percent of women needing the drug in that province was receiving it.

In early 2002, KwaZulu-Natal (KZN) and Gauteng provinces announced they would defy the national policy, which the Pretoria High Court had declared unconstitutional in December 2001, and provide nevirapine at non-pilot sites. Both provinces had good reason to expand nevirapine distribution: roughly 28 percent of Gauteng citizens and 37 percent of KZN residents are HIV positive (UNAIDS 2002c). Yet, the two provinces differed in their access to resources and their politics. Several international NGOs already had begun PMTCT programs in KZN, and the province received GFATM money in 2002 (*InterPress Service*, July 19, 2002). The Inkatha Freedom Party, headed by ANC-rival former Home Affairs Minister Mangosuthu Buthelezi, controlled the KZN provincial government (Maré 1999). Buthelezi publicly broke ranks with the ANC over nevirapine, saying: "Our nation is dying of AIDS. This is the time to act in the full measure of our capacity" (*South African Press Association*, February 12, 2002).

In contrast, the ANC controlled the Gauteng provincial government. When Premier Mbhazima Shilowa, the most senior ANC premier, announced he would provide nevirapine, the Mbeki government saw the action as a direct challenge. A party spokesperson said Gauteng had "jumped the mark," and another ANC official claimed Shilowa was "opportunistic" (*BBC News*, February 21, 2002). But Shilowa's actions were very popular and the national government was put on the defensive. Eventually Gauteng negotiated with the national government and then announced the province would provide the drug at public hospitals within the next year (*Business Day*, February 25, 2002).

The nevirapine incident illustrates the uncertain role decentralized institutions can play in AIDS policymaking. The provincial leaders' actions were intended to meet the needs of their citizens. Defiance was possible in KZN, because of its relative political independence and because it had gained access to external resources. (Such defiance may end with the ANC victory in the 2004 provincial government elections and Buthelezi's removal from the national cabinet.) In Gauteng, Mbeki's need to maintain political control limited the province's ability to immediately affect the nevirapine policy. However, in the long run, the negative media coverage the ANC received led to the public perception that the government was callous to society's most vulnerable citizens, pregnant women and infants (*Financial Times*, February 22, 2002). By April 2002, the national government announced a major reversal of the policy, to include universal rollout of nevirapine by the end of 2002 (Steytler 2003).

## The Judiciary

Similar to African legislatures and subnational governments, judiciaries have provided few opportunities for participation and accountability in AIDS policymaking. In established democracies, independent courts have helped to advance the rights of PLWHAs. For example, several US federal and state court cases in the late 1980s developed precedents on protection against discrimination in employment and housing for PLWHAs (Smith 2001, 183). On the other hand, most African judiciaries have yet to develop what Kwasi Prempeh (2001, 265) terms a "jurisprudence of constitutionalism." Although most constitutions in Africa's new democracies have included the protection of civil liberties and the promotion of human rights, courts rarely have been willing to challenge executive actions that undermine these provisions. South Africa provides an exceptional case. Justice Edwin Cameron (2005) maintains that courts in that country have asserted their independence, particularly since the end of apartheid. The Constitutional Court has issued important rulings protecting the rights of PLWHAs and their children, and it has gone against the executive in some rulings. For example, in 2000, the Court prohibited irrational discrimination against job applicants with HIV or AIDS. As the next chapter illustrates, some civil society organizations in South Africa have utilized the independent judiciary as a means to shape AIDS policy.

Outside of South Africa, judicial protection of the rights of those affected by HIV/AIDS has been inconsistent, even within the same country. For example, in her testimony to a US congressional committee in 2003, Janet Walsh of Human Rights Watch argued that one of the obstacles to protecting Kenyan women's property after their husbands died of AIDS was ineffective courts. She said: "Lawyers and individual women often complain that Kenya's courts are biased, slow, corrupt and staffed with ill-trained or inept judges and magistrates. Several judges we interviewed outright admitted that they do not apply laws on inheritance and division of family property" (Human Rights Watch 2003a). The weakness of Kenya's courts is also evident in their inability to protect the rights of children who have lost parents to the disease (Human

Rights Watch 2001, 5). On the other hand, in January 2004 Kenya's High Court ruled that a public school in Nairobi must admit seventy-two HIV-positive students. Because the children lived in a nearby institution for abandoned children, they were assumed to be HIV positive. The children's lawyer praised the court: "Our judiciary has demonstrated its readiness to uphold and assert human entitlements of all shades, including those within the socioeconomic realm, as being due to all classes of the citizenry, no less the vulnerable, the weak and the voiceless" (*South African Press Association*, January 12, 2004). Kenya's experience shows the sometimes inconsistent role of the judiciary in the AIDS fight.

The overall underdevelopment of Africa's democratic institutions has hampered representation and accountability in AIDS policymaking. Although there have been isolated instances when judiciaries have protected the rights of HIV-positive citizens or decentralized institutions have challenged central state policies, Africa's new democracies still lack opportunities for citizen representation and checks and balances, not solely in the realm of AIDS policymaking, but in general. And while Africa's democracies have been more likely than nondemocracies to include civil society representatives in AIDS policymaking, the pattern is not strong.

## Democratic Governments and Spending on Health

The democracies-promote-health thesis argues that governments will devote money to public health because citizens demand more spending, governments are concerned about reelection, and civil society organizations and the media hold governments accountable. While health spending and spending on AIDS are not the same, as of 2006, there was no measure of African government spending solely on AIDS for all sub-Saharan African countries. A 1999 UNAIDS report provides data for select countries from 1996, but since this was before many African governments began to acknowledge the magnitude of the disease, these ten-year-old figures are not extremely helpful (Ernberg et al. 1999). Furthermore, it has been estimated that in countries such as Rwanda, Kenya, Zimbabwe, Ethiopia, and South Africa over 50 percent of government health spending is for AIDS (International Crisis Group 2001, 17). While I acknowledge that the proxy of health spending may exclude some government spending on AIDS outside of the health budget (such as through the ministries of labor, industry, or education), health spending provides the best measure currently available.

Table 3.3 gives Freedom House rankings for forty-eight sub-

**Table 3.3    Democratic Rankings and Health Spending as a Percentage of Government Budget, Selected Years**

| Countries | 1980 Democracy | 1980 Health (%) | 1990 Democracy | 1995 Health (%) | 2004 Democracy | 2002 Health (%) |
|---|---|---|---|---|---|---|
| Angola | 2.5[a] | | 7 | 7.6 | 5.5 | 4.1 |
| Benin | 6.5 | | 5 | 7.1 | 2 | 11.1 |
| Botswana | 2.5 | 5.4 | 1.5 | 6.6 | 2 | 7.5 |
| Burkina Faso | 5.5 | 5.8 | 5.5 | 9 | 4.5 | 10.6 |
| Burundi | 6.5 | | 6.5 | 6.4 | 5 | 2 |
| Cameroon | 6 | 5.1 | 6 | 6.4 | 6 | 7.9 |
| Cape Verde | 1 | | 1 | 3.6 | 1 | 11.1 |
| Central African Republic | 6 | 5.1 | 5.5 | 4.1 | 5 | 7.4 |
| Chad | 6.5 | | 6.5 | 13.1 | 5.5 | 12.2 |
| Comoros | 4.5 | | 5 | 7.6 | 4 | 8.2 |
| Congo | 6.5 | 5.1 | 6 | 6.9 | 4.5 | 6 |
| DR of Congo | 6 | | 6 | 13.7 | 6 | 16.4 |
| Côte d'Ivoire | 5.5 | 3.9 | 5 | 4.7 | 6 | 7.2 |
| Djibouti | 3.5 | | 5.5 | 6.4 | 5 | 10.1 |
| E. Guinea | 6.5 | | 7 | 11.2 | 6.5 | 9.8 |
| Eritrea | n/a | | 5.5[b] | 4.1 | 6.5 | 5.6 |
| Ethiopia | 7 | 5.1 | 7 | 5.8 | 5 | 7.6 |
| Gabon | 6 | | 4 | 8.5 | 4.5 | 6.3 |
| Gambia | 2.5 | | 2 | 13.7 | 4 | 12 |
| Ghana | 2.5 | 7 | 5.5 | 8.3 | 2 | 8.4 |
| Guinea | 7 | | 5.5 | 9.2 | 5.5 | 4.8 |
| Guinea-Bissau | 6 | | 5.5 | 9.6 | 4 | 8.5 |
| Kenya | 4.5 | 7.8 | 6 | 6.6 | 3 | 8.4 |
| Lesotho | 5 | 6.2 | 5.5 | 9.6 | 2.5 | 10.9 |
| Liberia | 6 | | 7 | 9.5 | 4.5 | 5.5 |
| Madagascar | 6 | | 4 | 9.2 | 3 | 8 |
| Malawi | 6.5 | 5.5 | 6.5 | 11.3 | 4 | 9.7 |
| Mali | 6.5 | 3.1 | 5.5 | 6.9 | 2 | 9 |
| Mauritania | 6.5 | | 6.5 | 9.5 | 5.5 | 10.1 |
| Mauritius | 3 | 7.5 | 2 | 8.9 | 1 | 8.3 |
| Mozambique | 7 | | 6 | 12.4 | 3.5 | 19.9 |
| Namibia | 5.5[c] | | 2.5 | 12.9 | 2.5 | 12.9 |
| Niger | 6.5 | 4.1 | 5.5 | 5 | 3 | 10 |
| Nigeria | 2.5 | | 5 | 1.7 | 4 | 3.3 |
| Rwanda | 6 | 4.5 | 6 | 14 | 5.5 | 13.4 |
| Sao Tome | 6 | | 5 | 2.9 | 2 | 14.5 |
| Senegal | 4 | 4.7 | 3.5 | 13.1 | 2.5 | 11.2 |
| Seychelles | 6 | | 6 | 8.2 | 3 | 6.6 |
| Sierra Leone | 5 | 9.1 | 5.5 | 7.1 | 3.5 | 6.8 |
| Somalia | 7 | | 7 | 4.1 | 6.5 | 4.2[d] |
| South Africa | 5.5 | | 4.5 | 12.6 | 1.5 | 10.7 |

*(continues)*

**Table 3.3    continued**

| Countries | 1980 Democracy | 1980 Health (%) | 1990 Democracy | 1995 Health (%) | 2004 Democracy | 2002 Health (%) |
|---|---|---|---|---|---|---|
| Sudan | 5 | 1.4 | 7 | 5 | 7 | 6.3 |
| Swaziland | 5 | | 5.5 | 8 | 6 | 10.9 |
| Tanzania | 6 | 6 | 5.5 | 14.7 | 3.5 | 14.9 |
| Togo | 6.5 | 5.3 | 6 | 4.9 | 5.5 | 7.8 |
| Uganda | 4 | 5.1 | 5.5 | 9.2 | 4.5 | 9.1 |
| Zambia | 4.5 | 6.1 | 5.5 | 11.5 | 4 | 11.3 |
| Zimbabwe | 3.5 | 5.4 | 5 | 10.1 | 6.5 | 12.2 |
| Average | 5.23 | 5.40 | 5.32 | 8.39 | 4.17 | 9.29 |

*Sources:* Compiled from Freedom House (1981, 1991, 2005b), World Bank (1993, 269–270), and the World Health Organization (WHO) (2002, 1–4; 2005, 1–4).

*Notes:* Democracy scores are the average of two Freedom House scores (each on a scale of 1–7) for political rights and civil liberties.

  a. First available data is 1983.
  b. First available data is 1993.
  c. Data from 1974 (data not found from 1974–1988).
  d. Data from 2001.

Saharan African countries for the years 1980, 1990, and 2004. I use 1980 as a benchmark, since that year was before many of Africa's democratic transitions of the late 1980s, but it was after Lusophone countries gained independence. In 1990, many countries began to hold multiparty elections; 2004 is the latest year with available data. These time periods are coupled with data on health spending as a percentage of the government budget in 1980, 1995, and 2002. The years for health spending measures were selected based on data availability, although data on health spending are only available for twenty-three countries in 1980. To better assess the link between democracy and spending, I use the percentage of the government budget spent on health, instead of health spending as a percentage of GDP, since health spending as a percentage of GDP also includes private and donor spending.

Table 3.3 reveals some general patterns. First, using the Freedom House "free" category to define democracy, the continent has become more democratic since 1980. The mean Freedom House ranking score was 5.23 in 1980, 5.32 in 1990, and 4.17 in 2004. Clearly, countries such as Ghana, Mali, Benin, and South Africa have made huge strides in democratization over the past fifteen years. Second, since 1980, health spending has increased, although the paucity of 1980 data means that the data between 1995 and 2002 provide a more reliable measure of this change. In 1995, the average percentage of budget spent on health was 8.39 percent; by 2002 it was 9.29 percent. However, a few countries such as Benin, Mozambique, and Niger with large increases probably skew these numbers. Additionally, seven of Africa's eleven free countries in 2004 (Benin, Botswana, Cape Verde, Ghana, Lesotho, Mali, and Sao Tome and Principe) augmented health spending between 1995 and 2002; one country (Namibia) kept spending at the same level, while three (Mauritius, Senegal, and South Africa) experienced a decline in spending. There are also increases among ten of the twenty countries that moved from the not free category in 1990 to the partly free category in 2004. These countries are Burkina Faso, Central African Republic, Comoros, Djibouti, Ethiopia, Kenya, Mozambique, Niger, Nigeria, and Tanzania. The other ten countries in the not-free-to-partly-free group (Burundi, Congo, Guinea Bissau, Liberia, Madagascar, Malawi, Seychelles, Sierra Leone, Uganda, and Zambia) decreased health spending (WHO 2005, 193–199).

Table 3.4 classifies all countries based on the relationship between change in democracy between 1990 and 2004 and change in health spending between 1995 and 2002. For the purposes of the table and a consistent assessment, any change, no matter how small, constitutes a change in democracy or health spending. Table 3.4 shows three impor-

**Table 3.4    Sub-Saharan African Countries Classified by Democratic Change and Change in Health Spending, 1990 to 2004**

| Country Classification | Number of Countries |
| --- | --- |
| Increasingly democratic and increased health spending | 18 |
| Increasingly democratic and decreased health spending | 17 |
| Increasingly democratic and static health spending | 0 |
| Decreasingly democratic and increased health spending | 5 |
| Decreasingly democratic and decreased health spending | 2 |
| Decreasingly democratic and static health spending | 0 |
| No change in democracy and increased health spending | 4 |
| No change in democracy and decreased health spending | 1 |
| No change in democracy and static health spending | 1 |
| Total number of countries with increased health spending | 27 |
| Total number of countries with decreased health spending | 20 |
| Total number of countries with static health spending | 1 |

*Sources:* Compiled from Freedom House (1991, 2005b) and WHO (2002, 1–4; 2005, 1–4).
*Note:* Any change in Freedom House democratic measures between 1990 and 2004 and any change in health care spending as a percentage of government budget between 1995 and 2002 was counted.

tant trends. First, while there are more countries that increased health spending, the continent is fairly divided between countries that increased and countries that decreased health spending between 1995 and 2002. Twenty-seven countries increased health spending, twenty decreased spending, and one had no change. Second, there are almost as many countries that became more democratic after 1990 that have raised health spending as those that have lowered health spending. In 2002, eighteen more democratic countries had higher health spending, and seventeen had lower spending, than in 1995. Third, there are five countries with declining democratic measures and four with no change in democracy that increased health spending between 1995 and 2002.

While Table 3.4 presents inconclusive evidence, Table 3.5 shows there is an overall correlation between democratization and increased government health spending. These numbers say nothing about the causal relationship between democracy and spending, and they do not elucidate if there has been public pressure for more health spending. Table 3.5 divides health spending percentages for the forty-eight states into the lowest, middle, and highest third, each category having sixteen cases. The table shows that less than one in ten free countries (9.1% of the "free" group) has spending in the lowest third, while two out of five partly free countries (40.9%) and not free countries (40%) fall into the lowest third in terms of health spending. More than three out of five free countries (63.6%) have spending in the highest third, while less than one in five partly free countries (18.2%) and only a third of not free countries (33.3%) do so. On the other hand, among those countries classified as "not free," approximately the same percentage of countries falls into

**Table 3.5    Levels of Health Spending and Democracy Ranking, 2004**

| Rank Health Care Spending | Democracy Rank | | |
|---|---|---|---|
| | Free | Partly Free | Not Free |
| Lowest third | 9.1% | 40.9% | 40% |
| Middle third | 27.3% | 40.9% | 26.7% |
| Highest third | 63.6% | 18.2% | 33.3% |
| Total | 100% | 100% | 100% |
| | N=11 | N=22 | N=15 |

*Source:* Calculated from data compiled from Freedom House (2005b) and WHO (2005, 1–4).

the lowest, middle, and highest third of health spending. No doubt relatively high levels of spending in Rwanda (13.4%), Chad (12.2%), the DRC (16.4%), and Zimbabwe (12.2%) contribute to this outcome.

Table 3.6 provides the correlations between health spending and democracy for free countries. The expected relationship is that as the Freedom House score declines (free countries receive a lower ranking on the 1–7 scale, that is, become more free), health spending will increase. The negative correlations indicate that the expected pattern exists, although none of the correlations presented are statistically significant. The highest correlation is between democracy and health spending in 1980, showing that those countries that were free in 1980 were more likely to spend on health. Moreover, those countries continued to spend on health (though at a slower rate) in 1995 and 2002. This finding suggests that democracy may need to become entrenched to gain long-run, incremental benefits for spending. Thus, although the relationship between democracy and health spending exists, it is somewhat weak.

While this chapter's goal is to examine the relationship between democracy and health, not to present a model that investigates the variables that shape government spending on health, it is important to mention other factors that may influence health-spending allocations. First, sub-Saharan Africa's poverty conditions all government policies. One-third of Africans are undernourished, and all of the world's twenty poorest countries are in the region (Hunter 2003, 55; UNDP 2004, 4). SAPs, which have required governments to cut subsidies to health and other social services in order to balance budgets, have contributed to poverty,

**Table 3.6    Correlations Between Health Spending and Democracy, Selected Years**

| Health Spending | Democracy ("Free" Ranking) | | |
|---|---|---|---|
| | 1980 | 1990 | 2004 |
| 1980 (N=23) | −.352 | — | — |
| 1995 (N=48) | −.193 | −.074 | — |
| 2002 (N=48) | −.153 | −.197 | −.222 |

*Source:* Calculated from data compiled from Freedom House (1981, 1991, 2005b), World Bank (1993, 269–270), and WHO (2002, 1–4; 2005, 1–4).

particularly for individuals living on the margins. Because of debt and poverty, African states simply have few resources to allocate for health. For example, Malawi is the world's twelfth poorest country. In 2002, its Human Development Index (HDI) was .388, a ranking lower than the median of .465 for sub-Saharan Africa. Because of drought and government mismanagement of food reserves, an estimated 29 percent of the population needed food in 2003. In 2002, Malawi's debt was $2.9 billion, 154 percent of the country's GDP (*Reuters*, February 8, 2005). Given these statistics, Malawi is relatively generous on health spending, with 9.7 percent of the government's budget devoted to health in 2002. Similarly, Benin (HDI of .421) and Mozambique (HDI of .354) have made impressive commitments to health spending (UNDP 2004, 146).

Second, political priorities influence whether or not governments choose to spend the finances they have on health or other things. We have seen a weak relationship between democracy and health spending, but that relationship says nothing about government spending priorities. Nicolas van de Walle (2001, 164) writes that health has often not been a priority for Africa's leaders: "As budget constraints have hardened, leaders have preferred to spend their money to keep their elite coalition together rather than invest in mundane activities like building schools or undertaking vaccine campaigns, particularly given the donor predilection for such thankless tasks." Spending on health, and particularly spending on AIDS, often has no visible, immediate benefit, unlike spending on roads or patronage jobs. The benefits of prenatal care, childhood immunizations, and nutrition programs are only apparent in the long term—in measles outbreaks that never occur, infant mortality rates that decline, or women that survive childbirth. Spending on programs most needed for AIDS prevention such as primary care clinics, antenatal HIV testing, STI treatment, and VCT centers targets the most marginal members of society, not the most powerful (Barnett and Whiteside 2002, 363). The political payoff for such spending is low. This is one reason that health spending on hospitals in urban areas has tended to be higher in Africa than is often warranted (Garbus 2003, 40; Benatar 2001). Furthermore, military spending may be necessary to appease regime hardliners or protect security. In 2004, Uganda increased defense spending to 21 percent of the budget to fight the LRA rebellion, although health care spending remained constant at 9 percent (*Monitor*, April 18, 2004).

Third, donors may provide needed resources, removing pressure for government to spend on health. The World Health Organization's definition of government health spending makes it difficult to analyze if spending on health reflects government priorities or if it reflects increased donor resources. WHO defines government health care spending as the sum of outlays on health paid for by taxes, social security contributions, and external resources such as "loans channeled through the federal budget and grants passing through the government" (WHO 2005, 162). In the case of the GFATM, an average of 50 percent of grant money goes directly to the government. Thus, in a hypothetical example, if Mali received $50 million to fight AIDS, $25 million would be channeled through government agencies. Such grants may increase government spending, but only because governments have new resources to use, not because government officials have prioritized health in the budget. It may be possible to assume that government officials who complete the arduous task of applying for a GFATM grant must believe public health is somewhat important, but there is no evidence to support or refute that assumption. Although WHO does not report the amount of a government's health budget that comes from external resources, it does provide the percentage of a country's total health expenditures from outside sources. Of the forty-eight countries listed in Table 3.3, external resources made up at least 20 percent of health spending in nineteen: Benin, Chad, Comoros, the DRC, Djibouti, Eritrea, Ethiopia, Gambia, Guinea-Bissau, Liberia, Lesotho, Madagascar, Malawi, Mozambique, Niger, Rwanda, Sao Tome and Principe, Tanzania, and Uganda. Because some of these countries, particularly Mozambique, Benin, the DRC, and Niger, also had large increases in government health spending, it is hard to know how much of this increase is from external sources.

The magnitude of the pandemic and the high cost of prevention, care, and treatment programs necessitate the involvement of donors in the AIDS fight. UNAIDS (2005c) estimated that by 2008, $22 billion will be needed annually to fight AIDS globally. In 2002, national governments in all developing countries spent $2 billion, only 6 percent to 10 percent of all AIDS expenditures. For example, the Malawian government will contribute roughly $14 million from 2003 to 2008 to HIV/AIDS; in contrast, donors will provide $77 million (Garbus 2003, 82). Mozambique, which has a 12.2 percent HIV prevalence rate and an annual GNI per capita of $220, depends on external sources for approximately 80 percent of its total AIDS spending. In Lesotho, donors provide 86 percent of AIDS money (Martin 2003).

Donor dependence has implications for the accountability and responsiveness of African leaders. Because policymakers and international donors have repeatedly called for political commitment to AIDS, though they have rarely defined what commitment looks like, African officials have given increased political attention to the pandemic (United Nations 2001). For example, some Malawians suspected that the 2004 presidential candidates talked about AIDS to impress donors, not out of genuine concern (*Guardian*, May 20, 2004). In 2001 African countries pledged to devote 15 percent of their national budgets to health at the African Summit on HIV/AIDS and Other Related Infectious Diseases in Abuja, Nigeria. The 15 percent pledge demonstrated to donors that African political leaders had committed to health (Patterson and Cieminis 2005, 180). Yet, as Table 3.3 illustrates, only Mozambique, with 19.9 percent, has met this goal. The low salience of AIDS, the nature of elections in Africa, and the underdevelopment of democratic institutions make it more difficult for African voters to hold their governments accountable for this promise, though there is a weak relationship between democracy and health spending.

The Abuja pledge and the Malawi election illustrate another implication of donor dependence for health spending. Political leaders may resort to low-cost symbolic actions such as speaking about AIDS, disclosing their family's AIDS experiences, or submitting to a public HIV test to demonstrate their commitment to fighting the disease. For example, President Kufuor of Ghana discussed AIDS in his first state of the union address, and both the president and first lady have urged citizens to show compassion to those with the disease (*allAfrica.com*, February 16, 2001; *Ghanaian Chronicle*, March 31, 2003; *Accra Mail*, October 2, 2004). Newly elected Kenyan President Kibaki starred in an anti-AIDS TV commercial in 2003 (*Nation*, May 31, 2003). In Botswana, over thirty traditional leaders underwent HIV testing to urge others to do the same (*AP/Topeka Capital-Journal*, May 26, 2004). I do not discount these actions, because they challenge the stigma associated with AIDS. Encouraging citizens to be tested for HIV is crucial for prevention efforts since 95 percent of those worldwide with HIV do not know they carry the virus (*New York Times*, February 10, 2004). Yet, if such actions satisfy donors and citizens, African states may not be forced to make the difficult budgetary choices about developing costly programs or building needed health care infrastructure. This may be particularly true when publics themselves are ambivalent about prioritizing AIDS.

### Democracy and the AIDS Fight: An Inconclusive Relationship

In this analysis of the argument that democracies promote health in the context of Africa's AIDS pandemic, it becomes clear that, in general, public opinion has placed low priority on government actions on AIDS. Because death from AIDS occurs years after HIV infection, public worries about the immediate needs of jobs, food, and housing trump concerns about AIDS. However, in a finding that seems to demonstrate the importance of politicizing AIDS, in countries with widespread public debate on the disease, public salience is higher. Additionally, in Namibia, Botswana, and South Africa, where the public is most likely to say AIDS should be a government priority, politicians discussed AIDS in the 2004 elections.

Overall, this chapter illustrated that elections have yet to punish or reward governments for actions on AIDS. The disease remains an issue that few parties discuss, partly because of the personal nature of the disease and partly because elections in Africa's democracies remain relatively noncompetitive. However, this trend may be changing in more recent elections: officials in both democratic and semi-democratic countries talked about AIDS in 2004, whereas politicians in Africa's democracies did not broach the subject in elections between 2000 and 2002. With the exceptional case of South Africa, democratic institutions such as legislatures, judiciaries, and local governments have played a minor role in AIDS policy development. This fact limits the number of arenas in which citizens can shape decisionmaking or hold government accountable. For institutions that are uniquely situated to make AIDS policies—namely the CCMs—representation of civil society can be uneven, though Africa's democratic countries are slightly more likely to include civil society representatives than partly and nondemocratic countries. Because AIDS has yet to become a public priority in many countries and because Africa's underdevelopment makes devoting resources to AIDS difficult, only about half of Africa's new democracies have increased spending on health, while the other half have decreased health spending. While the general pattern shows that democracies are more likely to spend on health, the overall results are inconclusive. Many African leaders have engaged in somewhat symbolic actions to demonstrate commitment to fighting the disease, and they have relied on donors to finance AIDS programs.

The picture painted here illustrates the book's three themes. First, while the magnitude of the pandemic is undeniable, it has yet to cause citizens to prioritize AIDS in the public sphere. Low public salience reveals that AIDS has yet to be institutionalized in African politics, since citizens in many countries appear to not have a stake in AIDS outcomes. Second, inequality in political representation, and the tendency of power to be centralized in the executive, mean that the groups most vulnerable to the disease are underrepresented in AIDS policymaking. However, this level of representation depends on the country, and Africa's democracies appear slightly more willing to broaden such representation. While this representation in democracies may indicate the long-term, entrenched interest of civil society in AIDS decisions, it is unclear at this point if that is the case. Third, the nature of Africa's democratic institutions shapes policy outcomes. Because African elections are relatively noncompetitive, legislatures are weak, and subnational institutions have few resources, they have rarely pushed executives in AIDS decisionmaking. The result has been that government responses to AIDS in Africa's new democracies have been haphazard: some democratic countries have spent more resources on AIDS and their politicians have campaigned on the disease. For those countries, such as Botswana, the impact of that commitment is politically significant to their citizens and the donors who fund their programs. However, at this point, it is impossible to say that democracy guarantees that governments will institutionalize concerns about AIDS into all of their activities.

## Notes

1. A country is free if it receives a score of 1–2.5 on a combined measure of political rights and civil liberties, partly free if the score is 3–5, and not free if the score is 5.5–7. Freedom House rates countries on a seven-point scale, with one representing the most free and seven representing the least free. Political rights include the right to form parties and to compete for office. Civil liberties include religious, ethnic, economic, and gender rights, freedom of the press, and freedom of association. In 1972, Freedom House reported on thirty-nine countries; in 2004, it reported on forty-eight. There were no reports in 1972 on Seychelles, Djibouti, Sao Tome and Principe, Eritrea, Guinea Bissau, Angola, Mozambique, Cape Verde, and Comoros because those countries had not yet gained independence.

2. Throughout the chapter, I refer to democratic countries as those countries Freedom House classifies as free; partly or semi-democratic countries as those countries Freedom House terms partly free; and nondemocratic countries as those countries Freedom House classifies as not free.

3. For this analysis, I examined newspapers during an election year. If countries had separate legislative and presidential elections, I looked at presidential, not parliamentary, elections. Presidential candidates are more likely to receive media coverage of their campaigns and they are more likely than parliamentary candidates to discuss national problems such as AIDS.

4. Nelson Mandela has provided more leadership on AIDS in his post-presidency than during his presidency.

5. Even among whites, 93 percent believed government should provide ARVs for PMTCT and 87.7 percent thought government should provide universal access to treatment (Human Sciences Research Council 2002, 91).

6. The first round of the presidential election was much closer, with Mills winning 45 percent of the vote and Kufour winning 48 percent.

7. Despite these efforts to counter stigma, an editorial in the *Ghanaian Times* on September 18, 2003, argued that before Ghanaian consulates give visas to individuals, consul officials should examine an applicant's physical appearance for signs that he or she is HIV positive. The editorial was in response to stories that a Dutch tourist had been visiting Ghana for several years, intentionally spreading HIV among women.

8. Anonymous Malawian NGO representative, email correspondence with author, July 9, 2004.

# 4

---

# Civil Society's Influence on the Politics of AIDS

IN 2001, DELEGATES to the United Nations General Assembly Special Session on HIV/AIDS highlighted the significant contribution of civil society organizations in fighting AIDS (United Nations 2001, par. 33). Although civil society has advocated for resources for AIDS, provided care to HIV-positive people, and shaped national AIDS plans, civil society's role in the politics of AIDS is mixed and uneven. In some countries and on some issues related to HIV/AIDS, civil society has participated in policy development; at other times, civil society has been a more problematic political actor. This chapter examines two distinct, but interrelated, questions about civil society: (1) Why are some AIDS organizations internally strong? (2) What enables some organizations to influence AIDS policies? It is necessary to ask both of these questions. Organizational strength shapes how, or if, a group influences AIDS policies. While it may be possible for weak associations to shape isolated policy outcomes, it is more likely that strong associations will have a long-run effect on government actions. However, organizational strength may be insufficient for groups to influence policy if external factors such as state repression or political culture hamper them.

Strong organizations are defined quite broadly here as those with continuous operations and well-defined structures for doing the organization's business. Thus, an organization that rarely meets, does not engage in activities, has no institutions for decisionmaking or communication, and has an inactive membership is not considered organizationally strong. Organizational strength is a continuum, and ebbs and flows with time, leadership, external events, and resources. The chapter focuses on three factors that contribute to organizational strength: adequate financial resources, the human capacity of members and leaders, and internal structures that facilitate transparency and accountability. I operationalize an organization's influence on policy as activity that leads to changes in national and/or international AIDS programs. I analyze four factors shaping influence: the political system in which a civil society group operates, the political culture surrounding the organization, the domestic and international coalitions the association forges, and the group's relations with the state.

Civil society is the array of people's organizations, voluntary associations, self-help clubs, interest groups, religious bodies, nongovernmental development organizations, foundations, and social movements, which may be formal or informal in nature, which are not part of government, and which are not established to make profits (Fowler 1997, 8). Many civil society groups such as unions, business organizations, and human rights groups are intermediaries between the state and the family or individual. Others do not serve such an intermediary role, but do tasks, such as promoting music in a community, that are neither the state's nor the family's primary responsibility (Skillen 2004, 21). Individuals form groups to represent their interests, to hold government accountable, to get their members elected (or appointed) to positions of power, to provide services to their members, and/or to carry out a mission they support. Civil society is diverse; organizations vary in their relationships with the state, differ in their resources, and operate within unique political and cultural contexts.

Although this chapter focuses on organizations whose primary issue is AIDS, business groups, student clubs, local development organizations, religious associations, and women's groups also have been involved in the AIDS fight. Multilateral and bilateral donors and African states have relied heavily on multinational and indigenous NGOs to develop and implement AIDS programs. As early as 1987, Jonathan Mann, then the head of the GPA for WHO, sought to bring civil society into policy discussions about AIDS. As a result, civil society groups have formal avenues for participation in UNAIDS and the GFATM (Söderholm 1997, 137, 155). This incorporation mirrors academic debates that emphasize civil society's participation in development and democratization (Ndegwa 1996, 2–5; Harbeson et al. 1994, 1; Bratton and van de Walle 1992; Putnam 1993). Emmanuel Gyimah-Boadi (2004b, 100–105) asserts that civil society in Africa has challenged authoritarianism, uncovered abuses of power, fostered citizenship, provided for citizens' material needs, and incorporated marginalized groups such as women into politics. Lowell Ewert (2004, 104–106) maintains that civil society facilitates the realization of basic human rights such as participation and free speech. As Chapter 5 illustrates, this scholarship has policy implications since bilateral and multilateral donors have relied on local and multinational NGOs to design and/or implement many AIDS programs in Africa.

This chapter concentrates its empirical investigation on the Treatment Action Campaign (TAC), because the group's transparency has facilitated widespread research on the organization, and because it is considered the strongest and most influential AIDS organization in Africa (Webb 2004). TAC is contrasted with other AIDS organizations, particularly the Zimbabwe National Network for People Living with HIV/AIDS (ZNNP+), South Africa's National Association of People with AIDS (NAPWA), the Ghana HIV/AIDS Network (GHANET), and the Ghana AIDS Treatment Access Group (GATAG). Though there is limited academic research on these organizations, I choose them because they provide points of comparison with TAC. Also, the environments in which they operate vary, since Ghana and South Africa are democracies and Zimbabwe is not, and since South Africa and Zimbabwe have HIV prevalence rates around 20 percent, while Ghana's is roughly 3 percent (UNAIDS 2004a).

## The Organizations

TAC was formed in 1998, with the objective of "campaign[ing] for greater access to treatment for all South Africans by raising public awareness and understanding about issues surrounding the availability, affordability and use of HIV treatments." It also campaigns against "the view that AIDS is a 'death sentence'" (TAC 2006a). As of 2004, it worked primarily in three South African provinces—Gauteng, Western Cape, and KwaZulu-Natal. Its successes include pressuring the Pharmaceutical Manufacturers' Association (PMA) to drop its lawsuit against the South African Medicines Act, winning court cases demanding drugs for PMTCT, negotiating with Pfizer for donations of fluconazale, and advocating for universal access to ARVs for all South Africans needing them (Cameron 2005; TAC 2006a; Friedman and Mottiar 2004; Butler 2005).

As of late 2005, Zimbabwe's NGO Network Alliance (2005) reported that ZNNP+ had "suspended its operations until further notice," clearly making it a weak organization. It was formed in 1992, and it reported a membership of 1.5 million by 2000, making it one of the oldest and largest AIDS associations in Africa. Its objectives were to advocate for AIDS programs and spending, to provide counseling for members, to increase awareness of HIV/AIDS, and to demand representation of PLWHAs on government AIDS institutions. Its two biggest successes were gaining representation on the National AIDS Council and lobbying the government to pass the AIDS levy, a tax to provide money for AIDS programs (Batsell 2005, 68).

NAPWA was formed in 1994, as the magnitude of AIDS started to become apparent in South Africa. Though various reports put it between 70,000 and 300,000 members, it is one of the largest AIDS groups in the country (*Sowetan*, October 12, 2004; *Business Wire*, March 8, 2005; Harvard School of Public Health 2004; SANGONet 2006). Its goals are relatively broad: it seeks to fight AIDS discrimination, promote HIV/AIDS education, provide care and support for PLWHAs, and advocate for AIDS spending (NAPWA 2003). Its policy successes have included advocacy for human rights and nondiscrimination for PLWHAs, the development of care and support networks for PLWHAs and their families, increased government spending on HIV/AIDS, and, in 2004, partnership with the US-financed Harvard School of Public Health treatment adherence program in South Africa. Though NAPWA worked with TAC until 1999, the two have diverged in their goals and competed for members and the political spotlight since 2001.

Formed in 1996, GHANET is an umbrella association that represents 150 member organizations on the Ghana AIDS Commission (GAC) and on several technical working groups, including the country's CCM and the UNAIDS working group. Its goals are to fight AIDS discrimination, to act as a pressure group for PLWHAs, to serve as a broad-based forum for exchanging information on AIDS, and to train member associations to write grant proposals and manage AIDS programs (GHANET 2005). GHANET's successes have included its ability to shape GFATM grants and its recognition by donors and government as a national voice on AIDS. In contrast, GATAG is much newer (formed in 2002) and smaller (in 2003, the leadership hoped to reach 300 PLWHAs, but it is unclear if this has been achieved).[1] Ghanaians seeking access to affordable treatment formed the organization. Its biggest success has been to put treatment on Ghana's AIDS agenda, since the country has primarily focused on prevention. Part of this effort was a 2002 campaign to get Coca Cola bottling in Ghana to provide ARVs for its HIV-positive workers (GATAG 2005).

### What Makes a Strong AIDS Organization?

Civil society organizations vary in their internal dynamics and resources: some are financially well endowed, while others are in debt;

some have thousands of members, while others may have only a handful of participants. Some have hierarchical decisionmaking structures, and others are participatory. While there are many variables that shape internal dynamics, three are analyzed here: financial resources, human capacity, and internal structures that foster transparency, leadership accountability, and group unity. Table 4.1 categorizes organizations from the strongest (TAC) to the weakest (ZNNP+), and illustrates that TAC is relatively strong in all of these areas. The table is not intended to provide rigid categorization, but to allow for comparisons.

### Adequate Financial Resources

Group strength partly derives from financial resources, and while group leaders maintain it is impossible to ever have "enough" funds, it is clear that some groups are better endowed than others.[2] Funding enables organizations to hire staff members; to rent office space; to purchase communication technology such as phones, mailings, computers, and Internet access; to conduct membership drives; to complete projects that serve members; and to send representatives to international conferences. These tools can facilitate internal transparency and communication and can help publicize group successes to members and nonmembers. These tools also increase the likelihood that an organization can shape policy: professional staff can lobby government; attendance at conferences encourages the building of domestic and international

**Table 4.1    Factors Shaping Organizational Strength**

| Group[a] | Adequate Financial Resources | Capacity (Members) | Capacity (Leaders) | Internal Structures |
|---|---|---|---|---|
| TAC | Strong[b] | Strong | Strong | Strong |
| NAPWA | Weak | Strong | Strong | Weak |
| GHANET | Weak | Weak | Weak | Weak |
| GATAG | Weak | Weak | Weak | Weak |
| ZNNP+ | Weak | Weak | Weak | Weak |

*Source:* Compiled by author.

a. Associations are listed from strongest to weakest in terms of organizational strength. (Organizational strength is defined as a group with continuous operations and well-defined structures for meeting its objectives.)

b. For each variable, organizations are rated weak or strong. Although there is variation among organizations with the same rating, my purpose is to demonstrate the relative strength or weakness of different groups.

coalitions; communication technology facilitates interactions with the media.

A common problem among African civil society organizations is fundraising. Most local associations lack the experienced personnel to write grant proposals to donors and they cannot easily fundraise among an impoverished general public. Most do not engage in for-profit activities, such as consulting, because these ventures "can expose organizations to the risk of being diverted from their civic action" (Gyimah-Boadi 2004b, 109). This means that many local organizations either have no resources or they must rely on external funds for programs and organizational capacity. For example, the *Economist* reported that 111 of 120 Kenyan NGOs established between 1993 and 1996 received all of their funds from foreign governments (January 29, 2000, p. 25). This external involvement reflects an ongoing crisis of capacity within Africa's NGOs (Webb 2004, 29), and this reliance can be risky since funding cuts may mean the end of local programs. This happened to the Network of Zambian People Living with HIV/AIDS, which had to terminate its food distribution program for HIV-positive individuals when it lost multinational NGO financing (*UN Integrated Regional Information Networks*, May 26, 2005). Another option is for groups to forge connections with expatriates in the West who finance the group, a strategy the Ark Foundation Ghana uses.[3] For some organizations, such as GATAG, funding is highly contingent on the close connections their leaders have forged to donors or other NGOs.[4] However, for their long-run sustainability, AIDS organizations need to diversify their fundraising activities to include external grants, member dues, philanthropic donations from the country and the West, and profit-making services such as consultancy. Not only will this ensure financial independence, but it will also foster autonomy in decisionmaking.

TAC uses this multipronged approach to fundraising, though over 90 percent of its income in 2004 came from multinational NGOs and foundations in industrialized countries. TAC members do not have to pay dues, though in a few of TAC's branches they do. In 2004, TAC reported an income of R14,429,363 ($2,409,346). It received grants in 2003 and 2004 from Bread for the World ($667,952), Atlantic Philanthropies ($704,680), the Open Society Forum for South Africa ($233,687), American Jewish World Service ($17,159), the Rockefeller Foundation ($80,568), Oxfam ($15,142), Médicins sans Frontières (MSF; Doctors Without Borders) ($189,633), the Kaiser Foundation ($42,943), and an anonymous international rock star ($39,996) (TAC 2005, 4, 9, 11).[5] TAC does not accept money from the South African government, pharmaceutical companies, or some official government aid organizations, such as USAID (Friedman and Mottair 2004, 5). Additionally, the TAC website (www.tac.org.za) allows people world-wide to donate and sells merchandise priced in US dollars, such as the "HIV-positive" t-shirts made famous when Nelson Mandela was photographed wearing one. Another fundraising venture launched in 2004 was the sale of *Telling Tales*, edited by South African writer Nadine Gordimer. Twenty-one authors contributed their stories to the anthology for no profit, and all revenue goes to TAC. Between 2002 and 2004, TAC's income doubled.

TAC contrasts with ZNNP+ and GHANET. Before 2004, ZNNP+ received most of its funding from multinational NGOs and bilateral donor agencies such as the US Centers for Disease Control. In April 2004, the Zimbabwean Ministry of Health and Child Welfare advised donor organizations to stop funding ZNNP+ because of corruption, a recommendation that cut off the group's finances and may have contributed to its inactive status (*Herald* [Harare], April 30, 2004). NAPWA also experienced budgetary problems in 2004, which led to closing its national office from November 2004 until February 2005 (*Business Wire*, March 8, 2005).

GHANET's experience lies between those of TAC and ZNNP+. GHANET receives most of its money from the European Union and Irish Aid, and the GAC-administered Ghana AIDS Response Fund (GARFUND). Member organizations are supposed to pay dues, which has caused some groups to leave the network. Donor funding has been used to purchase a printer and office supplies. GARFUND money, on the other hand, must be used for specific AIDS-related projects, not advocacy. Fund applicants receive grants either through direct application or through allocation by district AIDS committees. However, this money comes with requirements: local NGOs must contribute 10 percent of project costs themselves (Patterson and Haven n.d., 10–11; GHANET 2005). GHANET's tentative financial situation has made it difficult to meet some of its goals, such as setting up regional offices throughout the country.

In a comparison of the five organizations, TAC is the strongest financially. NAPWA and ZNNP+ have experienced budgetary problems. GHANET has links to donors and the state, but not enough resources to meet its goal of linking the country's AIDS groups. GATAG relies on the potentially tenuous personal networks its president has forged for revenue.

TAC demonstrates the benefits that derive from financial resources.

First, funds enable TAC to communicate with members through its website and to disseminate information at its treatment workshops. Its email subscription list sends timely messages about scientific research on ARV treatment, TAC meetings, government policies, and other issues affecting TAC members. While AIDS organizations may not need the Internet to communicate with their members who are illiterate or who lack access to technology, websites and email communication give groups international legitimacy and facilitate fundraising beyond national borders. TAC communication contrasts with NAPWA and GHANET. GHANET has only slowly developed a membership directory, an essential tool for an organization that is supposed to facilitate networking. In early 2006, the organization's website provided a relatively incomplete membership list. As of January 2006, NAPWA's website was outdated—with its most recent announcements from 2003.[6]

Second, resources enable groups to hire full-time personnel. In 2004, TAC had forty staff (Friedman and Mottiar 2004, 2), and NAPWA had sixty, though financial problems affected NAPWA's staffing situation in 2004 (*Sowetan*, October 12, 2004). In contrast, GHANET finally had enough funding in 2005 to hire one staff member; before then it was volunteer run. Likewise, GATAG is volunteer based. ZNNP+'s staff situation was uncertain as of late 2005. TAC personnel conduct research, write newsletters, lobby government, interact with the media, and organize campaigns. In volunteer-run organizations, leaders with other employment obligations may not have the time for such activities. In 2003, a GHANET official explained that to compensate themselves, volunteers participated in donor-funded workshops to get stipends (Patterson and Haven n.d., 15).

Third, financial resources facilitate coalition building, since groups without funds cannot easily participate in Internet discussions or attend international conferences. Throughout Africa, AIDS groups are intensely aware of how a lack of money prevents them from participating in meetings where they might network with Western NGOs. Although GATAG's president Israel Asamoah does attend some conferences, GATAG leaders made this point in 2003, after they could not afford to attend an AIDS conference in Uganda (Haven 2003).[7] Before the 2003 International Conference on AIDS and STDs in Africa (ICASA), one African NGO representative said of the conference's $500 registration fee:

> To be charging $500 U.S. dollars as registration fees in Kenya is outrageous. As a matter of fact the highest GNI/GDP per capita in Africa is about 400 dollars in a year. Tell me who are these conferences meant for? Who are the people who always learn at these conferences? The

poor NGOs who are focused and committed but have little or no funding? Who are the people who always get the scholarships for these conferences even though they can afford to pay for it? We all know the answer! (AF-AIDS at http://archives.healthdev.net/af-aids/threads.html, September 2, 2003)

As the NGO representative hinted, the well-funded groups that already have connections to donors or multinational NGOs are the ones that can afford to attend conferences (Shaffer 2000). This fact caused one African NGO representative at a GFATM-organized event at the 2004 International AIDS Conference to comment that attendees seemed to be "insiders," or those who knew donors and multinational NGOs, rather than "outsiders," or small indigenous NGOs (PartnersGF eForum at http://forum.theglobalfund.org/en, November 5, 2004).

Although representatives of GHANET, GATAG, ZNNP+, and NAPWA have attended global conferences and tried to build coalitions, TAC's resources have enabled it to do more of these activities. TAC hires staff members to coordinate with AIDS activists globally. TAC officials have traveled to Thailand and Brazil to learn about those countries' treatment programs. Evidence of these international connections was apparent on World AIDS Day, December 1, 2005. TAC was the only African AIDS organization featured in a *New York Times* insert entitled "We all have AIDS." Nelson Mandela, Bishop Desmond Tutu, and TAC founder Zackie Achmat were the only Africans among the twenty-five AIDS activists photographed.

Financial resources are crucial for civil society organizations engaging in the politics of AIDS. However, it must be acknowledged that not every organization working on AIDS deserves large amounts of funding. Some groups may have incompetent leaders or corrupt practices. In countries that have received large amounts of external money to fight AIDS, some groups have formed rapidly to access these finances. Sadly, some know little or nothing about AIDS or organizational management. My point is not that all AIDS groups deserve large amounts of funding; rather, I argue that TAC is a relatively exceptional African AIDS organization in its financial resources, one factor making it more likely that TAC can affect the policy process.

*Human Capacity*

Organizational strength also derives from the devotion, skills, and experiences of group members and leaders. Before I analyze how the groups differ, it is important to acknowledge how AIDS similarly affects all of them. Members of AIDS groups share common experiences: they may be HIV positive; they may have lost family and friends to the disease; they may face AIDS-related discrimination. TAC leaders estimate that between 50 percent and 70 percent of group members are HIV positive, though members do not have to disclose their HIV status. For HIV-negative members, most have lost loved ones or friends to AIDS (Friedman and Mottiar 2004). Although there is little empirical research on this topic, these experiences may motivate members' participation in AIDS groups.[8] Because TAC and GATAG campaign specifically for access to lifesaving ARVs, participation in these two groups is literally about life and death. Edwin Cameron (2005, 158–160), an openly gay, HIV-positive justice in South Africa, describes how one TAC member, Christopher Moraka, fought in 2000 for access to fluconazale, a drug used to treat esophageal candidiasis.[9] The drug was too expensive for widespread use because its maker Pfizer had a patent for its production. Moraka testified to a parliamentary committee on medicine pricing:

> To underestimate [Christopher's] courage in [testifying] would be wrong. A few seats to Christopher's right sat representatives of the pharmaceutical industry—well-suited professional public relations experts with a job to do. In front of him sat members of the committee . . . Outside the committee chamber, tea and crust-less miniature sandwiches were being served. But neither tea nor bread, however served, were of much use to Christopher. He was desperately ill. He was also addressing the committee in his second language. No one of them shared his living circumstances. . . . But Christopher persisted. For him, this was about life and death—his life and his death, and that of many thousands of others . . . A few short months after testifying in Parliament Christopher was dead.

The willingness to endure such pain and public humiliation for a larger cause can be a source of group strength for all AIDS organizations.

The specific nature of AIDS shapes the work of these associations. Because the primary means of HIV infection, sexual transmission, is linked to debates on promiscuity, prostitution, and, in the West, homosexuality, PLWHAs face stigma. Experienced, observed, and feared stigma discourages people from getting tested or from disclosing their status, and this discrimination places an immense burden on PLWHAs and their families, friends, and caregivers (UNAIDS 2003, 31). Edward Green (2003b, 168–169) argues that levels of stigma vary across countries, with citizens in Ugandan focus groups exhibiting a "striking[ly] positive attitude about people with AIDS." Yet, even though stigma appears to be less in Uganda, this does not mean people with AIDS are immune to discrimination.

Stigma may make it less likely that individuals, regardless of their serostatus, will join AIDS organizations or play an active role in them. An urban female student in Ethiopia explained how even discussing the possibility of getting tested could result in negative consequences: "The students rejected me only because I *talked* about [the] test" (Stigma-AIDS at http://archives.healthdev.net/stigma-aids, April 27, 2004; emphasis added). A South African development NGO official said: "If one or a number of your leaders have AIDS, it becomes a problem to attract people to your organization. The belief is that he/she is negligent and dirty" (Manning 2002, 11). Stigma is even present within the United Nations system, where discussions about AIDS and AIDS projects are at the forefront. It is estimated that 5 percent of the roughly 10,000 UN employees are HIV positive. Yet as of 2004, fewer than twenty individuals had openly discussed their HIV status (Stigma-AIDS at http://archives.healthdev.net/stigma-aids, June 28, 2004).

Stigma intersects with power inequalities to limit mobilization of people most needing representation through AIDS organizations, since stigma makes it less likely that members of marginalized groups will disclose their status (Stigma-AIDS at http://archives.healthdev.net/stigma-aids, May 12, 2004). Edwin Cameron (2005, 58, 73) contrasts his power to disclose his HIV status with the powerlessness of many South Africans to do the same. As a white, well-educated, middle-class man with a constitutionally secure job, Cameron could choose to live openly with AIDS. In contrast, those without privilege may have no choice but to forgo help, testing, treatment, or membership in organizations like TAC. TAC officials acknowledge that the group's membership is lower than it potentially could be because stigma discourages participation (Friedman and Mottiar 2004, 3).

In addition, AIDS creates economic, emotional, and social stresses that curtail people's time and energy for civil society participation (Whiteside et al. 2002). For many AIDS NGOs, and indigenous NGOs in general, the disease has negatively impacted their organizations, as HIV-positive personnel become sick and HIV-negative coworkers must deal with overwork and the emotional turmoil of losing colleagues. For example, of fifty-nine NGOs surveyed in South Africa's Kwazulu-Natal province in 2002, forty-five said that AIDS had impacted their organization. As leaders die, organizations lose institutional memory and the personal ties that leaders may have with the state, multinational NGOs, donors, and other civil society groups. The death of members means a loss of workers, resources, and political clout. Even before individuals die, they may lose hope. One South African NGO representative said: "[HIV-positive people] don't participate in community activities, because they think they will die soon" (Manning 2002, 10–11). And the sheer number of member deaths in a country like South Africa is bound to impact any organization. For example, within three months in 2003, TAC lost one hundred of its members (*Sunday Times*, October 12, 2003). The disease itself may weaken AIDS organizations.

Despite these common experiences, AIDS groups differ in their human capacity. One source of human capacity is group size, and the five associations vary considerably. NAPWA is the largest with between 70,000 and 300,000 members. Although ZNNP+ reported over one million members in 2000, by 2005, it appears its membership had greatly dwindled. GHANET's size is difficult to determine because its members are organizations, not individuals. However, it has the potential to be several thousand people. In 2003, GATAG had a small membership of roughly three hundred. In 2004, TAC's membership was roughly 9,500. Perhaps a more crucial issue is change in membership. Organizations with increasing numbers of members may have more potential to mobilize people for political action. Increasing membership also may demonstrate some level of organizational success, since unsuccessful organizations are unlikely to attract participants. In comparison to ZNNP+, NAPWA, and GHANET, TAC's membership increased from 8,000 in 2003 to 9,500 in 2004. In contrast, GHANET's membership dropped from 450 organizations in 1996 to 150 organizations in 2004 (Patterson and Haven n.d.).

Members' political experiences and education levels also affect human capacity. TAC's membership tends to be unemployed and urban; many members' ability to communicate in complex policy debates in English is limited (Friedman and Mottiar 2004, 7). Both TAC and NAPWA have trained local members, so participants have gained leadership experience. NAPWA and TAC also are similar in that some of their members were involved with mass mobilization against apartheid before 1994. In contrast, members of Ghana's organizations do not have this larger experience with mass mobilization, since civil society activism was not crucial in Ghana's democratic transition. Finally, literacy rates among adults in South Africa (86%) and Zimbabwe (90%) are higher than in Ghana (73%), a fact that may affect the different groups' capacity (UNDP 2004, 141). For example, GHANET acknowledges how its members' limited education and management experiences have hampered some of its efforts (GHANET 2005). To sum up, TAC and

NAPWA are strong in terms of human capacity because of their size and/or growing membership, some members' experiences with political mobilization under apartheid, and the relatively high literacy rate in South Africa. GHANET, GATAG, and ZNNP+ are weaker because of smaller or, for ZNNP+ and GHANET, diminished memberships. Their members also have less experience with overall mass mobilization. In Ghana, relatively lower literacy rates present challenges.

Visionary leaders are another element of human capacity: leaders can motivate members, build coalitions, facilitate fundraising, and attract members. All five groups have charismatic leaders. Former ZNNP+ head Frenk Guni is dynamic and bold, which might have contributed to the ZNNP+ clashes with the government outlined below. GHANET's president in 2003, Sam Anyimadu-Amaning, was a charismatic leader, as is GATAG's president (Haven 2003). NAPWA's founder Peter Busse was recognized for his tireless energy. TAC leader Zackie Achmat is an HIV-positive, gay South African, whom Edwin Cameron (2005, 55) describes as "a man of immoderate intelligence, personal magnetism and courage" with a "steely sense of strategy." Illustrating his willingness to take risks, in 1999 Achmat began a "drug strike" in which he refused to take his ARVs until 2003, when the government announced the medications would be available to all South Africans who need them. His action helped TAC gain international support and it demonstrated his solidarity with millions of HIV-positive South Africans. Achmat's gutsy moves, his outspokenness, and his charisma have benefited TAC.

But the leaders of the two South African organizations have another asset that is less apparent in the other three groups. They gained political experiences during the apartheid period working in the gay rights movement, the community-based United Democratic Front, and the outlawed ANC. They learned to organize civil disobedience campaigns (i.e., campaigns in which they peacefully broke the law, but accepted the consequences) and to build international coalitions, skills TAC officials utilized in the group's 2003 treatment campaign. During apartheid, future TAC and NAPWA leaders became adept at locating their arguments for gay rights in a larger framework of human rights, and some of these individuals formed organizations to work on these issues. For example, in 1994, Achmat founded the National Coalition for Gay and Lesbian Equality to lobby for inclusion of gay rights into the South African constitution. Achmat then worked with the AIDS Law Project (ALP) at the University of Witwatersrand, an organization founded in 1993 predominantly to provide free legal assistance to individuals facing discrimination because of HIV/AIDS. The language of human rights has been particularly crucial for how TAC frames its arguments for universal treatment. Finally, these leaders gained experience negotiating with government and other civil society groups at the 1992 National AIDS Conference on South Africa and through the AIDS Consortium Project (Mbali 2004; Power 2003a, 58).

### Internal Structures to Facilitate Transparency and Accountability

Internal structures that promote participation, transparency, and accountability can also shape organizational strength. If members distrust their leaders, they may be less willing to follow the decisions those leaders make. If group decisionmaking processes are viewed to be illegitimate, members may leave the organization. Without internal transparency, corruption and financial mismanagement can occur.

TAC's structure seeks to encourage participation, transparency, and accountability.[10] Its basic unit is the branch, and each province has an executive committee. There are monthly meetings at each of these levels. Branches nominate and members elect the national executive. The national leadership makes the major strategic decisions, though it consults with the provinces and each province has a national representative. Provincial, branch, and national leaders have varied perspectives about communication between national leaders and the grassroots. For example, provincial leaders in Western Cape complained that the national secretariat undermined their authority when it changed plans for protests at a speech by then deputy president Jacob Zuma (Friedman and Mottiar 2004, 8–10). In contrast, other leaders insist that provincial officials can influence national strategies. In an organization as large as TAC, this variety of opinions is not surprising. NAPWA has a similar structure in terms of the use of branches and provincial officials, but its communication among levels is less transparent. In contrast, GHANET has suffered internal dissent, poor communication, and undefined relationships with member organizations. Member groups are uncertain about meeting times, the goals of the organization, or GHANET's funding sources (Patterson and Haven 2005, 86).

Internal structures also shape leadership accountability. TAC and NAPWA officials at each level are elected in regular elections. However, to ensure transparency, the Independent Electoral Commission oversees TAC's national executive elections. More informally, members have the opportunity to speak openly and frankly about TAC leaders: "There is no disciplinary procedure for people who hold dissenting views . . . TAC has a culture of speaking openly" (Friedman and Mottiar 2004, 11). This tolerance contrasts with GHANET, whose members (and some leaders) were hesitant to speak to researchers about the organization (Haven 2003). The open communication also differs somewhat from GATAG, which primarily uses its membership email list to convey information. However, over half of the members on this list are academics, international NGOs, and other Ghanaian AIDS NGOs.[11] The email list became a venue for confusion about the GATAG leadership in 2005, when someone claimed the president had been replaced. In response, the real GATAG president sent an email message to members announcing that someone was posing as the group's president with alleged support from local police. The president said the "impersonator's" objective was to discredit the organization and its president by raising questions about accountability and transparency. The problem was resolved out of the public eye, but it confused members and demonstrated uneven communication in the organization.[12]

Regular elections, open discussions, and institutional checks and balances that enable members to limit leaders' power are important in any civil society organization. Otherwise, there is the danger that key personalities will dominate, a possibility that can be exacerbated if an association depends heavily on the skills and charisma of its leaders (Ndegwa 1996). AIDS groups such as ZNNP+, GATAG, and GHANET that rely on personal leadership may face similar challenges. This possibility exists within TAC too, though Friedman and Mottiar (2004, 11) assert, "the fact that TAC does have functioning democratic structures is in itself an important guarantee that members retain a voice since they build in mechanisms which force leadership to respond to membership."

Part of accountability includes financial transparency. Of the five organizations, TAC is the most open about its finances. It posts its audits on its website, including its lists of donations. It also requires each province to submit a monthly budget and, once approved, the executive transfers funds to the province. TAC officials say these tight financial controls are necessary for donor grants, to retain trust in the organization, and to enable auditors to quickly detect any misappropriation of funds (Friedman and Mottiar 2004, 10). Similarly, GHANET and NAPWA require annual financial audits, but this information is not accessible on their websites (GHANET 2005; NAPWA 2003).

TAC contrasts with ZNNP+, which I discuss below, and with NAPWA, which was accused in 2004 of misappropriating funding it received from the Department of Health's HIV/AIDS NGO funding source. In two October 12, 2004, *Sowetan* articles, journalist and former

South African National AIDS Council (SANAC) member Lucky
Mazibuko described how NAPWA reached a funding crisis in late 2004,
and managers were unable to pay staff for several months. However,
managers paid their own salaries, something employees and organizational members did not know about until later. Similarly, there have
been reports of Kenyan and Ghanaian AIDS groups that disappeared
after they received government grants (Patterson and Haven 2005,
85–90; *East African Standard*, July 3, 2003). While few in number,
these incidents illustrate that at times AIDS groups may have limited
transparency. To summarize, the internal structures of TAC are strong;
they promote financial transparency, allow for regular and transparent
elections, and encourage open discussion and criticism. While the other
organizations may have some of these aspects—NAPWA has regular
elections and GHANET's constitution requires annual financial audits—
they do not have all of them.

In groups with diverse members, leaders must work to build bridges
across race, class, and gender lines, and internal structures that facilitate
transparency and accountability can help do this. Otherwise such divisions can become tools of power and inequality in AIDS organizations,
just as they may be in other civil society groups (Fatton 1995; Patterson
1998). Although none of the five AIDS groups has been immune from
some of these divisions, these issues have received considerable attention in TAC, because of the group's successes and because race continues to shape South African politics and society (Friedman 2004, 241;
Gibson and Gouws 2003, 53, 61).

TAC's membership is primarily poor and black: an estimated 80
percent of members are unemployed and 90 percent are black South
Africans. However, its leadership is middle class and Mark Heywood,
TAC's national secretary, is white. Heywood, who also works for the
ALP, has a long history of activism with the ANC's exile branch in the
United Kingdom and, after 1989, in South Africa (ALP 2004).
Individuals within the South African government and society have
repeatedly criticized Heywood based on his race. For example, in March
2004, NAPWA said Heywood was "the white racist who has succeeded
in dividing black people." When the chair of the AIDS Consortium tried
to intervene, he was labeled part of the "black bourgeoisie" (TAC
2004a; *Business Day*, April 1, 2004). This followed a 2003 attack from
Health Minister Manto Tshabalala-Msimang, in which she said that people "come with buses and go to commissions where they wait for the
white man to tell them what to do . . . Our Africans say: Let us wait for

the white man to deploy us." Because these statements resonated with some TAC members, group leaders have had to become more sensitive about racial issues (Friedman and Mottiar 2004, 5).

Gender divisions also shape TAC, since an estimated 70 percent of members are women. TAC operates within a larger environment of patriarchy that limits women's political and social advancement. Women are more active at the branch level of TAC, possibly because women are more likely to be HIV positive than men. There are differences in women's representation depending on the level of the organization: most in provincial management are women and, since 2003, the four-person national secretariat is half female. However, only about one-third of all TAC office bearers are women. And TAC's public face is male, since high-level women have yet to acquire the public profile of Achmat and Heywood (Friedman and Mottiar 2004, 8–9).

What differentiates TAC from many AIDS organizations with similar cleavages is its conscious commitment to addressing the divisions not only rhetorically, but also through internal structures. TAC gives branch and provincial leaders, many of whom are poor women, opportunities to organize local activities, to manage funds, and to advance to national-level positions. The organization educates its male members about women's rights in treatment workshops and its national campaigns. After three men and one woman were elected to the national secretariat in 2003, one of the men agreed to be replaced by a woman to create a more gender-balanced executive. And the national executive has set gender parity as a goal in leadership positions (Friedman and Mottiar 2004, 9). In contrast, it is unclear that GHANET, GATAG, ZNNP+, and NAPWA have such explicit goals.

This section has argued that TAC is a strong organization because of its access to adequate financial resources, its human capacity, and its internal structures. It has asserted that TAC is not the only AIDS group with some of these assets, and that groups vary in how well developed these factors can be. For example, GHANET's president is dynamic, but overall its members lack much political experience. NAPWA is large and its leaders have wide political experience, but the 2004 corruption scandal hints that its internal structures are not very transparent.

Why do these elements of organizational strength matter for organizational effectiveness? Financial resources make it easier to mobilize members, to use communication technology, to hire staff, and to forge coalitions. A 2004 study showed how human capacity affects AIDS groups, particularly on CCMs, the national committees composed of representatives from government, civil society, and donor organizations that write proposals to the GFATM and oversee GFATM grants. Low educational levels, lack of professional skills, and limited leadership experience prevented civil society members from achieving their goals in Cameroon, Malawi, and Nigeria (GNP+ 2004, 11). Leadership experience also matters: TAC has successfully used civil disobedience because its leaders understand how to frame such campaigns to gain public support and how to shape the media agenda (Mbali 2005, 45).

Finally, internal structures facilitate or hamper accountability and transparency, two aspects crucial for member participation and external support. Because multinational NGOs must be accountable for their resources, they are unlikely to support an indigenous AIDS organization whose members do not participate or whose leaders are not accountable (Patterson 2003b). AIDS groups with disillusioned members have little ability to shape policy, since African civil society has affected political change by mobilizing large numbers of people, not by lobbying majoritarian institutions (Bratton and van de Walle 1992). A lack of accountability and transparency can breed division, even though, as Steven Talugende, coordinator of the National Forum of PLWHA Networks in Uganda, argues: "Unity among civil society members is essential" to fight AIDS (PartnersGF eForum at http://forum.theglobalfund.org/en, November 20, 2004).

### What Makes an AIDS Organization Influential?

Civil society's ability to shape AIDS policies depends not only on the internal aspects of organizations, but also on the context in which they operate. In this section, I will examine four contextual factors that may increase civil society's ability to influence the politics of AIDS: (1) a democratic political system; (2) a political culture that supports the activities of AIDS groups; and (3) domestic and international coalitions. The fourth factor—civil society's relationship with the state—also shapes influence but I do not conclude that one type of state-civil society relationship has more potential to make civil society influential than another type. Table 4.2 highlights differences among the five organizations in terms of these four variables. It illustrates that South Africa's democracy, the country's political culture, and coalitions have shaped TAC's effectiveness. Unlike the other organizations, TAC has sought a dual strategy in relations with the state, sometimes cooperating with and sometimes confronting it.

**Table 4.2    Factors Affecting Group Influence on Policy**

| Group[a] | Political System | Political Culture Supports AIDS Activities | Coalitions (National) | Coalitions (Global) | Relations with State |
|---|---|---|---|---|---|
| TAC | Democratic | Strong | Strong | Strong | Cooperation & Confrontation |
| NAPWA | Democratic | Strong | Weak | Weak/None | Cooperation/Capture |
| ZNNP+[b] | Authoritarian | Strong | Weak | Weak/None | Confrontation |
| GHANET | Democratic | Weak | Weak | Weak/None | Cooperation |
| GATAG | Democratic | Weak | Weak | Weak | Confrontation |

*Source:* Compiled by author.

a. Organizations are listed from most to least influential.

b. I base ZNNP+'s effectiveness on its participation in civil society's advocacy for the AIDS levy. Since 2002, the organization has become increasingly ineffective.

## A Democratic Political System

Advocates of the "democracy facilitates health" thesis assert that democracy enables civil society to influence government health policies. Although Africa's democratic transitions have been notoriously uneven (Joseph 1999, 10; Bratton and van de Walle 1997, 3), AIDS organizations have benefited from the increased freedom of association that has accompanied the spread of democracy in several African countries. For example, in 1999, there were approximately 54,000 NGOs in South Africa; in 2004, this number was estimated to be as high as 80,000, with TAC and NAPWA among them (Gyimah-Boadi 2004b, 112; James and Caliguire 1999, 88). The emergence of GHANET after Ghana's 1992 multiparty election, and GATAG, after that country's 2000 alternation in power, was possible in an increasingly open political environment. Political liberalization also has enabled associations that previously concentrated on the promotion of democracy to now focus on AIDS (Bryant 2004, 13).

Africa's democratic transitions have led to more than political space for advocacy. They also have created independent courts, subnational governments, and legislatures through which some AIDS organizations have challenged state policies. Yet, as Chapter 3 argued, these institutions provide a relatively underdeveloped avenue for representation and participation; as a result, in Ghana, GHANET and GATAG have not utilized them. In contrast, TAC has used the civil liberties outlined in the 1996 South African constitution and the country's independent judiciary to achieve policy goals. It must be recognized, though, that the decision to do this was partly rooted in the political experiences of TAC's leaders. For example, some had been involved in antidiscrimination court cases for HIV-positive individuals before 1998 (Mbali 2004). Also, TAC's close alliance with the ALP facilitated their legal strategy. NAPWA, which works in the same political system as TAC, has not incorporated a legal strategy, partly because of its relatively cooperative relationship with the government. It has, though, utilized marches to raise AIDS awareness (NAPWA 2003).

Use of the legal strategy brought TAC one of its most important policy successes. In 2001, TAC sued the government to provide either AZT or nevirapine for PMTCT.[13] This lawsuit occurred at the same time that some provincial governments were challenging the national nevirapine policy. In 2001, the Pretoria High Court ruled that the constitutional right to health care required the government to provide nevirapine to all HIV-positive pregnant mothers. The government appealed, arguing that the policy was an encroachment on executive power. It lost its appeal to the Constitutional High Court in 2002.

Since then, government policies on nevirapine, and TAC responses to those policies, have vacillated. In July 2003 the South African Medicines Control Council, the government agency charged with drug approval, reported that it may deregister nevirapine based on results from Ugandan and South African studies (*New York Times*, August 7, 2003). Two months later, the council rescinded the statement and supported the use of nevirapine (*South African Press Association*, September 13, 2003). One year later, the council recommended against giving HIV-positive women a single dose of nevirapine, based on the finding that between 30 percent and 50 percent of women taking nevirapine may develop resistance to combination therapies containing the drug. At the 2004 International AIDS Conference, the South African health minister strongly hinted that the government had adopted single-dose nevirapine because of the TAC-sponsored lawsuit, not scientific evidence (*New York Times*, July 14, 2004, p. A11). In response, TAC quickly issued press releases that cited WHO's support for single-dose nevirapine and explained scientific studies of the drug's potential risks and benefits. TAC further asserted that "public confidence in the current single-dose nevirapine regime has been undermined needlessly" because of the government's actions (TAC 2004b). Approximately one month later, the health minister announced that nevirapine monotherapy would continue until further research was completed (*South African Press Association*, August 12, 2004).

This saga illustrates both the ability of TAC to use the judiciary and the weakness of relying solely on the courts for policy development. Because the executive must implement judicial rulings, the courts provide a limited means through which to change policies (Butler 2002, 8). In reality, the underlying power of court decisions may be their influence on public opinion. This power depends on how (or if) AIDS organizations publicize decisions, oversee their implementation, and engage the policy process. At every point in the nevirapine debate, TAC has issued press releases, held marches, and disseminated well-researched reports. Again, these actions have been possible because the organization has the financial resources to hire staff to conduct research, to communicate with journalists, and to mobilize coalition members. As judicial autonomy and capacity slowly develop in other African democracies such as Botswana, Mali, and Ghana, courts may provide institutional avenues for more civil society challenges to AIDS policies (Prempeh 2001, 260).[14] TAC has been willing, and able, to take advantage of South Africa's new democratic structures, while other AIDS associations in Africa's new democracies have not.

### A Political Culture That Supports Activities of AIDS Groups

As TAC illustrates, democratic institutions that provide avenues to challenge state policies may be an asset. However, a comparison among ZNNP+, GATAG, and TAC shows that while democracy may be important, it is neither necessary nor sufficient. Ghana is democratic, while Zimbabwe is not (Freedom House 2005b). Yet, AIDS groups in Zimbabwe have been viewed as more active (and until roughly 2002, more successful) than similar groups in Ghana. This is because civil society associations are situated within unique political cultures. Political culture is a society's overarching beliefs about politics and the role of the state; these beliefs stem from a country's historical and social experiences and are reflected in political behavior and attitudes. Civil society groups that are congruent with their particular political cultures are more likely to shape policy than those that are not (Swidler 2001). In addition, the AIDS stigma is another dimension of political culture that can impact AIDS organizations. In countries with relatively low HIV prevalence rates, AIDS is often viewed as a disease of "other people"

(Oppong and Agyei-Mensah 2004, 78). This attitude, and the lack of experience citizens may have with the disease, may contribute to a political culture that disdains public mobilization against AIDS.

While it still functioned, ZNNP+ operated within a political system of increasing repression. Yet, it successfully lobbied for the AIDS levy and for representation on the National AIDS Council. More broadly, Zimbabwe's AIDS organizations, and their international NGO partners, have developed programs that contributed to the country's decline in HIV prevalence from 24.6 percent in 2003 to 21 percent in 2004 (UNAIDS 2005e, 20). In another undemocratic country, Uganda, AIDS organizations have worked closely with government to shape AIDS programs (Barnett and Whiteside 2002, 323). How has this influence been possible? While success depends partly on organizational resources (particularly in Uganda), political culture has supported civil society's involvement on AIDS in those two countries. High prevalence rates— 4.1 percent in 2003 for Uganda (though in the 1990s, it was over 15%) and 21 percent in 2004 for Zimbabwe—have meant that citizens have more personal experiences with AIDS. The Ugandan president also has facilitated open discussion of the disease (Green 2003b; UNAIDS 2005e, 22).

Though not among the associations this chapter investigates, AIDS groups in Botswana, a democracy with an HIV prevalence rate of 37.3 percent in 2003, provide a contrast, since they have played a minor role in pushing AIDS policies (Morrison and Hurlburt 2004, 4). There are several reasons for this. First, political activity reflects the belief that authority rests in the state and the paramount chiefs; Botswana's *kgotla* governance system provides limited space for civil society groups to shape policy. Second, state officials have increasingly brought business groups and labor unions into corporate governance to develop national economic plans, making it less necessary for these groups to overtly advocate for social welfare policies (Molutsi 2004, 162–169). Third, since President Festus Mogae came to office in 1998, the government has been proactive on HIV/AIDS. The president has increased AIDS spending and, most notably, announced in 2002 that the country would provide ARVs to all HIV-positive citizens who need them. This action, as well as his willingness to speak openly about AIDS almost every day, has made his country attractive to bilateral and multilateral donors and private organizations, all of which have provided millions of dollars to the country (Morrison and Hurlburt 2004, 3). This is not to say there are no AIDS organizations in Botswana, because groups like the Botswana Network of People Living with HIV/AIDS do important work for

PLWHAs. However, because of the political culture and state actions, these groups have had marginal involvement in policy development, despite the country's democratic political system and its high prevalence rate.

Differences in South Africa's and Ghana's political cultures and HIV prevalence rates may explain why the protest strategies TAC (and sometimes NAPWA) has effectively used have been ineffective for GATAG. Because of President Mbeki's actions on AIDS, AIDS has a level of public attention in South Africa that it does not have in Ghana. Additionally, because of apartheid and its long duration, South Africa has a political culture of protest that Ghana lacks. TAC and NAPWA leaders gained experience in the United Democratic Front, the Congress of South African Students, and the Congress of South African Trade Unions (COSATU), which organized strikes, work stoppages, boycotts, and large-scale marches to oppose apartheid (Deegan 2001, 57–60). Since its founding, NAPWA has organized some marches and protests, though its recent efforts have not been as massive as those of TAC. In 2003, TAC mobilized over 30,000 protesters for its treatment access campaign, during which it charged the health minister and the minister for trade and industry with culpable homicide for failing to prevent approximately six hundred AIDS-related deaths each day. TAC members interrupted the health minister's speeches and they criticized the government for failing to sign an agreement to provide ARVs from the country's arbitration body, the National Economic Development and Labour Council. In response, police arrested over one hundred activists in Cape Town and used water cannons to disperse crowds in Durban (*Agence France Presse*, March 20, 2003; *South African Press Association*, March 25, 2003; *South African Press Association*, March 20, 2003).

In contrast, GATAG has found that similar protest tactics are ineffective, because they do not resonate with Ghana's political culture, in which the majority of citizens are unwilling to overtly challenge authority. The GATAG president said: "We [in the organization] are advocates; we didn't want to use the word 'activist' because in Ghana we are, by our nature . . . not an aggressive people" (Patterson and Haven 2005, 87). Only about one-fifth of Ghanaians participate in unions, professional organizations, or voluntary associations, while over half belong to a religious association. Ghana's authoritarian past and citizens' concern about meeting their daily needs may help explain this pattern of participation (Gyimah-Boadi and Mensah 2003). Additionally, Ghana's low HIV prevalence rate makes it difficult for AIDS groups to gain widespread support. Thus, despite Ghana's democratic political system, its political culture does not support protest politics, particularly for AIDS organizations like GATAG. GHANET's nonconfrontational style has resonated more in that country's political culture.

### National and International Coalitions

Alliances with other organizations can increase political influence, though the ability to forge such coalitions often depends on a group's financial resources and human capacity. TAC illustrates the potential power of coalitions, since it has collaborated with domestic and international groups to shape policies on ARV treatment. NAPWA has worked in coalitions with some other AIDS groups, though by 2001 it had voted to "distance itself" from TAC. Increasingly eclipsed by TAC, its relations with other AIDS organizations have frayed and it has forged a stronger relationship with the state and the South African Traditional Healers Association, particularly to support nutritional and vitamin supplements for PLWHAs (Mbali 2005; Heywood 2004). Jake Batsell (2005, 71) describes the limited coalition building among Zimbabwe's AIDS groups: "More cooperation among AIDS NGOs ultimately could lead toward better cooperation with the government in fighting HIV/AIDS." There are no signs ZNNP+ forged strong global alliances. In Ghana, GHANET's domestic and international networking ability has been limited because of its organizational weakness. GATAG is not listed as a GHANET member, though in 2003 its president said it was (Haven 2003); its president also maintains ties to the Pan-African Treatment Movement (PATAM).

Alliances are a key part of TAC's strategy. And alliances are rooted in Achmat's past activist experiences, which taught him the value of "united fronts despite differing views" (Friedman and Mottiar 2004, 21). TAC works with the major trade union COSATU, the South African Council of Churches, other faith-based organizations, physician associations, nurses organizations, women's groups, the South African Communist Party (SACP), and the ALP. Some of these are predictable allies, such as health care providers or faith-based organizations. COSATU's participation also makes sense given the fact that AIDS has disproportionately affected union members.

These TAC alliances were important in mobilizing action for universal access to ARV treatment in South Africa. As Chapter 2 illustrated, the South African president and health minister have expressed doubt about ARV efficacy and safety, and they have argued that the drugs' high cost prohibits their widespread distribution by government

(Furlong and Ball 2005, 143). In August 2002, TAC and COSATU held a National HIV/AIDS Treatment Congress that over eight hundred individuals from various domestic and international organizations attended. Delegates produced a resolution stating: "There is a need to boldly take advantage of the best scientific knowledge about HIV/AIDS, including treatments for HIV. People in the developed world should not be the only people who benefit from breakthroughs in medical research" (COSATU 2002). In response, the South African Cabinet announced that it would investigate the costs and benefits of ARVs. When the cabinet delayed discussion of its report in early 2003, the coalition (led by TAC) leaked the report's key aspects to the press, including the prediction that between 2003 and 2010, almost two million lives could be saved if ARV treatment was available. The coalition then kept pressure on the government through organized marches and protests (*Financial Times*, July 15, 2003; TAC 2003). In late 2003, the government announced its plans for universal access to ARVs, starting with delivery to 50,000 people by March 2004. The coalition, with TAC as its leader, was widely credited with pressuring government until it provided treatment (*Sunday Times*, November 30, 2003, p. 21).

After the 2003 announcement, the coalition has continued to hold the government accountable for its promised treatment plan. In March 2004, TAC threatened litigation against the minister of health if she did not authorize immediate procurement of ARVs (*SABC News*, March 16, 2004). In July 2004, TAC and the ALP issued a report entitled "Our people are suffering, we need treatment," which detailed continued problems with the ARV rollout, including lack of funds, drug procurement hindrances, and little public information on accessing treatment (TAC and ALP 2004). At approximately the same time, the AIDS Budget Unit at the Institute for Democracy in South Africa, an independent public interest organization, reported that the government's plan was underfunded (AIDS Budget Unit 2004). In November 2004, TAC organized countrywide protests demanding more information on the government program (TAC 2004e). In late 2004, the government responded that it would not meet its 2004 treatment goal (*Washington Post*, November 30, 2004, p. A1).

Well-developed communication links and overlapping membership among coalition groups have helped TAC coordinate these activities. Several TAC leaders, including Achmat, are members of the ANC. As of 2005, Heywood was a leader in the ALP and TAC, and he had served as chairperson of the Law, Ethics and Human Rights Task Team of SANAC. COSATU and the SACP are part of the tripartite alliance with the ANC, a fact that has made it more difficult for the government to ignore their demands for ARV access.

While coalitions can increase an organization's political voice, they are not cost free. Alliances require that groups reject purism and adopt compromise. They also assume that various groups can find common ground, despite their differences. For example, TAC has worked with the Catholic Church, despite church opposition to, and TAC support for, condom use to prevent the spread of HIV (Friedman and Mottiar 2004, 20). Conflicts over strategy also affect alliances: the South African Nursing Council withdrew from TAC activities after March 2003 because it did not like the tactics being used (*Panafrican News Agency*, April 7, 2003). Although they were allies until 1999, NAPWA and TAC have become rivals. Animosity between the two groups was so high by 2005 that fifteen TAC "plants" in NAPWA were expelled at the group's national conference. NAPWA also has repeatedly referred to TAC as a "pharmaceutical industry lobby" (*Business Wire*, March 8, 2005). As this conflict suggests, current (and former) alliance members may compete for members and resources (Staggenborg 1986), sometimes through rather base tactics and rhetoric.

AIDS groups can also forge international coalitions. For example, GATAG tried to mobilize international support for its Coca Cola campaign, and some global activists pressured the company to drop arrest charges against the GATAG activists, but the level of mobilization has been somewhat limited. In contrast, Steven Friedman and Shauna Mottiar (2004, 22) write, "TAC's most strategically important alliance may have been that with international allies." TAC has partnered with MSF to support treatment projects in poor neighborhoods, the results of which helped TAC argue that treatment is feasible. TAC also has worked with the New York–based Treatment Action Group, which has run treatment workshops for members (Cameron 2005, 190; TAC 2006a).

Although globalization is often accused of hampering social equality in many ways, it has been a resource for TAC, since easy Internet communication and relatively cheap transportation have made it possible to mobilize activists in developed countries to support TAC campaigns. Civil society representatives, policymakers, PLWHAs, and academics can exchange ideas through online discussion groups such as AF-AIDS or the Global Fund's Partnership eForum.[15] Meetings such as the ICASA and the International AIDS Conference enable activists to forge working relationships. Globalization has made it possible to sustain international coalitions without having TAC representatives permanently stationed abroad. Three lessons about global coalitions can be drawn from TAC's efforts.

First, successful coalitions develop momentum that enables them to attract more members, tackle new issues, and build on past policy victories (Hertzke 2004, 29). Although the call for ARVs for citizens in poor countries started after the 1998 International AIDS Conference in Geneva (Smith 2002; D'Adesky 2004), activist demands gained greater attention at the 2000 International AIDS Conference in Durban, South Africa. TAC played a crucial role in mobilizing protests during and after the conference that targeted both pharmaceutical companies and Western governments that enforced the TRIPS Agreement. The movement gained additional strength in 2001 when the PMA dropped its lawsuit against the South African Medicines Act of 1997. The law allows South Africa to engage in compulsory licensing of medicines in health emergencies (Halbert and May 2005, 195). Between 1997 and 2001, the South African government and the pharmaceutical companies had been deadlocked in litigation. However, in 2001, TAC, using the independent judiciary, submitted an *amicus curiae* (friend of the court) brief, which turned a "dry legal contest into a matter about human lives" (Cameron 2005, 177).

These litigation efforts were coupled with public demonstrations in South Africa, the United States, Brazil, Europe, and Asia in March 2001. Many of the protests were organized by the Health Global Access Project (Health GAP), an ad hoc coalition formed in 1998. Although now an independent organization, Health GAP's founding members included the AIDS Coalition to Unleash Power (ACT UP), Search for a Cure, Health Action International, Doctors Without Borders, Partners in Health, TAC, the AIDS Treatment Data Network, and Ralph Nader's Consumer Project on Technology. Many of these groups also held loud, raucous protests at US presidential campaign events for then Vice President Al Gore, actions that embarrassed the Clinton Administration and disrupted the well-scripted Gore campaign (Behrman 2004, 151–159). Because of the efforts of TAC and its global partners, the conventional wisdom on treatment changed from the belief that treatment was impossible in poor countries to the realization that both treatment and prevention are essential to fight AIDS. Delegates to the United Nations General Assembly Special Session on HIV/AIDS unanimously agreed to this point in June 2001 (Patterson and Cieminis 2005, 173–175).

With the movement's 2001 successes, there was even more momentum for treatment. In 2002, Bono, U2 rock music star and cofounder of Debt, AIDS, Trade, Africa (DATA), toured the United States to raise AIDS awareness and advocate for treatment among Americans, particu-

larly evangelical Christians (Behrman 2004, 276).[16] The Global AIDS
Alliance, formed by Paul Zeitz, a doctor and former USAID official in
Zambia, became an increasingly vocal treatment advocate in
Washington, DC. In 2002, Zackie Achmat and Milly Katana of
Uganda's Health Rights Action Group formed PATAM, with which
GATAG is allied, to increase continent-wide efforts to gain ARV access
(PATAM 2004).

A second aspect of the global treatment movement is that its participants have framed AIDS treatment in multiple ways. The loosely
defined goal of "social justice" has become the master framework for
appealing to many organizations (della Porta and Tarrow 2005, 12;
Smith and Bandy 2005, 6). Treatment access has been tied to the
antiglobalization movement, which demands that the TRIPS Agreement
allow states with high HIV prevalence levels to produce or import cheap
generic ARVs (Smith 2002). Antiglobalization groups such as Public
Citizen/Global Trade Watch and People's Global Action viewed ARV
access as one of many issues in their antiglobalization protests at the
1999 WTO meeting in Seattle and the 2001 Group of Eight conference
in Genoa. Human Rights Watch and Physicians for Human Rights see
ARV treatment through the lens of universal human rights treaties that
guarantee a right to health care. DATA, Global Justice, Jubilee USA
Network, Bread for the World, and the Global AIDS Alliance tie AIDS
treatment and AIDS funding to debt relief for Africa. CARE, Africare,
and Oxfam have framed treatment as a development issue—without
access to ARVs, the pandemic will wipe away the continent's achievements in health and education. Faith-based organizations such as World
Vision and Samaritan's Purse have approached treatment through the
lens of religious, particularly Christian, teachings.[17]

A third lesson is that global coalitions often form around the least
politically controversial issues, not the most difficult ones (Smith and
Bandy 2005, 6–7). As the next chapter demonstrates, aspects of AIDS
prevention have become more divisive than AIDS treatment, particularly in the United States. Many of the above-mentioned groups differ
greatly in their approach to abstinence education, condom distribution,
women's empowerment, and legal reform to end discrimination against
PLWHAs. Although treatment programs face obstacles in drug distribution, costs, and health care capacity, it has been easier to generate political consensus globally—though not necessarily in South Africa—for
treatment than for comprehensive prevention programs.

Both domestic and international coalitions have great potential for
raising awareness on AIDS, pooling group resources, and pressuring

policymakers. The global treatment movement illustrates the possibilities for activists when they coalesce around an issue, but studies of other global movements show that such coalitions are often characterized by short-term collaboration on specific issues and limited intergroup communication (Smith and Bandy 2005, 2). Just like domestic alliances, these coalitions are not cost free. TAC has made decisions its international allies oppose, like when it decided to negotiate with GlaxoSmithKline and Boehringer Ingelheim for compulsory licenses to produce the drugs didanosine and stavudine instead of suing the two companies, as representatives from the Consumer Project on Technology urged (Cameron 2005, 181).

Furthermore, building organizational structures that overcome, not replicate, the inequalities between the First and Third Worlds may challenge global alliances. While TAC insists that groups in the developed world do not dominate the treatment movement (Friedman and Mottiar 2004, 22), this equal footing may not be possible for organizations without the same level of resources or leadership experience that TAC has. As treatment programs gradually become more established throughout Africa, the global coalition will be challenged to redefine its issues. One redefinition might focus on insuring transparency in ARV distribution programs, while another might concentrate on extending ARVs to the millions of children who are HIV positive but who have not thus far been central in the movement. No matter what issues the movement addresses, the process of deciding that focus will require negotiation and compromise between First and Third World organizations.

### Civil Society's Relations with the State

The state-civil society relationship may vary with time, the issue, and the organization. The state and civil society can operate independently; they can cooperate to achieve mutually beneficial goals; they can confront one another. Also, the state can capture, or control, civil society organizations to benefit its supporters or to increase its legitimacy. Captured organizations may receive state benefits, but the cost may be their autonomy (Azarya 1988, 6–7). The thousands of AIDS service organizations that care for orphans or provide support to PLWHAs without government assistance exemplify the pattern of state-civil society independence. Because of the relatively apolitical nature of these associations, I do not analyze them here. GHANET illustrates cooperation, while GATAG and ZNNP+ exemplify confrontation. NAPWA has cooperated with the government, though the relationship has elements of capture. Finally, in the opinion of TAC leaders, TAC has both cooperated with and confronted the state. State officials, particularly at the national level, view the relationship to be confrontational.

GHANET has national recognition, sitting on the GAC and the CCM. Thus it is a regular participant in developing AIDS policies and designing grant proposals for donors. It has benefited from grants from the GARFUND, and its representation on the CCM has helped to shape GFATM grants. Though there is a fine line between cooperation and capture, GHANET appears to work closely with, but somewhat autonomously from, the government. In contrast, the aforementioned protests by GATAG, its run-in with the police, and the 2005 accusations that it had been "infiltrated" demonstrate the confrontational nature of its relationship with the state.

ZNNP+ illustrates a pernicious outcome of state confrontation. Since its inception, the organization had challenged Robert Mugabe's AIDS policies. In 1999, ZNNP+ members blocked the president from leaving a Harare hotel. Frenk Guni boldly reported: "The secret forces were there, but we told them to shoot us" (cited in Batsell 2005, 68). In 2001, Guni voluntarily fled the country after he criticized Mugabe's plan to divert national AIDS funding to other political projects. In 2002, the Zimbabwean government accused Guni of embezzling state HIV/AIDS money. Guni's supporters believe that the government positioned people in the ZNNP+ to destabilize the organization (*Daily News*, October 4, 2002; *Standard*, June 15, 2003; Hyman 2003). By 2003, the government essentially controlled ZNNP+ in order to silence Mugabe's critics. After Guni left Zimbabwe, new AIDS networks similar to ZNNP+ suddenly appeared. This pattern of forming new organizations to counter the opposition parallels how the ruling party has dealt with other civil society critics (Zimbabwe Human Rights NGO Forum 2002). In 2004, the ZNNP+ lost most donor support and then in 2005 it suspended operations.

NAPWA has cooperated with the state on SANAC and to implement government-funded AIDS education programs. More recently, the relationship has shown elements of capture. NAPWA has depended on state finances for its operations (*Sunday Times*, July 27, 2003), which has meant that the ministry of health may have greater opportunity to use its ties to NAPWA to claim it represented PLWHAs, particularly during the 2003 debates over ARV treatment: "NAPWA became a perfect and convenient restorer of creditability in the government's continued legitimization [on AIDS] . . . NAPWA was strategically . . . manipulated by the [Department of Health]" (*Sowetan*, October 12, 2004). Although it is impossible to prove, these ties to government may have contributed to the racially based attack from NAPWA on Mark Heywood (TAC 2004a; TAC 2004d). More recently, at its 2005 general meeting, NAPWA members elected Nkululeko Nxesi as its national director; Nxesi has strong views on the crucial role of nutrition for PLWHAs and the "often devastating side effects of ARVs" (*Business Wire*, March 8, 2005). These views mirror those of the minister of health.

The TAC-state relationship has been both cooperative and confrontational. TAC has been represented on AIDS decisionmaking bodies. Although it was originally excluded from SANAC, by 2004 several council members were TAC leaders or sympathizers. (However, as Chapter 2 showed, SANAC's policymaking power is somewhat limited.) TAC members also participated in the task team to study the financial costs for ARV rollout in 2002. TAC officials realize that to achieve their treatment goal, TAC must work with government, because NGOs, private citizens, and international NGOs will be insufficient to make the ARV rollout work. Several TAC officials report positive relations with provincial health officials, an important fact since, in the South African quasi-federal structure, most health funding is distributed at the provincial level (Friedman and Mottiar 2004, 16; Hickey et al. 2004, 117). And at times, civil society activism can be an asset to the state, as TAC's activism against the PMA in 2001 demonstrates. Because of its leaders' membership with the ANC, and its role on SANAC, at times TAC has been criticized for working too closely within the corridors of power (Friedman and Mottiar 2004, 24).

However, from the national government's perspective, the TAC-government relationship is more hostile than cooperative, and national-level government officials have not shown much enthusiasm for partnering with TAC (Friedman and Mottiar 2004, 15). TAC has confronted the state in various ways, including the aforementioned lawsuits over PTMCT and the 2003 campaign for ARVs. TAC has used civil disobedience, such as when it has illegally smuggled in generic ARVs for its pilot treatment programs. These confrontational strategies have been effective partly because TAC has been able to set the media agenda: it has issued timely press releases containing medical arguments for ARVs and it has referred journalists to scientific experts for comments. In doing so, TAC has acted as a knowledge broker, challenging the role of the state as the center of policy expertise (Schneider 2002, 155, 158; Mbali 2005, 45).

Why has TAC been able to incorporate this dual strategy? First, it has the organizational strength to both challenge and cooperate with the state. Second, unlike NAPWA or GHANET, it is financially independent from the state and thus is not beholden to government. Third, TAC has supportive alliances that have mobilized global public opinion and provided funding. Fourth, TAC has adroitly built what its leaders term a "moral consensus" for ARV treatment. TAC's moral argument—that no one should die from AIDS because of a lack of affordable treatment, since there are available medicines that are proven to be effective—is a powerful motivator for action. However, many AIDS organizations make this point, so TAC's moral consensus is richer than just this platitude. It is rooted in the belief in a global right to human dignity, health, and well-being. By fighting the AIDS stigma and urging openness about HIV status, the organization affirms the humanity of PLWHAs. Group members report hope and self-worth since TAC emphasizes that it is possible with ARV treatments to live openly with AIDS. TAC's morality also is rooted in its financial transparency, open meetings, regular elections, open communication, and opportunities for grassroots members to advance in the organization. In seeking integrity throughout the organization, it has fostered legitimacy among members and nonmembers. Concern for integrity also shapes strategic decisions. Because the South African government is elected, TAC leaders do not take lightly decisions for actions of civil disobedience that defy the law (Friedman and Mottiar 2004, 13–14, 17).

The unique nature of the South Africa AIDS fight also enhances TAC's moral arguments. As the party that fought to end apartheid, the ANC has great moral stature. When TAC pointed out that the ANC government had failed HIV-positive citizens, many of whom are black, and when the government continued to argue that treatment access was too expensive, the government lost the moral argument. When the president questioned the HIV-AIDS link and the efficacy of ARVs, he limited the future for PLWHAs. That is, if science could not be trusted, there would be no way to fight AIDS; if ARVs had no efficacy, AIDS was an automatic death sentence. Edwin Cameron (2005, 121) writes: "[Questioning the existence and medical manageability of HIV] is a deeply pessimistic view: one that has not only restigmatised our understanding of the disease, but that has disempowered our understanding of our own capacity, as Africans, to intervene with immediate efficacy to stop appalling suffering." In contrast, TAC empowers millions of HIV-positive South Africans in the AIDS fight.

Small-scale AIDS service organizations, GHANET, GATAG, ZNNP+, NAPWA, and TAC exemplify the varied ways that civil society and the state can interact. These relations may be nonexistent, confrontational, cooperative, controlling, beneficial, or negative. At different points, the state-civil society nexus may exhibit all of these qualities. The relationship civil society has with the state affects its participation in AIDS decisionmaking, though it is impossible to say that a particular type of relationship makes a group effective, since a country's political context, a group's organizational strength, and political culture matter too. For example, the type of confrontation TAC has used led to ZNNP+'s demise because of Zimbabwe's repressive political system. GHANET's cooperation with the state has led to benefits for its NGO members, partially because the country's political culture values consensus building.

This section has examined some factors that help organizations influence AIDS policies. TAC has been particularly effective because of its ability to use South Africa's democratic system, its political culture of protest, coalitions, and a dual strategy of cooperation and confrontation with the state. While other organizations have had some successes, they have faced authoritarian political systems (ZNNP+), hostile (or ambivalent) political cultures (GATAG), state capture (NAPWA), and/or an inability to forge coalitions (GHANET).

## A Lack of Power?

The magnitude of the AIDS pandemic, as well as its potential for long-run economic and social destruction, has led to the formation of thousands of AIDS organizations across Africa. Civil society's growing self-awareness in democratic states and the long-term prognosis for AIDS in Africa mean these groups will continue to play a role in care, support, education, treatment, and advocacy activities. Like all civil society groups, AIDS organizations vary in strength, because of their financial resources, their human capacity, and their internal structures. While stronger organizations like TAC may be more likely to affect AIDS policies, weaker organizations may have some policy successes, as other groups in this chapter illustrate. The domestic political system, political culture, coalitions, and relations with the state also affect how influential AIDS groups can be, though there is no "magic bullet" for making a strong and/or influential AIDS organization.

In the long-term, part of civil society's influence in the AIDS debate will rest on how well, or even if, it seeks to address the underlying problems of poverty and global inequality that lead to higher HIV prevalence rates in poor countries, and that hamper poor countries from providing treatment, care, support, and prevention programs for their citizens

(Farmer 2005, 18–19). Globally, these power inequalities get played out in institutions such as the TRIPS Agreement. Locally, they are manifested in state capture of AIDS organizations or state policies that disempower PLWHAs. Activism on these structural inequalities means AIDS organizations must move beyond single-issue politics. TAC has tried to do this through its participation in South Africa's People's Health Campaign. But the strategy of a broad agenda also creates challenges, particularly if groups raise high expectations they cannot meet or if their coalition partners are unwilling to support these efforts.

Finally, AIDS groups face the dilemma of how to become institutionalized within the policy process. Protest politics calls attention to issues, such as the global treatment movement did, but that is insufficient for instituting a long-term response to the pandemic. Although she writes specifically about the African NGO community, Sarah Michael's assertions (2004, 14–15) apply broadly to civil society. Civil society often lacks power not only because the African state has asserted its supremacy in the state-civil society relationship, but also because civil society has had to fight for financial resources, international links, and access to political institutions to shape policy. Africa's AIDS groups need to overcome these challenges in order to counter state centralization or to utilize Africa's nascent democratic openings. With some notable exceptions such as TAC, with its internal strength and its ability to forge a moral consensus in a unique political environment, few groups have yet to accomplish these goals.

## Notes

1. Information on GATAG comes from interviews conducted with the president by Bernard Haven, then Calvin College student, in December 2003. Haven also has served as the manager for the group's website, though he does not provide website content. Bernard Haven, email correspondence with author, January 16, 2006.

2. For example, TAC, the most-endowed organization examined here, sent a plea for funding to its email list on January 17, 2006. It hopes to raise R10 million ($1,670,982) by March 2006. The message said, "If TAC does not urgently raise more funds we will have to scale back on our activities" (TAC 2006b). I use 1 US dollar=R5.989, the rate in January 2006 on http://www.oanda.com/convert/classic, for currency conversions. To ease reading, I provide many currency figures in US dollars.

3. Information on Ark Foundation comes from Catie Schierbeek, a Calvin College student who volunteered at the Accra, Ghana, organization during 2004. See also http://www.arkfoundationgh.org.

4. Bernard Haven, January 16, 2006.

5. Although the exchange rate fluctuated greatly between 2003 and 2006,

my goal is to demonstrate the relatively large amount of financial support TAC has received from various international and domestic foundations and NGOs.

6. An examination of major AIDS groups in Botswana, Cameroon, Ghana, Nigeria, Kenya, Malawi, Rwanda, Senegal, Tanzania, Zambia, and Zimbabwe reveals that websites for AIDS organizations can be uneven, incomplete, and relatively unhelpful. Organizations often have website links that do not work, outdated information, and incorrect email addresses for leaders. Some groups, though listed by USAID as major players in AIDS service or advocacy, have no website at all (USAID 2004).

7. Bernard Haven, January 16, 2006.

8. In a somewhat similar situation, Ram Cnaan (1999, 157–183) finds that a shared religious experience can unite members, create common goals, and foster efficiency and effectiveness in faith-based organizations.

9. Esophageal candidiasis is a fungal infection that is one of the AIDS-defining illnesses; its presence indicates a more advanced stage of HIV infection. The fungus causes ulcers on the esophagus that cause pain and difficulty in swallowing. For some, the infection prevents eating and contributes to wasting (Smith 2001, 278–280).

10. Steven Friedman and Shauna Mottiar (2004) interviewed over thirty members and leaders in TAC; much of this section on TAC's internal aspects is based on their rich examination.

11. Bernard Haven, January 16, 2006.

12. This exchange occurred through the email list serve on the GATAG website between February 4 and February 18, 2005. It can be found in the archives of the membership list at http://www.gatag.org.

13. Nevirapine is cheaper and easier to administer than AZT. One dose is given to the mother during labor, and one dose is given to the infant after birth (Hudson et al. 2002; Guay et al. 1999). Recent studies have shown that in the long run, infants treated with nevirapine are less likely to become HIV positive than those treated with AZT (*Reuters,* September 12, 2003).

14. Freedom House (2005b) provides information on judicial autonomy and capacity in African countries.

15. These two forums are coordinated by the Health and Development Networks Moderation Team, with financial support from the government of Ireland. They are available through join-partnersgf@eforums.healthdev.org and join-af-aids@healthdev.net.

16. Tom Hart, Director of Legislative Relations, Debt, AIDS, Trade, Africa (DATA), interview with author, Washington, DC, February 24, 2005.

17. Information on these organizations can be found on their websites: Public Citizen/Global Trade Watch (http://www.citizen.org), People's Global Action (http://www.agp.org), Human Rights Watch (http://www.hrw.org), Physicians for Human Rights (http://www.phrusa.org), DATA (http://www.data.org), Global Justice (http://www.globaljusticenow.org), Jubilee USA Network (http://www.jubileeusa.org), Bread for the World (http://www.bread.org), Global AIDS Alliance (http://www.globalaidsalliance.org), CARE (http://www.careusa.org), Africare (http://www.africare.org), Oxfam (http://www.oxfam.org), Samaritan's Purse (http://www.samaritanspurse.org), and World Vision (http://www.worldvision.org).

# 5

―――

# External Donors
# and Political Commitments

―――――――――――――――

THIS CHAPTER COMPARES two donor programs on AIDS: the Global
Fund to Fight AIDS, Tuberculosis and Malaria (GFATM) and the US
President's Emergency Plan for AIDS Relief (PEPFAR). The first,
formed in 2001, is a multilateral funding organization that provides
grants globally to address AIDS, tuberculosis (TB), and malaria. The
second is a bilateral effort that President George W. Bush announced
about halfway through his 2003 State of the Union address:

> To meet a severe and urgent crisis abroad, tonight I proposed the
> Emergency Plan for AIDS Relief—a work of mercy beyond all current
> international efforts to help the people of Africa. . . . I ask the
> Congress to commit $15 billion over the next five years, including
> nearly $10 billion in new money, to turn the tide against AIDS in the
> most afflicted nations of Africa and the Caribbean. (Bush 2003)

While the US president's high-profile announcement surprised many
viewers, and some debated the president's motives and timing, the PEP-
FAR initiative followed the growing global realization among bilateral
and multilateral donors about the seriousness of the AIDS crisis.[1] PEP-
FAR also illustrates increased US awareness and activism on AIDS, particularly among Bush supporters like evangelical Christians.

The United States is not the only bilateral donor giving considerable
sums for AIDS, although in 2004 it provided 45.4 percent ($1.62 billion)
of all bilateral commitments and GFATM contributions from the Group
of Seven and the European Commission.[2] Because as of 2004 this was
the largest percentage and dollar amount, Bernard Rivers, executive
director of AIDSPAN and editor of *Global Fund Observer*, refers to the
United States as the "one thousand pound gorilla" that has the potential

to shape the AIDS programs of other donors, African states, and multi-lateral NGOs (*All Things Considered*, NPR Radio, June 3, 2005).

However, the United States does not seem so generous if we compare the country's share of global GDP to its share of global AIDS funding. In 2004, the United States had 28.9 percent of the world's GDP, but gave only 17.4 percent of global AIDS resources. This contrasted with the United Kingdom, with 5.2 percent of the world's GDP and 7.7 percent of the world's share of AIDS funding, or Canada with 2.4 percent of the world's GDP and 3.1 percent of AIDS resources. The United Kingdom and Canada are more generous than the United States, and than other Group of Seven members such as Japan (with 11.5 percent of global GDP and 2.3 percent of global AIDS funds) and Germany (with 6.7 percent of global GDP and 1.9 percent of global AIDS funds). Most donors give money primarily through bilateral programs. In 2004, 83 percent of US funding, 94 percent of UK funding, 59 percent of Canadian funding, and 65 percent of Japanese funding was given bilaterally. An exception was France, which gave roughly 81 percent of its AIDS funding to the GFATM (Kates 2005, 11, 15).

The GFATM mobilizes money from bilateral donors, private foundations, corporations, and citizens to fight the three diseases worldwide. The fund stresses that "it is not an implementing agency" and that it "attaches no conditions to any of its grants" (GFATM 2005f). Since its first grants in 2003, the GFATM has approved over $4 billion for programs in 128 countries. (Of this amount, it has dispersed roughly $1 billion.) In its most recent round of grants, in December 2005, the Governing Board approved $382 million to twenty different countries for HIV, malaria, and TB programs. Over half (56%) of GFATM money has gone to HIV/AIDS programs, 31 percent to malaria programs, and 13 percent to TB. Sub-Saharan Africa has benefited greatly from the GFATM: 61 percent of grants have gone to the continent, dwarfing the 13 percent to East Asia/Southeast Asia, the 9 percent to Latin America, the 7 percent to Eastern Europe/Central Asia, and the 5 percent to the Middle East and North Africa. Governments are the biggest recipient of grants, and receive over 50 percent of GFATM money (GFATM 2006a). At the end of 2005, the GFATM reported that its financing had helped 384,000 people begin ARV treatment, one million individuals begin Directly Observed Treatment Short-Course (DOTS) Therapy for TB, and antimalaria programs distribute 7.7 million insecticide-treated bed nets (GFATM 2005d).[3]

PEPFAR promises $15 billion between 2004 and 2008. As of summer 2005, it had approved roughly $1.5 billion to fight HIV/AIDS in twelve African countries and it had dispersed $780 million (USAID 2005b; Kates 2005, 12).[4] In contrast to the GFATM, PEPFAR narrowly focuses on fifteen countries, twelve of which are in Africa. It also is more rigid in its funding allocations: its authorizing legislation stipulates that 55 percent of its funding for bilateral programs go for ARV treatment, 20 percent for prevention, 15 percent for care for PLWHAs and for those affected by HIV/AIDS, and 10 percent for orphans and vulnerable children. Most PEPFAR money goes to multinational NGOs and US academic institutions for AIDS programs.

Although PEPFAR was criticized in its first year for slow funding dispersal and financial shortfalls (*Kaiser Daily HIV/AIDS Report*, June 24, 2004; *Wall Street Journal*, January 27, 2005), by 2005 the program had important successes. ARV treatment programs in Zambia, Uganda, and Ethiopia have enrolled large numbers of patients, with drug regimen adherence rates near 100 percent (*Boston Globe*, May 29, 2005; Bass 2005). By its own account, PEPFAR had exceeded its June 2005 treatment goal of 202,000 patients on ARVs by over 30,000 (OGAC 2005a). Access to ARVs has provided crucial hope to Africans with the disease and, more broadly, to societies the pandemic affects (Tobias 2005). One official working in Zambia said that an additional, but intangible, benefit of PEPFAR was that it increased attention to AIDS: "When the leader of the world's most powerful country allocates $15 billion to a problem, people notice. In the long run this attention is helpful for addressing the problem because we need a greater global response. It has been positive . . . for hometown America to be aware."[5] This attention has translated into increased funding for the initiative from Congress for fiscal year 2006 (*Kaiser Daily HIV/AIDS Report*, June 17, 2005).

Because this chapter looks at donors, it is essential to clarify terminology. The donor community in developing countries is multilayered. Loosely defined, donors include both multilateral organizations that have governments as their members, like UNICEF and WHO, and bilateral government organizations like USAID and DFID. Multinational NGOs such as CARE, Oxfam, or World Vision, which work in several countries but are headquartered in industrialized countries, are sometimes included in the donor definition, although I will refer to them as NGOs. To add to the layers of the development community, multinational NGOs often hire host-country nationals and work with local partners, making it difficult to label them as "American" or another nationality. Local partners, sometimes referred to as indigenous NGOs, have their own members, goals, and institutions. The relationships between these layers—multilateral/bilateral donors and multinational NGOs and multinational NGOs and their local partners—are often complex and shaped by power inequalities and accountability issues. Indigenous NGOs must account for funds they receive from multinational NGOs and demonstrate they are meeting program goals, but because they fear losing money, they may be unable to shape program objectives through open, honest dialogue (Hoksbergen 2003). Multinational NGOs are accountable to the Western citizens who give them donations and the governments that provide their grants, sometimes making it problematic for them to respond to their local partners.

The purpose of this chapter is not to dispute the reported gains of the GFATM or PEPFAR. Instead, I examine the potential of each program to foster what policymakers often term "political commitment" to AIDS. World leaders agreed in 2001 in the United Nations Declaration of Commitment on HIV/AIDS that political commitment is essential for fighting the pandemic (Patterson and Cieminis 2005, 175). I define political commitment as: (1) increased spending on HIV/AIDS; (2) accountability to those affected by or infected with HIV/AIDS;[6] and (3) accountability to those who fund AIDS programs. I question how the GFATM and PEPFAR foster these three elements of political commitment for both African leaders and the two donor institutions themselves. Although other definitions of commitment could be used, I choose these three aspects because spending is essential to combat AIDS, policies are more likely to be legitimate and effective in the long term if decision-making processes incorporate the voices of people AIDS affects, and without financial accountability, spending for AIDS may dwindle.

Because of the newness of these programs, my assertions focus on their potential to achieve these three outcomes. In terms of African officials, neither the GFATM nor PEPFAR have means to prod leaders to spend more money on AIDS. But, the GFATM has structures to foster the accountability of African leaders to people the pandemic affects and to encourage accountability of African leaders to the GFATM itself. In contrast, PEPFAR does not have institutions to encourage African leaders to be accountable to those AIDS affects. While PEPFAR can urge accountability of African leaders for the grants that government ministries directly receive, since most grants do not go to African state agencies, this is a relatively moot point. In terms of the donor institutions themselves, both the GFATM and PEPFAR encourage accountability to those providing their financing. (For PEPFAR, this is the US Congress; for the GFATM, primarily Western governments.) However, PEPFAR may have more potential to encourage the US Congress to allocate more money to AIDS than the GFATM has to urge its donors to provide it with more resources. In contrast, GFATM structures are more likely to make the GFATM accountable to the people AIDS affects than PEPFAR is to make that program accountable to the same individuals.

## The Emergence of the GFATM and PEPFAR

The formation of the GFATM followed growing attention to AIDS in the new millennium. Greg Behrman (2004, 217–271) details the lost opportunities on AIDS in the late 1990s, particularly under the Clinton Administration. In 2000, the World Bank developed the MAP initiative, to channel loans through newly instituted national AIDS commissions in AIDS-affected countries. The 2000 UN Security Council discussion of AIDS and the 2001 UN General Assembly Special Session on HIV/AIDS demonstrated increased concern about the disease among multilateral donors. The multilateral GFATM was initially an idea of Jeffrey Sachs and UN Secretary-General Kofi Annan. In 2001, the Group of Eight industrial countries approved the idea, contingent on its being a private entity and not under the direct control of the United Nations. Western donors, particularly the United States, feared that a UN-directed program would be mired in inefficient bureaucracy. Even before UN member states endorsed the GFATM at the UN Special Session on HIV/AIDS in June 2001, the United States made a founding pledge of $200 million to the organization. In subsequent negotiations over the GFATM's structure, Western countries insisted that the organization have a small secretariat; they did not want another donor agency doing AIDS projects, but an organization to raise and allocate money. African countries insisted that the GFATM be independent from the World Bank, because of its involvement with structural adjustment programs. African countries also wanted grant awards to be contingent on technical merit, not political considerations (Patterson and Cieminis 2005, 172–173; Behrman 2004, 251–255).

The passage of PEPFAR builds on this growing interest in AIDS among donors. It also reflects increased domestic concern about AIDS, particularly among Republican Party coalition members. By the late 1990s, a loose coalition of activists began to agitate for more funding for AIDS and for access to ARV treatment (Irwin et al. 2003, 170–183). At the same time, evangelical Christians, many of whom voted for President Bush in 2000 (Guth et al. 2001), had become more involved in international development and human rights issues. Focus on the Family, Family Research Council, the National Association of Evangelicals, the US Conference of Catholic Bishops, Christian

Solidarity Worldwide, Christian Federation Worldwide, World Vision, Salvation Army, Anglican Communion, and International Justice Mission lobbied to pass the 1998 International Religious Freedom Act, the 2000 Trafficking Victims Protection Act, and the 2002 Sudan Peace Act (Hertzke 2004, 9). These successes emboldened the faith-based coalition and motivated their involvement in debt forgiveness and PEP-FAR (*New York Times*, October 26, 2003, p. A1).[7] One advocacy group representative explained:

> [Debt relief legislation in 2000] was something with a clear religious message—Leviticus and the forgiving of debts every fifty years, in the Jubilee year. [Some conservative Republicans] became passionate on the issue, and it became a political moment when conservatives could take a risk on an international development issue. But then policymakers began to question how debt relief benefited Africa if millions of Africans were dying of AIDS.[8]

At about the same time the GFATM was being formed, Senators Jesse Helms and Bill Frist introduced legislation to provide $500 million over three years for PMTCT in select African countries. Yet AIDS activists, such as Paul Zeitz of the Global AIDS Alliance, and Democrats John Kerry, Richard Durbin, and Patrick Leahy criticized the effort as meager, given the size of the pandemic. In response, staffers for Senators Frist and Kerry worked on a more comprehensive AIDS package, basing their ideas on the work of the HIV/AIDS Task Force at the prestigious Center for Strategic and International Studies. At the same time, the White House developed PEPFAR with input from a few individuals: Senator Frist; Joe O'Neil, the director of the Office of National AIDS Policy; and Anthony Fauci, director of the National Institute of Allergy and Infectious Diseases. In secret meetings, these officials asked technical experts working on public health in poor countries if a large-scale AIDS program with a major treatment component was feasible. In these discussions, some public health officials urged greater support to the GFATM instead of developing a US bilateral program.[9] Because of the proposal's rapid development, there was limited interagency vetting or input from interest groups. Anne Peterson, then assistant administrator for Global Health at USAID, did not know about the program until the announcement, and neither did US Ambassador for Global AIDS, Jack Chow (Behrman 2004, 281–294).[10]

Unlike the GFATM's formation, when African leaders such as Kofi Annan, Nigerian President Olusegun Obasanjo, and other representatives from Africa at the UN Special Session on HIV/AIDS influenced the fund's eventual outcome, African leaders were relatively absent from PEPFAR's policy development. The *New York Times* (July 14, 2004, p. A1) reported that some countries did not know they had been chosen to participate until after the 2003 announcement: "Mozambique was simply informed that it would be one of 12 African nations, and 15 countries overall, awarded substantial financial assistance." Zambian officials claimed they were unaware of the policy. Likewise, there was limited lobbying by African embassies to pass PEPFAR or amend its provisions.[11] However, Dr. Peter Mugyenyi, a Ugandan physician who heads the Joint Clinical Research Centre in Kampala, a crucial organization in Uganda's AIDS fight, provided input on treatment and prevention programs (Behrman 2004, 307). The administration also said it based its ABC policy (Abstinence, Being Faithful, and, if A and B are not possible, Using a Condom) on Uganda's successful prevention messages (OGAC 2005b, 12).

By 2003, people in the United States had become more aware of the AIDS pandemic, as celebrities such as Ashley Judd, Bono, and Brad Pitt traveled to Africa, toured the United States to educate citizens on AIDS, and spoke on network television. By 2004, one year after PEPFAR's passage, Americans were very aware of AIDS: Of 2,900 adults surveyed, 51 percent said they had seen a lot of media coverage on AIDS in Africa in the previous year (Kaiser Family Foundation 2004b); 59 percent of Americans told a *Wall Street Journal* poll that HIV/AIDS had "gotten worse" in the past five years (*Wall Street Journal*, August 2, 2004). Growing awareness translated into political action, and a variety of groups, including the aforementioned religious organizations, became involved in advocating for PEPFAR and for amendments to the legislation. Family Research Council, a conservative Christian organization, successfully lobbied for one-third of the HIV prevention money to go for abstinence education (Abraham 2003). World Vision contacted roughly 450,000 of its supporters, telling them to urge their senators and representatives to support PEPFAR; roughly 10 percent of these individuals responded. As Serge Duss, Director of Public Policy and Advocacy, World Vision, reported:

> [World Vision] had at least one person in each of the 435 congressional districts contact their representative. That is huge. I have been told that if a congressman gets ten letters on a foreign issue that carries a lot of weight. It is an avalanche because the public usually doesn't contact on foreign affairs, and particularly not the representatives who aren't on the foreign relations committees.[12]

In the end, PEPFAR passed overwhelmingly by voice vote in the Senate and by a 375 to 41 margin in the House. President Bush signed the authorizing legislation into law on May 27, 2003, less than five months after he announced his AIDS plan during the State of the Union address.[13] The rapid passage of PEPFAR was highly unusual in the context of the US policymaking process.

### Varying Approaches to AIDS: An Emergency or a Development Problem?

AIDS can be framed in different ways: as a health issue, a human rights issue, a reflection of gender inequalities, a short-term humanitarian emergency, or a long-term development problem. These perspectives are not mutually exclusive, but the way the problem is framed leads to certain policy or program outcomes. For example, those who view AIDS solely as a health issue will search for technical solutions, such as providing condoms for prevention, and they will situate funding and program decisions in the ministry of health. Although development officials, and member states at the UN General Assembly Special Session, have argued that fighting AIDS requires an integrated framework that incorporates AIDS policies into poverty reduction, economic growth, and good governance programs, there has been relatively little attention to this approach among all donors. However, a comparison of PEPFAR, the GFATM, and the United Kingdom's AIDS programs in DFID demonstrates some variation on this point (de Waal 2004, 5).

PEPFAR's rapid passage reflects the fact that US citizens and policymakers viewed AIDS in Africa to be an emergency, not a long-term development problem. In 2004, 70 percent of people in the United States said that AIDS was a serious global problem; 49 percent said that the world was losing ground on AIDS; and 55 percent said the United States was not doing enough to fight AIDS (Kaiser Family Foundation 2004b). While this data does not measure US *priorities* on AIDS spending, it does demonstrate a general level of support in the United States for US leadership on the disease. It also contrasts with the data presented in Chapter 3, in which countries with high HIV prevalence rates and people who had lost multiple friends and family members to AIDS often did not view the disease as a national priority. US public opinion about foreign aid demonstrates that US citizens see AIDS as a short-term emergency, not a long-term development problem. In 2004, 62 percent of people in the United States thought the United States spent "too much" on foreign assistance (Kaiser Family Foundation 2004b). Given this perception of foreign aid, it is likely that if US citizens perceived the pandemic to be a development problem instead of an emergency, then over 55 percent of respondents would not think the United States should do more on AIDS. A June 16, 2005, vote in the US House Appropriations Subcommittee on Foreign Operations mirrors this view: the committee allocated *more* to PEPFAR than President Bush requested and *less* to the president's major development initiative, the Millennium Challenge Account, than he wanted (*Reuters*, June 17, 2005).[14]

Framing AIDS as an emergency (a word the program's title incorporates) has several implications. Emergencies often arise without warning, although this is not true of the pandemic. In 1990, the CIA projected in an interagency report that there would be forty-five million HIV infections by 2000, with most in Africa (*Washington Post*, July 5, 2000, p. A1). Although US policymakers did not take the prediction seriously, today we know that it was not inaccurate. Emergencies require quick attention, but the implication is that an emergency can be fixed relatively rapidly, as evidenced in PEPFAR's five-year time frame.

To address emergencies, individuals (or countries) often need outside help. President Bush's 2003 State of the Union message illustrates this theme: "Human dignity has been a part of our [US] history for a long time. We [the United States] fed the hungry after World War I. This country carried out the Marshall Plan and the Berlin airlift . . . It's nothing new for our country. But there's a pandemic which we must address now, before it is too late" (Bush 2003). PEPFAR's authorizing legislation is entitled the United States Leadership Against HIV/AIDS, Tuberculosis, and Malaria Act of 2003 (P.L. 108-25), reflecting the belief that, as the world's only superpower, the United States is crucial for the AIDS fight. This emergency focus is manifested in PEPFAR's structure, its narrow approach, and its orientation toward rapid, quantifiable results.

At first glance, the GFATM does not appear to differ much from PEPFAR in how it frames the AIDS issue. While it does not highlight the "emergency" nature of AIDS and it does not focus on "saving" AIDS-afflicted countries, it also tends to downplay the long-term development issues surrounding AIDS. An examination of GFATM-funded projects does not include many that seek to address the relationship between AIDS and poverty, conflict, human rights violations, gender inequalities, or governance. There are a few exceptions, such as a project to empower civil society organizations in Nigeria for AIDS advocacy or a project to provide education and worker training to at-risk youth displaced in the Colombian civil war (GFATM 2006a).

On the other hand, the GFATM may not be as narrow in its approach as it first seems. Its mission statement says, "Programs underwritten by the Global Fund build upon existing poverty-reduction strategies and sector-wide approaches that have been developed to improve public health" (GFATM 2005f). To back up this rhetoric, the GFATM has allocated 20 percent of its funding to human resources and training and 13 percent to physical infrastructure (GFATM 2006a). The GFATM also requires a country to explain how its grant proposal helps the country meet some of the goals outlined in its Poverty Reduction Strategy Paper.[15] In contrast, while PEPFAR has provided training on AIDS prevention, care, treatment, and strategic information management, the program has not spent one-third of its resources on human capacity or infrastructure (OGAC 2005b, 65, 102). Additionally, the GFATM does not have a specific time frame. PEPFAR is authorized for five years, reflecting the hope that within that period, US money can help to stem the AIDS emergency. The GFATM assumes it will exist as long as there is a need to finance AIDS, TB, and malaria projects, and as long as it has funding for those projects.

Finally, by paying for TB and malaria programs, the GFATM recognizes the crucial link between AIDS and other diseases. It was estimated that roughly 30 percent of HIV-positive individuals worldwide at the end of 2001 were co-infected with TB, and TB accounted for up to one-third of AIDS deaths worldwide. In some African countries, 70 percent of people with TB are HIV positive. Since so many HIV-positive people develop TB, and TB has an adverse effect on HIV progression, WHO asserts that TB care and prevention should be integrated into HIV/AIDS programs (WHO 2006b). The links between malaria and HIV are less clear, although studies show serious implications for co-infected pregnant women and their unborn children, such as maternal anemia and low birth weights. HIV levels for pregnant women also increase with malaria infection. More broadly, malaria kills approximately one million Africans annually, is the leading cause of under-five mortality, accounts for 40 percent of Africa's public health expenditure, and costs the continent roughly $12 billion each year in lost GDP (Roll Back Malaria 2005; GFATM 2005e). To fully address the pandemic, the GFATM realizes that TB and malaria cannot be ignored. To be fair, the PEPFAR legislation is supposed to include resources for TB and malaria, but 93 percent of PEPFAR funding in fiscal years 2004 and 2005 went for AIDS (Copson 2005).[16]

PEPFAR also contrasts with DFID's AIDS programs. The British agency has made a concerted effort to analyze the socioeconomic impact of HIV/AIDS on development and to incorporate an AIDS perspective into all its development programs. In particular, DFID has sought coherence between policies for macroeconomic stability and AIDS by recognizing that the unpredictability of aid flows and an over-reliance on loans instead of grants have hampered African states from developing long-term AIDS programs (de Waal 2004, 6). To address this problem, DFID has begun to rely more on grants than loans in its macroeconomic policies.

## Goals and Structures of PEPFAR and the GFATM

These various approaches to AIDS have led to different program structures for PEPFAR and the GFATM. Because AIDS has been framed as an emergency in the United States, and because US politicians must respond to this understanding of the pandemic, PEPFAR's structures and requirements reflect the need to assure Congress that money will be spent wisely and that program recipients will be able to demonstrate results quickly. Without such qualities, skeptics in Congress probably would not have voted for PEPFAR, believing AIDS in Africa to be too difficult to address. The president requested a large amount of new money, $10 billion, during a period in which foreign aid spending has been relatively constant. In fiscal year 2002, foreign aid was roughly $17 billion; by fiscal year 2003, it was $23.6 billion, although almost all of the 2003 increase was for Afghanistan and Iraq. In fiscal year 2002, spending on global HIV/AIDS programs for all US agencies was only $454 million (CRS 2004, 10, 16). The PEPFAR funding request was a bold initiative.

To reassure Congress, PEPFAR adopted a relatively narrow approach. It focuses on only fifteen countries: Botswana, South Africa, Tanzania, Nigeria, Côte d'Ivoire, Uganda, Rwanda, Kenya, Mozambique, Namibia, Ethiopia, Zambia, Guyana, Haiti, and Vietnam.[17] This does not mean that the United States does not work on HIV/AIDS in other nonfocus countries; rather, the vast majority of the new PEPFAR money goes to the fifteen focus countries. The Bush Administration hopes that the fifteen can model successful AIDS programs to nonfocus countries (Tobias 2005). These countries were chosen for several reasons. It was crucial that the partner country be engaged on the AIDS issue and be interested in meeting the targets quickly in an accountable and transparent way, two criteria a country like Zimbabwe could not meet. To meet PEPFAR's overarching goal of treating two million people with HIV/AIDS, a country had to have a large number of HIV-positive people. While Swaziland and Lesotho have very high HIV prevalence rates, they have small populations (UNAIDS 2004b, 191); thus they were excluded. A country also needed to have Centers for Disease Control and Prevention (CDC) and USAID missions to facilitate rapid implementation, something absent in Congo and Angola, though present in the politically unstable Côte d'Ivoire.[18] Underlying all of these requirements, though, is the US desire to use its money wisely, and country choice would facilitate that. In contrast, any country or NGO (with its host country's approval) may apply to the GFATM. The fund's Technical Review Panel evaluates grant proposals based on their technical merit and recommends proposals for funding to the Governing Board. The Technical Review Panel is composed of twenty-six experts in the fields of public health and medicine who come from industrialized and developing countries.

The GFATM also compares to PEPFAR in that it does not set concrete targets it hopes to meet in a set time period. On the other hand, by 2008, PEPFAR plans to provide treatment for *two* million people living with HIV/AIDS, prevent *seven* million new infections, and provide care for *ten* million people infected with and affected by HIV/AIDS, including orphans. The "2-7-10 goals" create program urgency, require the Office of the US Global AIDS Coordinator (OGAC) to quantify activities, and drive PEPFAR's decisionmaking structures. They also make it easier for Congress to monitor progress. Annual country targets for treatment, care, PMTCT, capacity building (e.g., training health care workers), and prevention are derived from the larger 2-7-10 goals (OGAC 2004a).

OGAC officials argue that reaching quantifiable results will foster global optimism on AIDS: "The world needs hope. And in order to have hope, we need to be able to point to results and progress" (Tobias 2005). OGAC's first report to Congress explains how PEPFAR has more than exceeded its targets during its first year in the areas of treatment and care (OGAC 2005b, 12–13). Similarly, the GFATM has not been immune from quantifying its achievements in reports, particularly for the number of individuals its grants have put on ARV treatment. However, the emphasis on numbers, particularly with PEPFAR, comes with costs. One NGO worker involved in the AIDSRelief consortium, a PEPFAR-funded program to provide ARV treatment in nine countries, said: "There has been a push to get the numbers [of people] required treated by hook or by crook by the end of Year 1, which was February 28, 2005. We were as much as told that if we did not, our continued funding could be in jeopardy."[19]

PEPFAR's numerical emphasis also reinforces the understanding of AIDS as an emergency, instead of viewing AIDS as a reflection of uneven global development, gender inequalities, or human rights inequities. For example, PEPFAR has tended to ignore the gender dimension of AIDS, even though in sub-Saharan Africa 57 percent of those who are HIV positive are women (UNAIDS 2004b, 3). Gender empowerment through girls' education, microfinance, and legal reform can decrease women's vulnerability to HIV, but PEPFAR's focus on short-term results makes it difficult to engage in these long-term development projects (Fleischman 2005). PEPFAR also has tended to focus on easily measurable prevention strategies, such as the number of people trained in abstinence education or exposed to HIV-prevention mass media messages (OGAC 2005b, 19–22). These measures say little about how these interventions prevent HIV infections or decrease risky sexual behavior (Kates and Nieburg 2005, 3).

The allocation of 55 percent of PEPFAR funding for treatment further illustrates the need to quantify results to Congress.[20] It is easier to measure treatment successes than prevention successes, since it is difficult to measure risky sexual behavior that does not occur (Kates and Nieburg 2005, 4). This does not mean that implementing treatment is easy, because the limited number of health care personnel and inadequate health care facilities have complicated treatment programs in Africa. When Botswana, a relatively well-developed African state, received $100 million from Merck Pharmaceutical Company and the Gates Foundation in 2001 for a five-year program to provide universal treatment, it took eighteen months to put five hundred people on ARVs. As of 2004, the country had spent only one-third of the project's money. However, Botswana also illustrates that once programs conquer these logistical challenges they can scale up operations rapidly (*Boston Globe*, June 12, 2005).

In order to meet its numerical goals, PEPFAR needed a streamlined and centralized decisionmaking structure. OGAC oversees and coordinates resources for all US international AIDS activities, including PEPFAR focus countries. Technically, OGAC is situated within the US State Department, but the director Randall Tobias has a direct line to the president and holds ambassador status.[21] In the focus countries, OGAC works through the US embassy, where the US ambassador forms a team from the host government, multinational NGOs, and US agencies such as USAID, CDC, Department of Defense (DOD), Peace Corps, Department of Labor (DOL), and Health and Human Services (HHS). OGAC sets the country's targets for prevention, care, and treatment programs, and the country team devises a strategy to meet those targets (OGAC 2004b, 12). On the positive side, this approach facilitates communication and coordination among US agencies. In reality, agencies sometimes have continued to approach AIDS programs from their own agency's paradigm, such as CDC through the lens of public health and USAID through the lens of long-term development (Bass 2005). On the down side, the structure puts pressure on the US embassy to meet deadlines, and some embassies have been stretched beyond their capabilities (Nieburg, Kates, Morrison 2004, 4). Some US ambassadors and agency representatives also have felt implicit pressure to accept unrealistic targets. More broadly, the structure gives no special voice to African state leaders and, until quite recently, it made limited efforts to consult with African state officials or work within each country's public health system. One public health official working in Rwanda summarizes how PEPFAR began: "PEPFAR got off to a rough start. Consultations with countries and stakeholders were foregone for political and programmatic expediency."[22]

The GFATM is more decentralized than PEPFAR. To apply for a GFATM grant, a country must set up a country coordinating mechanism (CCM). CCMs are intended to facilitate representation from societal sectors affected by and/or working on AIDS: government, bilateral and multilateral donors, local and multinational NGOs, FBOs, businesses, academic institutions, and people with the disease(s). The CCM seeks to encourage a grassroots, consultative process in which all affected sectors reach consensus on how the country will address AIDS, TB, and/or malaria. The process is supposed to foster transparency and accountability, although Chapter 3 illustrated potential problems with civil society representation on some CCMs. Governments designate a principal recipient for GFATM grants, such as the ministry of health, and local NGOs are subrecipients. Since principal recipients tend to be government agencies, public officials have a relatively large stake in the process. Unlike PEPFAR, the GFATM does not "impose on African states what their AIDS, TB, or malaria projects have to look like, just that they have to be technically sound. It doesn't say what is right or wrong in AIDS programs or institutions."[23]

As of early 2006, three Africans sat on the GFATM's Governing Board, which decides grants based on recommendations from the Technical Review Panel. This representation gives African states more ownership in the fund, and it creates political capital for those voices on the board, since they have a stake in voting and decisionmaking. A relatively small secretariat of 135 employees in Geneva supports the

GFATM and its Executive Director, Dr. Richard Feecham from the United Kingdom. The Governing Board chooses a president for a two-year term, with former US Secretary of Health and Human Services Tommy Thompson serving from 2003 until April 2005. Dr. Carol Jacobs, chairman of the National HIV/AIDS Commission in the Office of the Prime Minister in Barbados, followed Thompson as the board president.

## The GFATM and PEPFAR:
## Different Approaches to NGOs

Both PEPFAR and the GFATM view civil society as crucial for the fight against AIDS, although because of its need to rapidly scale up activities PEPFAR has relied heavily on multinational NGOs and US academic institutions to meet its targets. While it gives some grants directly to African government agencies, the majority of what OGAC terms its prime partners are NGOs. For example, only four of twenty prime partner grants in 2004 in Ethiopia went to government agencies; of the approximately 360 PEPFAR prime partners, a little over 10 percent were African government agencies (OGAC 2005c). On this point, PEPFAR differs from DFID and the GFATM. In most cases, DFID provides direct budgetary support to governments, a process that gives governments a stake in funding (de Waal 2004, 1). Because CCMs applying to the GFATM define their own programs, the involvement of NGOs varies with the country proposals. Also, since government agencies tend to be the principal recipients of grants, there is less involvement of multinational NGOs, though some multinational NGOs have applied directly to the GFATM for grants. (For example, the Lutheran World Federation received roughly $485,000 in 2003 to educate religious leaders globally about the pandemic.) In 2005, the GFATM reported that 51 percent of its funding went to governments; 25 percent to NGOs and community-based organizations; 4 percent to people living with the disease(s); 5 percent to academic institutions; 5 percent to faith-based organizations; 5 percent to the private sector; and 5 percent to other associations (GFATM 2006a).

There are three overall reasons why PEPFAR depends on multinational NGOs and US academic institutions to meet its numerical objectives. First, organizations such as CARE, Salvation Army, Family Health International, Africare, Interchurch Medical Assistance, World Vision, Catholic Relief Services, the Columbia Mailman School, and the Harvard School of Public Health were already working in Africa before

PEPFAR, and they had the ability to scale up their activities relatively quickly. Second, there is a prevailing view among US policymakers that private organizations are a largely untapped force to do development work efficiently and effectively (Putzel 2004; Adelman 2003; Kolbe 2003). Third, US policymakers felt political pressure to address AIDS, but they were unwilling to directly give money to African governments because of fears of corruption. Research that demonstrates that only democratic, transparent countries use aid to effectively foster development has discouraged direct assistance to governments (Burnside and Dollar 2000; Collier and Dollar 2002). Because democracy is uneven in the fifteen focus countries—only four were considered "free" in 2005 by Freedom House—there was not much confidence in providing PEPFAR money to governments (Freedom House 2005a).

Although African state officials are represented on the country teams, few, if any, indigenous NGOs are. Instead, OGAC encourages its prime partners (most of whom are multinational NGOs or academic institutions) to allocate small grants to their local partners (subpartners) and to provide management training for these groups. For example, one multilateral program in Zambia gives grants of anywhere from $5,000 to $40,000 to over one hundred local partners to work with orphans and vulnerable children.[24] Multinational NGOs also receive more points for their grant applications if they demonstrate how they will work with local partners. The idea behind this grant specification is that PEPFAR "needs to build national capacity so that at some time in the future, the countries [will] have at least the skill sets to sustain programs."[25] OGAC (2005b, 13) reported that "in the Plan's first eight months, 80 percent of the more than 1,200 partners working on the ground were indigenous organizations." The hope is, however, that eventually local NGOs will be able to replace multinational NGOs, because US audit, financial accountability, and reporting requirements are more rigorous than is the norm in these countries, it will take time for this to occur.[26]

While PEPFAR is supposed to incorporate local NGOs into its AIDS programs via multinational NGOs, some local NGOs may lack the capacity or ability to forge ties to these large NGOs to access PEPFAR resources. As the following example of a Kenyan NGO illustrates, some of these groups may represent the poorest and neediest Africans:

> [On a fact-finding trip to Kenya] we heard about this group and this was very poignant about the PEPFAR process. [The country team] has to show [to OGAC] they are giving a good faith effort to give money to groups, so in Kenya, USAID put an ad in the paper about grants that

are available to NGOs, it outlined the guidelines, the time frame, etc. So, there is a set of small NGOs in Kenya with staff members which, if they get paid at all, are only part time. One of these groups works with HIV-positive people who are blind and disabled. These are the marginalized of the marginalized that this group serves. This NGO downloaded the forty-five page document off the USAID website and spent over one and one-half weeks putting together a proposal for a grant, only to be told that they weren't eligible. They lack capacity and organization. Basically no organizations their size are being considered, because most of these grants are at least one million dollars. And certainly this NGO wouldn't have the absorptive capacity to be able to use that money. That is the point: No NGO in the truest fashion of the word—in terms of being grassroots and really participatory—can meet these criteria.[27]

Of course, one could argue that if such a group lacks the capacity to write a grant proposal or to complete financial reports, it should not receive money since it clearly cannot manage a large-scale project. This may be true, but the interviewee's larger point should not be ignored: many NGOs that are participatory and grassroots are not incorporated into the PEPFAR granting process. OGAC argues that this inclusion will occur through grants from multinational NGOs to their partners, not by groups such as this Kenyan NGO getting $1 million. But this assumption relies on two conditions: (1) local NGOs have ties to a multinational NGO (or have the ability to forge such ties); and (2) the partnership between multinational NGOs and local partners facilitates consultation about what partners need. The Kenyan NGO clearly lacked ties to such a multinational NGO, hence its futile attempt to apply for a grant that it could not administer. But the next interviewee, Jacqui Patterson of Interchurch Medical Assistance, demonstrates that PEPFAR's rapid scale-up makes meeting the second condition more difficult. She described the challenges of getting PEPFAR funding for the AIDSRelief consortium:

> We [the consortium] had only about twenty days to get a grant proposal together for over two hundred facilities, 100,000-plus patients, five years, and nine countries. This was a challenge. . . . To be able to get a certain number of people on treatment by X date has probably been at the expense of a quality program. And it was at the cost of focusing much time on meaningful, consultative capacity building. This type of consultation was compromised.[28]

The difficulties of PEPFAR's rapid scale-up have the potential to not only affect program quality, but also to influence the long-term relationships between multinational NGOs and their local partners. A multinational NGO official in Zambia said: "Partnership needs trust, transparency, and an equal playing field and that is a challenge when you are trying to quickly meet objectives."[29] Africa's future ability to fight AIDS will depend in part on the quality of these relationships, since changing sexual behavior, empowering women, and fighting the AIDS stigma are not activities that outside organizations can do without the cooperation of Africans. For multinational NGOs to effectively facilitate these changes, they must build strong relationships with African AIDS organizations so that they fully understand local issues (Webb 2004, 20). Does the GFATM do a better job of incorporating local NGOs? The evidence is scant, but the CCM structure does require some local NGOs or AIDS groups to be involved. Although Chapter 4 showed that AIDS organizations vary in influence, their institutional presence on the CCM theoretically provides some opportunity to build consensus among all stakeholders.

## The Relationship Between the GFATM and PEPFAR

Although the GFATM and PEPFAR have different structures and time frames, officials at both insist that the two entities complement each other. GFATM grants are given to non-PEPFAR focus countries and to programs such as TB and malaria treatment for PLWHAs. The GFATM may provide a way to fund some prevention activities, such as work with prostitutes and condom distribution, which, as the next section demonstrates, have become politicized under PEPFAR.[30] The GFATM also provides a way for smaller donors that lack the capacity to carry out large, multicountry AIDS programs to participate in the AIDS fight (Copson 2005). Though the relationship between the two entities was rocky in 2003 and 2004, consultations increased in 2005 under Tobias and former GFATM President Tommy Thompson. In its 2005 report to Congress, OGAC describes its cooperation with the GFATM positively (OGAC 2005b, 86–88).

US funding to the GFATM has not always reflected this positive relationship. The 2003 PEPFAR legislation authorized up to $1 billion to the fund between 2004 and 2008. In 2004, the United States gave roughly $350 million. In late 2005, the US House and Senate appropriated approximately $450 million for the fund, twice what the Bush Administration had requested (Copson 2005). However, US contributions to the GFATM cannot exceed one-third of all GFATM donations, a provision intended to encourage other countries to contribute. Because of this provision, the GFATM did not receive $87 million that Congress had approved for fiscal year 2004. To ensure this situation was not repeated, European countries increased pledges to roughly $1.6 billion for 2006 and 2007. While these pledges are good news for the GFATM in the short term, the problem is that the GFATM needs increasing resources to continue financing its approved proposals and to launch new rounds of financing. For 2006, the fund estimates a $1.1 billion shortfall and for 2007, $2.6 billion. At the end of 2005, the fund received some last-minute pledges from six European donors and Australia, allowing it to prepare for a sixth round of grants for 2006 (GFATM 2005d). The GFATM's awkward financial situation raises questions about the institution's long-term prognosis.

## Ideological Issues That Distinguish PEPFAR from the GFATM and Other Donors

It is important to remember that PEPFAR is the AIDS program of *one* country. As such, it reflects some of the most heated debates in US politics, particularly cultural clashes over sexuality and questions about the involvement of religious groups in the public arena. In contrast, these are not issues central to European politics; there has not been mass mobilization of conservative Christians in European elections or extensive political debates over abortion or sexual freedom in West Europe (Anderson 2004; Christodoulides 2005). This divide between the United States and Europe has meant that PEPFAR looks very different in its requirements from the AIDS programs of other bilateral donors in Europe. For example, DFID does not stress abstinence as a major means for preventing HIV transmission. Likewise, because the GFATM allows CCMs to develop their own policies and evaluates those based on technical merit, not ideological criteria, its decisions do not reflect the religious, cultural, and moral debates surrounding PEPFAR. Because PEPFAR is unique in some of its policy requirements, it is worth focusing on four of those differences.

### Generic Drugs for Treatment Programs

PEPFAR requires that ARVs used in the program meet the same safety standards established for drugs sold in the United States. In effect, this means that the Food and Drug Administration (FDA) must approve all ARVs in PEPFAR-funded treatment programs. While brand-name ARVs have FDA approval, as of August 2005 nine generic combination drugs had been approved. The US Government Accounting Office reported in January 2005 that the FDA-approval requirement meant that PEPFAR provides a smaller selection of recommended first-line ARVs than the GFATM. Prices for PEPFAR-purchased drugs are higher than generics, and the annual price per person could greatly increase the cost of putting two million people on treatment (GAO 2005). Although Ambassador Tobias created an expedited review process for generic ARVs, critics assert that FDA approval is redundant for drugs with WHO approval (*Washington Post*, January 26, 2005, p. A10). Critics also claim that US reliance on brand-name drugs reflects Randall Tobias's close ties to the pharmaceutical industry, since he was previously the chief executive officer of Eli Lilly & Co. (*Washington Post*, July 2, 2003, p. A2). One outcome of this policy has been that PEPFAR workers in the field lack clear guidelines on procuring ARVs and coordinating with national AIDS programs (GAO 2004, 3).

In an interesting turn of events, Uganda, Nigeria, Ethiopia, and Tanzania refused to accept FDA approval for ARVs in 2005 and demanded that these drugs have WHO approval. These countries also wanted FDA-approved generics without WHO approval to be registered in their national registries. The action sparked a three-month negotiation that resulted in an agreement that the FDA will share its confidential information on approvals of generic AIDS drugs with WHO. The sharing of information will expedite WHO review and, thus, African acceptance of some FDA-approved generics (*Boston Globe*, August 29, 2005). The action of African state leaders was a concrete, though somewhat limited, attempt to voice their disapproval of PEPFAR's mandated use of US products for treatment. The action seemed to indirectly tell the United States that it needed to work within multilateral health structures that African states recognize, namely the WHO approval process, instead of requiring a separate bureaucratic process for African states involved with PEPFAR.

### The Antiprostitution Pledge

As of May 2005, US recipients of grants for HIV/AIDS programs must pledge to oppose prostitution and sex trafficking in return for federal funds.[31] This issue is important because of the central role of commercial sex workers in the spread of HIV. Supporters of the pledge say it ensures that grant recipients comply with US laws to prevent sex trafficking and that the pledge will not hinder AIDS prevention efforts. Moral perspectives also shape the issue. Pia de Sollenni, director of women's issues at the conservative Family Research Council said, "Giving money to groups that turn a blind eye to prostitution is unacceptable. If you're turning a blind eye to it, then you're supporting it" (quoted in *Baltimore Sun,* August 28, 2005). Conservative lawmakers such as Senators Rick Santorum (Pennsylvania Republican) and Tom Coburn (Oklahoma Republican) have criticized some NGOs, such as the well-respected CARE, for "pro-prostitution and anti-American" activities.

Critics fear that the pledge further stigmatizes sex workers who risk HIV infection or who already have AIDS. They argue that stigma prevents people from being tested for HIV and discourages participation in prevention education programs (*Wall Street Journal,* February 28, 2005; *USA Today,* June 10, 2005). Over two hundred AIDS organizations, scholars, and activists signed a letter to the White House summarizing these concerns (Human Rights Watch 2005c). In response to the requirement, the BBC World Service Trust suspended a $4 million, US-funded HIV prevention campaign in early 2006 rather than sign the pledge (*Guardian,* January 23, 2006). Similarly, Brazil, which is not a PEPFAR focus country, refused $40 million in US AIDS grants. While Brazil can afford such action—it receives only about 3 percent of its AIDS resources from the United States—it is doubtful poorer African countries could do the same (*Wall Street Journal,* May 2, 2005).

In June 2005, USAID issued a policy directive (AAPD 05-04) mandating each group that receives grants from USAID for HIV/AIDS must agree to oppose prostitution (USAID 2005a). USAID changed its criteria for grant selection for HIV-prevention programs in Central America to downplay the goal of increasing condom usage, a move that de facto limits working with prostitutes (*Baltimore Sun,* August 28, 2005). These policies have three outcomes. First, the reporting requirements increase the bureaucratic red tape for grant recipients. Second, detailing work with prostitutes can be nebulous since sex work can be difficult to define. Some women in poor countries engage in survival sex but do not consider themselves to be prostitutes. Yet, these women are still at risk for HIV infection, and must be educated about HIV prevention. Should groups receiving US funds count their interactions with these women? Finally, the increasing bureaucratic requirements, and the threat of being castigated on the floor of the US House or Senate, may make some groups reconsider their AIDS programs with prostitutes. For example, officials at Population Services International, a nonprofit health organization, worry that working with prostitutes has become too controversial. Yet, HIV prevention programs with prostitutes are crucial to fight the pandemic. Since AIDS first appeared in the early 1980s, significantly higher rates of HIV infection have been documented among sex workers than other population groups, and sex work is often a significant means of HIV infection entering the general population. Studies also have demonstrated that sex workers are likely to respond positively to HIV education programs, primarily through increasing condom use and STI testing (UNAIDS 2002b). If NGOs limit their work with prostitutes, the policy's critics assert, the larger AIDS fight may suffer.

### Grants to Faith-Based Organizations

PEPFAR seeks to foster competition for grants by encouraging applications from a variety of groups, including FBOs. In 2005, $82 million, or nearly 10 percent of all federal AIDS funding, went to FBOs (*Baltimore Sun*, August 28, 2005); FBOs total roughly 20 percent of all groups getting PEPFAR money (*AP/Yahoo News*, January 30, 2006). Supporters of FBOs argue that these groups have fought HIV/AIDS in Africa since the pandemic's beginning. African religious organizations have provided care for their HIV-positive congregants and religious leaders have devised HIV prevention messages (HIV/AIDS: The Faith Community 2003; Messer 2004, 5). Also, many large-scale multinational NGOs with AIDS programs are faith-based, such as World Vision, American Jewish World Service, Catholic Relief Services, Church World Service, and the Salvation Army. FBO supporters claim that these organizations are cost effective and have extremely dedicated personnel (Hill 2005).[32]

Critics raise concerns. African FBOs *and* small-scale US FBOs often lack the capacity to do large-scale projects. Even World Vision, one of the world's largest development NGOs, struggled organizationally when it received millions of new dollars in 2004.[33] Critics question the ability of some FBOs with no international or public health experience to do effective AIDS projects. They point to groups such as the Concerned Women for America, a conservative Christian lobbying organization with limited development experience, which received $113,000 to teach Mexican church officials to combat sex trafficking (*Wall Street Journal*, February 28, 2005). Opponents fear that FBOs will not transparently use PEPFAR money for HIV/AIDS programs, but to proselytize (CHANGE 2004, 16–17).

Because PEPFAR only began in 2004, there was little research at the time of this writing on how FBOs have used PEPFAR money. One study of a $5 million, PEPFAR-supported abstinence education program through the Ethiopian Orthodox Church found that the church positively reinforced its members' beliefs in abstinence. On the other hand, the abstinence messages meant little to the one-quarter of church members who reported having engaged in premarital or extramarital sex. Further, the programs did not address gender inequality, an important omission since inequality may push women into risky sexual relations. Most broadly, though, there was little evaluation of the church's programs and their appropriateness for the social, cultural, and economic situation of all church members (Fenio 2005).

While debates about grants to FBOs reflect secular and religious perspectives about who can and should implement development programs, these grants also should be situated in a larger context of Washington politics, where budget deficits intensify competition over government money and partisan politics is heated. Because PEPFAR provides the largest amount of US money for AIDS in the history of the disease, it has made HIV/AIDS an appealing issue to work on for a variety of US government agencies and multinational NGOs. While money for other development programs such as environmental projects has remained stagnant, HIV/AIDS funding has grown from $454 million in fiscal year 2002 to roughly $3 billion for fiscal year 2006 (CRS 2004, 10). PEPFAR also is rooted in the post–Cold War paradigm of foreign policy, which blurs the line between international and domestic issues. Foreign aid is no longer the sole domain of agencies like USAID, but now involves, among others, DOD, CDC, HHS, and DOL (Lancaster 2000, 14). The formation of OGAC, theoretically free from entrenched interests or bureaucratic turf wars, provides additional opportunities for Washington interest groups, including FBOs, to access resources and shape policies. In the process, agencies like USAID and organizations such as CARE or Population Services International have experienced heightened criticism.[34]

Additionally, support for FBOs must be put in a political context in which conservative groups such as the Heritage Foundation and Family Research Council gained political power after the 2000 election.[35] President Bush, most Republicans, and some Democrats believe FBOs should receive access to US money to deliver social services domestically and internationally. Since 2001, President Bush has made it easier for these groups to apply for and get US dollars through executive orders 13198, 13199, and 13279 (Black et al. 2004, 297–308). However, smaller FBOs, and their congressional supporters such as Illinois Republican Congressman Henry Hyde, have continued to complain about the relatively limited amount of PEPFAR money going to FBOs; they assert that liberal groups dominate global health funding and continue to receive most PEPFAR money (*Wall Street Journal*, February 28, 2005; Hyde 2005). There could be important implications for these views. According to Richard Cizik of the National Association of Evangelicals, continued evangelical support for PEPFAR partly depends on whether or not "[evangelicals] feel they are getting the money for [their] programs."[36] The debate about money for FBOs puts OGAC in a difficult position. To meet its targets it must work with large-scale NGOs, only some of which may be FBOs.

### The ABC Prevention Policy

Of all of PEPFAR's aspects, none has been more contentious than the ABC policy, and particularly its AB focus. The PEPFAR strategy is "specifically designed to . . . use evidence-based prevention programs, such as the ABC approach of Abstinence, Be faithful, and as appropriate, the correct and consistent use of Condoms" (OGAC 2004b, 8). Congressional amendments to the authorizing legislation earmarked 33 percent of the prevention money for AB programs, or those that educate about abstinence until marriage and promote marital fidelity (*New York Times*, April 30, 2003). Critics of ABC assert that since only 20 percent of PEPFAR money goes for prevention, and since 33 percent of that amount must be for AB education, there is not much funding for prevention programs that work such as PMTCT, VCT, or blood supply protection. Opponents argue that targeting youth with an abstinence message is inappropriate since at least 50 percent of African girls marry by age eighteen and abstinence is impossible in marriage. Since marriage is a risk factor for women in countries with high prevalence rates, women's marital fidelity will not necessarily protect them from HIV infection (Baylies 2002, 356).[37]

Additionally, opponents point to the mixed research findings on the effectiveness of US abstinence-only programs. This research shows that youth who make "virginity pledges" are less likely than nonpledgers to have sexual intercourse, although the pledge effect depends on age and context. However, if pledgers do have intercourse, they are less likely to use contraception, and their STI infection rates do not differ significantly from their nonpledging peers (Bearman and Brueckner 2001, 2005). Another criticism opponents make is that the ABC policy has led to the development of piecemeal prevention programs: "Instead of giving people consistent and comprehensive information on abstinence, monogamy, negotiating sex, how STIs are spread, and condom use— information that people can use in different ways at different points in their reproductive lives—[PEPFAR] has tended to see these things as separate and distinct programs."[38] Because of the focus on A and B, the policy makes condoms selectively available for "at risk" groups. Critics complain it is difficult to define who is at risk in high prevalence countries where most people do not know their serostatus (CHANGE 2004, 9–10). Moreover, opponents assert that qualifying condoms as a strategy to be used "as appropriate" (a phrase that OGAC employs) has created a stigma against condom use. One Ugandan AIDS activist reported: "Those of us who are promoting condoms are looked at as immoral people." This backlash allegedly contributed to a reported condom shortfall in Uganda in early 2005 (*Boston Globe*, September 8, 2005).

By late 2005, reports had started to emerge about tangible funding outcomes of the ABC policy. Some organizations with comprehensive sexual health programs in Africa say they have seen their grants withdrawn under PEPFAR guidelines for ABC (Walgate 2004). For example, Population Services International, which has been involved in condom distribution programs for years, has now started to implement AB programs because of funding requirements. With PEPFAR, abstinence-only programs can receive grants, while condom promotion programs that do not mention abstinence are no longer eligible for funding (*The World*, BBC/WGBH Boston, July 21, 2005).

Supporters of ABC present counterarguments. They maintain that AB programs are "culturally appropriate" (Ssempa 2005). By this, they argue that the messages of abstinence and being faithful resonate with African traditions that value family and commitment. My goal is not to dispute or support these claims, but to point out that this is one argument ABC supporters make. They also argue that the ABC policy is rooted in African ideas about prevention, particularly the public statements of Ugandan President Yoweri Museveni. The Ugandan government has been the biggest supporter of the ABC policy (OGAC 2004a, 54), and in 2004, it worked with USAID to develop a new AB curriculum based on US abstinence-only materials. President Museveni had publicly encouraged "zero grazing" since the late 1980s, but some critics argue that Uganda's emphasis on abstinence is a relatively recent phenomenon (Human Rights Watch 2005a, 2). AB critics also maintain that as one of PEPFAR's biggest recipients, Uganda, which got $125 million in 2005, has learned to appease conservatives in Washington.[39]

ABC proponents say PEPFAR supports AB programs that countries such as Uganda and South Africa were already doing, and they maintain that critics have narrowly defined the B strategy, since being faithful also includes partner reduction and wise partner selection (i.e., knowing a partner's serostatus) (OGAC 2004a). Ambassador Tobias asserts that condoms continue to be widely distributed with PEPFAR money; since mid-2004, he has often repeated: "Abstinence works; being faithful works; condoms work." Finally, proponents point to other research on US abstinence-only programs that found that youth who took virginity pledges had *lower* rates of acquiring STIs and engaged in fewer risky sexual behaviors than nonpledgers (*New York Times*, June 15, 2005, p. A16; Johnson and Rector 2005).

Much of the debate about ABC has focused on Uganda's decline in HIV prevalence from approximately 20 percent in 1991 to 5 percent in 2001 (Peterson 2003; Green 2003b, 141).[40] Opponents and proponents of ABC have used different scientific studies to bolster their arguments. AB proponents claim that partner reduction and fidelity in marriage or relationships contributed to Uganda's decline (Low-Beer and Stoneburner 2004, 170; Green et al. 2002). They also cite data indicating that youth have delayed their first sexual experiences in Uganda (Kiirya 1998).

In contrast, AB critics point to a 2005 study that argues that deaths from AIDS and increased condom use contributed significantly to HIV decline (*Washington Post*, February 24, 2005, p. A2; Wawer et al. 2005). (In response to this research, the Ugandan ambassador to the United States wrote in a March 14, 2005, letter to the *New York Times* that the study was "misleading and dangerous" because it is "widely known" that the AB strategy has worked in Uganda.) These debates about prevention led more than 140 public health and NGO officials to sign a short statement in the *Lancet* that argued for common ground on prevention. The statement called for a locally endorsed, comprehensive approach to HIV prevention that promotes risk avoidance for youth through abstinence, delayed sexual onset, and when appropriate, condom use; that encourages mutual fidelity and partner reduction; that educates about correct and consistent condom use for sexually active adults; and that builds on community-based approaches (Halperin et al. 2004).

The aforementioned policies on FBOs, generic drugs, prostitution, and prevention put PEPFAR at odds with other bilateral donors and the GFATM. They also illustrate larger themes about policymaking and implementation. First, policy development is difficult when different ideological viewpoints utilize various scientific studies to support their own perspectives. The lack of definitive findings on what has caused Uganda's decline in HIV prevalence exacerbates these ideological differences and makes the country a problematic model for other prevention programs (Schoepf 2003; Farmer 2003). Second, these divisions create confusion among policy practitioners.[41] An example from the 2005 Addis Ababa meeting of PEPFAR officials is illustrative. Edward Green, author of *Rethinking AIDS Prevention*, a book that asserts that Uganda's HIV reduction was because of increased fidelity and partner reduction, not greater condom use, delivered the meeting's keynote address on prevention. Senior USAID officials spent $100,000 to buy four hundred copies of his book for conference participants. Although Green has spoken often about how all aspects of ABC are needed, according to the *Boston Globe*, at the meeting he downplayed condom effectiveness, even for sero-discordant couples. In contrast, when Carolyn Ryan, PEPFAR's senior technical advisor on prevention, spoke to the group, she said, "Consistent condom use reduces risk by approximately tenfold" (*Boston Globe*, May 31, 2005). Practitioners received different messages at the same conference about the efficacy of condoms.

A third implication of these divisions is that they have forced policymakers, AIDS activists, and NGOs to build coalitions around aspects of the AIDS fight that are less controversial than many prevention issues. As Chapter 4 illustrated, a global coalition emerged for treatment, not prevention. For PEPFAR, the outcome is a policy that many public health officials argue overemphasizes treatment at the expense of prevention (*Boston Globe*, May 31, 2005; *New York Times*, June 11, 2004, p. A8).[42] In reality, prevention and treatment are intertwined: increased treatment makes citizens more likely to be tested for HIV; increased testing increases the likelihood that people will get treatment; HIV-positive people who know their status and can access treatment are the best advocates for prevention. Over the long term, a comprehensive combination of treatment and prevention can contribute to a decline in HIV (Farmer 2003). But, politically controversial interventions that might decrease HIV infections have been marginalized in the AIDS debate. The *Lancet* reported in 2002 that spending $10 billion annually on prevention activities like comprehensive school-based AIDS education, peer education, PMTCT, outreach programs for sex workers, condom promotion, treatment of STIs, VCT, needle exchange programs for intravenous drug users, and outreach programs for homosexual men could prevent twenty-nine million people globally from being infected with HIV by 2010 (Stover et al. 2002). However, several of these interventions are so politically divisive that civil society coalitions have been unable to mobilize around them.

A fourth implication is that since these policies, particularly the antiprostitution pledge and the ABC policy, put the United States at odds with other donors, they hamper a global approach to AIDS. If UNAIDS and WHO officials report that condoms are an essential part of the AIDS fight, but major US NGOs receiving PEPFAR grants will not distribute condoms because they fear losing grant money, a coherent AIDS prevention message is lost. Furthermore, if some governments and NGOs become squeamish about condom distribution or developing programs for sex workers because of US policy stipulations, they may self-censor their HIV prevention programs. In Ghana, which is not a PEPFAR focus country, government policies on prevention now focus on abstinence (Patterson and Haven 2003). These outcomes may mean that citizens receive either conflicting messages or incomplete information about how to prevent HIV transmission. For governments, the lack of policy coherence increases demands on state institutions that already lack capacity. For example, difficulties harmonizing Tanzania's national government AIDS plan (partly funded by the GFATM) and the PEPFAR strategy have meant that doctors in one Arusha hospital have nine forms they must fill out monthly for each ARV patient in donor-funded treatment programs. Overworked health care personnel pay the price for a lack of coordination between donors.[43]

On the other hand, while these spirited policy discussions may contribute to confusion in the field and incomplete HIV/AIDS prevention policies, they do mean that AIDS is on the political agenda. Debates over which groups get money and how they use it engage policymakers, civil servants, activists, and the public health community in continued dialogue about AIDS. Future research will need to investigate what this political jockeying will mean for the long-term AIDS fight in Africa.

### Building Political Commitment to AIDS Among African Leaders

The record of success in fighting AIDS—which as of late 2005 was admittedly thin—demonstrates that in countries such as Uganda and Senegal *state* leaders were crucial actors. In such cases, the state was not an afterthought, or only one more participant to be consulted; it was a central player in AIDS policymaking (Putzel 2004, 1138). This section evaluates the potential for PEPFAR and the GFATM to shape three aspects of political commitment among African state officials: (1) increased funding for AIDS; (2) accountability to those AIDS affects; and (3) accountability to those funding AIDS programs, namely the GFATM and the US government. First, some critics of the GFATM and

PEPFAR claim neither has forced African leaders to make hard political decisions about putting their own country's money into fighting HIV/AIDS since neither requires state contributions.[44] And African democracies have not necessarily increased health spending. There is no evidence that either PEPFAR or the GFATM has specifically urged governments to spend more on AIDS or health. However, an example from Nigeria suggests the GFATM might be willing to move in this direction for some countries.

In November 2005, the GFATM threatened to cancel its $107 million grant to Nigeria because of questions about reporting data and missed program targets. Though the GFATM eventually approved the grant, there was speculation that some board members thought the country should spend more of its own money on AIDS because of its increased oil revenues and debt relief. This debate coincided with an MSF report that found that almost 50 percent of Lagos patients in the government's ARV program experienced an interruption in treatment because they were required to pay part of the costs (*Globe and Mail*, December 16, 2005). Roughly one week after the GFATM debate and the MSF report, the government announced it would provide free AIDS drugs in 2006. While impossible to prove, it appeared that the combination of indirect GFATM pressure and civil society advocacy influenced the government policy (*Reuters*, December 24, 2005).

Second, how do the GFATM and PEPFAR encourage African governments to be accountable on AIDS to people the disease affects? The GFATM has the potential to foster this accountability through the required CCMs. State officials often chair CCMs and, as of November 2004, all CCMs must involve people living with and/or affected by AIDS, TB, and/or malaria (PartnersGF eForum at http://forum.theglobalfund.org/en, November 21, 2004). The GFATM's website lists CCM membership, so that there is some transparency in terms of who devises and oversees grants. Of course, this does not mean that each CCM incorporates PLWHAs or civil society organizations fully into decision-making. Since governments are usually the principal recipients of GFATM grants, state leaders must build coalitions for spending decisions, and they can claim credit for that spending. Since grant amounts are publicized on the GFATM's website, AIDS groups can track funding and hold governments accountable for progress. While AIDS groups may not do this, the GFATM makes such actions possible.

In contrast, PEPFAR's structure may make it more difficult for government to be accountable to citizens affected by AIDS, because it does not require African governments and these groups to build consensus about priorities and it gives governments very few, if any, resources for which they are directly accountable. While consensus may emerge between multinational NGOs getting PEPFAR money and their local partners, this is not the same as the CCM consultation between African governments and civil society over how to allocate resources and the accountability that potentially emerges from that consultation. In some countries where governments built such consensus *before* PEPFAR emerged, PEPFAR goals have replaced agreed-on priorities. Jennifer Cooke (2004, 21) writes about Ethiopia, "There is a sense that this sudden shift [to US policy priorities with a new emphasis on treatment], and the sizeable resource flows that accompany it, may be driving the Ethiopian government to shift its priorities and resources to treatment as well ... External pressure and resources may shape, rather than complement or strengthen, the Ethiopian response." Alex de Waal (2004, 4) echoes this observation, when he reports that PEPFAR officials showed up in Ethiopia without consulting the country's national plan for health sector expansion.

In such a situation, government accountability to citizens affected by AIDS is blurred. Are African governments accountable for their own priorities or those of PEPFAR? If government-PEPFAR priorities are similar, but PEPFAR provides much of the money needed to meet them, who gets the credit for successes or the blame for failures? These theoretical dilemmas were played out in an exchange between Botswana and OGAC officials. In June 2005, OGAC claimed there were over 32,000 Batswana receiving treatment because of PEPFAR. In response, Segolame Ramotlhawa, director of Botswana's treatment program, called the US figures "a gross misrepresentation of the facts" and reported that no patient was dependent on PEPFAR for treatment. In one sense, the debate illustrated the complexity of determining who benefits from which program. OGAC counted any patient who benefits indirectly from US assistance, a process that may credit PEPFAR with what are primarily government initiatives. More basic, though, is that the various components of ARV treatment programs have been funded by different actors: the Gates Foundation has built AIDS clinics; Merck Pharmaceutical Company has donated ARVs; the government pays doctors and nurses; PEPFAR money has purchased lab technology; and Harvard University has trained lab technicians. Politically, the credit claiming was important to OGAC because it needs to show progress to the US Congress. It was important in Botswana's democracy because President Festus Mogae promised universal treatment in 2002 and he has made AIDS one of his top issues. Thus, Botswana did not want its citizens to think that the United States was the only one responsible for the country's treatment successes (*Washington Post*, July 1, 2005, p. A1).

Third, how do the GFATM and PEPFAR encourage accountability of African state leaders to the two institutions? The GFATM Governing Board, with equal representation from wealthy and poor countries, can approve or reject grant proposals and suspend funding. In August 2005, the board temporarily suspended five grants to Uganda citing evidence of serious mismanagement. While the grants were eventually restored, the fund insisted on new management procedures (*Kaiser Daily HIV/AIDS Report*, August 25, 2005).

To be fair, PEPFAR tries to avoid these accountability issues by providing few grants directly to governments. Instead, many government agencies are subpartners, making them directly accountable for funds to the prime partner, such as a multinational NGO or US academic institution (OGAC 2005c). For African government agencies that do receive grants, such as Uganda's ministry of health, they must fully detail their use of funding to OGAC. Yet, even though PEPFAR does not directly hold most governments accountable for specific grants, it still could threaten to end PEPFAR funding to a country if government officials refused to cooperate with NGOs or a government came into power that was explicitly anti-American. On the flip side, PEPFAR's presence in a country can be a tool to reinforce US foreign policy goals, though I do not mean that US interests are the primary reason PEPFAR works in some countries. For example, Uganda and Nigeria, two PEPFAR countries with recent accountability problems with the GFATM, are important for US interests: Uganda supported the 2003 invasion of Iraq, and as of October 2005, Nigeria was the fourth largest supplier of crude oil imports to the United States (Oloka-Onyango 2004; DOE 2005). PEPFAR may reaffirm US ties to those countries.

Only time will tell if the GFATM will encourage African states to be more accountable to those the disease affects. The CCM structure and the outside review process have the potential to do this. In contrast, PEPFAR claims to "foster indigenous leadership" by training individuals in organizational development, program management, and strategic information (OGAC 2005b, 14). While such skills are important, they do not encourage state and nonstate actors to work together to make difficult political decisions such as how much a country will spend on treatment for HIV-positive adults, what a country will stress in its AIDS prevention programs, or if AIDS orphans will become a priority. These are tough political questions, but PEPFAR's focus on multinational

NGOs and US agencies takes this decisionmaking out of the hands of African state officials and may blur lines of responsibility for results.

## Building Political Commitment to AIDS Among Donors

It is not solely African leaders who must commit to fighting AIDS. To deal with the magnitude of the pandemic, donors also must commit. How do PEPFAR and the GFATM encourage increased spending on AIDS, accountability to people AIDS affects, and accountability to those who provide their funds? First, both PEPFAR and the GFATM provide new money for AIDS. Public health officials who have worked on AIDS since the 1980s welcome this increase. Despite this, funding remains inadequate. UNAIDS (2005c) estimates $22 billion will be needed by 2008 to fight AIDS globally. If donors continue to give at the level they did in 2005, there will be a $13.7 billion shortfall in 2008 (Kates 2005). The most often mentioned way to address this shortfall is for the United States, Germany, Japan, and France to spend money (bilaterally or multilaterally) at levels closer or equal to their share of global GDP. That is, wealthier countries should pay their "fair share" of the cost of fighting AIDS. Does each institution have the potential to encourage greater (or even sustained) giving? In an odd way, PEPFAR's structure may facilitate this commitment. PEPFAR gives US NGOs, academic institutions, and government agencies a stake in AIDS spending. To protect their programs, budgets, and interests, these groups may lobby the US Congress for more, or at least sustained, funding. Indeed, many development NGOs such as World Vision, CARE, Africare, and Christian Children's Fund have advocacy offices in Washington to do just that. On the other hand, such lobbying only works if lawmakers view some level of public support for AIDS spending, as they did in 2003. Because AIDS has been portrayed as an emergency—a short-term problem to be fixed—it may be more difficult to sustain this public support. For Congress to continue funding the initiative after 2008, activists will have to maintain pressure on lawmakers, policymakers will have to believe the program is working, and the public will have to know and care about the human cost of program cuts.[45]

The GFATM may have a harder time encouraging donors to commit funding to its multilateral efforts, because it has no built-in constituency with political power. US (or French, German, or Japanese) agencies and NGOs do not receive the bulk of its grant money. While the organization Friends of the Global Fight Against AIDS, Tuberculosis and Malaria advocates for the GFATM in Washington, Japan, and Western Europe, the group faces challenges building domestic constituencies to lobby governments for more GFATM money. The fact that the GFATM often has financial shortfalls that have had to be met with last-minute donations may also demonstrate its limitations in encouraging donors to commit to AIDS through a multilateral endeavor.

Second, through its decisionmaking structure, the GFATM is more accountable than PEPFAR to the millions of people affected by AIDS. In early 2006, of the twenty voting members of the GFATM Governing Board, two represented NGOs and one represented an AIDS organization. Furthermore, the GFATM's Partnership Forum allows PLWHAs and civil society organizations to communicate with each other and to lobby the fund for changes (GFATM 2006b). The transparency of the GFATM website makes the institution more accountable to people AIDS affects, since they can easily access information about grants.

In contrast, PEPFAR does not have these requirements for civil society representation at OGAC. Similarly, it does not have mechanisms to ensure that indigenous AIDS organizations are incorporated into decisionmaking about strategies in the focus countries. It also lacks the level of transparency of the GFATM. OGAC has been slow about releasing reports, sharing information on its grant awards, or detailing the amount of money consultants receive for PEPFAR projects.[46] As of January 2006, the OGAC website did not detail successful proposals, though it did provide a list of its prime partners and subpartners for each focus country (OGAC 2005c). To be fair, these transparency problems are not unique to PEPFAR, but are consistent throughout many bilateral donor programs (Easterly 2002; *Financial Times*, June 20, 2005, p. G8).

PEPFAR presents a paradox: it gets US agencies and NGOs entrenched in AIDS work, which probably leads them to pressure Congress for continued (or more) funding. But, to have this interest in long-term AIDS funding, PEPFAR compromises some of its accountability to people affected by the disease. For example, 70 percent of PEPFAR funding in Nigeria goes for US goods and contractors, giving them a huge stake in that program. But, Abdulsalim Nasidi, director of special projects in Nigeria's Ministry of Health, hints at the inequality of that practice: "Of course we'd like that money to go for Nigerian supplies and personnel, but those are the rules" (*All Things Considered*, NPR Radio, June 13, 2005). This inequality between the donor and recipient makes it less likely that an honest partnership between the two can be forged. That type of partnership is needed to conquer AIDS, as one multinational NGO official said: "The issue [of local partners participating and buying into program goals] will emerge more and more in the future, because it will be important to bring our partners along for the long-run success of our project."[47] But, partnership is not only crucial for the recipient; it also has the potential to rejuvenate the donor's financial commitment. Because of PEPFAR's five-year focus, some African officials worry that thousands of HIV-positive Africans will be put on ARVs that their governments cannot afford after 2008, when Congress must reauthorize PEPFAR (Cooke 2004, 22).[48] Equal partnership can enable the United States to see both the costs and benefits of its program.

Finally, both the GFATM and PEPFAR are relatively accountable to their financial donors. PEPFAR gets money from the US Congress, which appropriates tax revenue to the program. Governments are the primary donors to the GFATM, although individuals, businesses, and foundations also have contributed. OGAC provides detailed reports to Congress on PEPFAR's progress to the 2-7-10 program goals and OGAC officials regularly testify before congressional committees. The GFATM gives extensive information on its website.

## Donors, Inequality, and the Global AIDS Fight

The GFATM and PEPFAR both provide new money for HIV/AIDS, a health and development problem long ignored. The ability of various organizations and individuals to get the pandemic on the political agenda globally and in Washington reflects a growing concern about the pandemic's size and what that magnitude will mean not only for Africa, but also for global security (*New York Times*, January 29, 2003). The magnitude necessitates donor involvement to fight AIDS, because of Africa's poverty and underdeveloped health care capacity. This dependence, though, can marginalize the voice of African states in decisionmaking, particularly in the case of PEPFAR. The fact that PEPFAR effectively doubles the US foreign aid budgets for several African countries makes equal partnership more difficult. While Mozambican and Rwandan officials have challenged decisions to use PEPFAR money for brand-name drugs, Zambian leaders had little interaction with the country's PEPFAR team until several months after PEPFAR was announced (*New York Times*, July 14, 2004, p. A1; Kerry 2005). And although leaders in Botswana disputed OGAC's treatment numbers, they also stressed in the *Washington Post* their gratitude for the millions of US dollars the country had received (see also *Washington Post*, July 14, 2005).

These two donor programs highlight another element of inequality: wide variation among African countries receiving AIDS funding. Table

5.1 lists external AIDS funding for thirty-one sub-Saharan African countries.[49] The table provides PEPFAR grants for 2004 and 2005 for focus countries, and GFATM grants approved for four funding rounds between 2002 and September 2005. I use GFATM approved, not dispersed, funds, because the PEPFAR money reported is also planned not dispersed. Because nonfocus countries may receive US money through USAID for health and HIV/AIDS, the table also includes those amounts from 2004 through September 2005. Some countries receive HIV/AIDS funding through USAID for multicountry programs. Examples include Lesotho within the Southern Africa Regional HIV/AIDS Program or Togo within the West African Regional Program. USAID does not delineate country totals, and I do not include these amounts because they are relatively small (e.g., $7.5 million for twelve southern African states in 2005; $15 million for nine central African states; and $19.5 million for nineteen West African states) (USAID 2005b). The table excludes MAP money since the MAP initiative provides loans, not grants.

Although the trends are not completely consistent—South Africa, Nigeria, and Mozambique are exceptions—most PEPFAR focus countries received more money per HIV-positive person than nonfocus countries. Zimbabwe and Djibouti were outliers: Zimbabwe, for reasons discussed in Chapter 2; Djibouti, because of its small HIV-positive population and its $7.2 million GFATM grant. Uganda, Rwanda, Zambia, and Namibia were clear winners in terms of funding, receiving large amounts from PEPFAR and the GFATM. A comparison between Rwanda and Burundi, countries the same size with roughly the same level of HIV prevalence, also illustrates this disparity: Rwanda received $456 per HIV-positive person while Burundi received $35. The relatively low amount for South Africa, $54 per person, reflected the country's higher level of economic development and its ability to spend more on AIDS programs than other African countries.

Table 5.1 reaffirms the point made by an official working with the GFATM that donors reward countries with the capacity to write and administer grants.[50] For example, donors say Rwandan officials have been open to outside assistance and they have sought to improve management practices. In contrast, political divisions and lack of communication in the Nigerian National AIDS Commission have affected GFATM grants.[51] Thus, the funding disparities of Table 5.1 reflect not only donor preferences, but also uneven state capacity and governance across the continent. While these funding differences may not be surprising, since donors want resources to be used efficiently, they do illustrate how politics in recipient countries shapes the AIDS fight. That is,

**Table 5.1    PEPFAR, USAID, and GFATM Funding for Selected Focus and Nonfocus Countries in Sub-Saharan Africa**

| Country | Population with HIV/AIDS | Adult HIV Prevalence (%) | PEPFAR Funding[a] ($US millions) | USAID Funding[b] ($US millions) | GFATM Funding[c] ($US millions) | Total Funding Amount ($US millions) | Funding Per HIV+ Person ($US) |
|---|---|---|---|---|---|---|---|
| Angola | 240,000 | 3.9 | | 18.1 | 27.6 | 45.7 | 190 |
| **Botswana** | 350,000 | 37.3 | 67.4 | | 18.6 | 86 | 246 |
| Burkina Faso | 300,000 | 4.2 | | x | 7.1 | 7.1 | 24 |
| Burundi | 250,000 | 6 | | x | 8.7 | 8.7 | 35 |
| Cameroon | 560,000 | 6.9 | | x | 20.9 | 20.9 | 37 |
| Central African Republic | 260,000 | 13.5 | | x | 12.9 | 12.9 | 50 |
| Chad | 200,000 | 4.8 | | x | 7.4 | 7.4 | 37 |
| Democratic Republic of Congo | 1,100,000 | 4.2 | | 8 | 34.8 | 42.8 | 39 |
| **Côte d'Ivoire** | 570,000 | 7 | 63.6 | | 19.1 | 82.7 | 145 |
| Djibouti | 9,100 | 2.9 | | 0.2 | 7.2 | 7.4 | 813 |
| Eritrea | 60,000 | 2.7 | | 4.6 | 8.1 | 12.7 | 212 |
| **Ethiopia** | 1,500,000 | 4.4 | 118 | | 97.3 | 215.3 | 144 |
| Gabon | 48,000 | 8.1 | | x | 3.2 | 3.2 | 67 |
| Ghana | 350,000 | 3.1 | | 12 | 14.2 | 26.2 | 75 |
| Guinea | 140,000 | 3.2 | | 5 | 4.8 | 9.8 | 70 |
| **Kenya** | 1,200,000 | 6.7 | 228.6 | | 39.6 | 268.2 | 224 |
| Lesotho | 320,000 | 28.9 | | x | 10.6 | 10.6 | 33 |
| Liberia | 100,000 | 5.9 | | x | 7.6 | 7.6 | 76 |
| Malawi | 900,000 | 14.2 | | 22 | 41.8 | 63.8 | 71 |
| **Mozambique** | 1,300,000 | 12.2 | 92.1 | | 29.7 | 121.8 | 94 |
| **Namibia** | 210,000 | 21.3 | 64 | | 26 | 90 | 429 |
| **Nigeria** | 3,600,000 | 5.4 | 179.8 | | 28.2 | 208 | 58 |

*(continues)*

**Table 5.1** continued

| Country | Population with HIV/AIDS | Adult HIV Prevalence (%) | PEPFAR Funding[a] ($US millions) | USAID Funding[b] ($US millions) | GFATM Funding[c] ($US millions) | Total Funding Amount ($US millions) | Funding Per HIV+Person ($US) |
|---|---|---|---|---|---|---|---|
| **Rwanda** | 250,000 | 5.1 | 90.6 | | 23.3 | 113.9 | 456 |
| **South Africa** | 5,300,000 | 21.5 | 221.5 | | 66.1 | 287.6 | 54 |
| Sudan | 400,000 | 2.3 | | 3 | 16.6 | 19.6 | 49 |
| Swaziland | 220,000 | 38.8 | | x | 68.9 | 68.9 | 313 |
| **Tanzania** | 1,600,000 | 8.8 | 175.5 | | 134.9 | 310.4 | 194 |
| Togo | 110,000 | 4.1 | | x | 25.7 | 25.7 | 234 |
| **Uganda** | 530,000 | 4.1 | 215.1 | | 119.3 | 334.4 | 631 |
| **Zambia** | 920,000 | 16.5 | 196.7 | | 117.1 | 313.8 | 341 |
| Zimbabwe | 1,800,000 | 24.6 | | 21.2 | 10.3 | 31.5 | 18 |

*Sources:* Compiled by author from WHO (2004), OGAC (2004a), UNAIDS (2004a), GFATM (2006a), and USAID (2005a).

*Notes:* PEPFAR focus countries are listed in boldface type.

x = No available country budget for fiscal years 2004, 2005. Some of those countries received funding through regional programs, or their health programs do not include explicit HIV/AIDS components.

a. PEPFAR funding is for fiscal years 2004 and 2005 and includes USAID funding for HIV/AIDS in those countries.

b. USAID funding is for fiscal years 2004 and 2005 and includes USAID funding specifically for health and HIV/AIDS for fiscal years 2004 and 2005. Health spending that does not include specific allocations on HIV/AIDS is not included. Since USAID delineated funds for child survival, maternal health, and family planning programs from its HIV/AIDS spending, I do not include those in the AIDS amount.

c. GFATM funding is approved, not dispersed; HIV/AIDS funding total is for four funding rounds between 2002 and September 2005.

because of political factors—a lack of government transparency, corruption, and/or the unwillingness of politicians to invest in the state capacity needed to get grants—citizens suffer from a lack of resources for AIDS treatment, care, and support programs.

The table hints at another potential inequality. As of mid-2005, the GFATM had approved approximately $1 billion to the thirty-one countries. Yet if the GFATM does not continue to get financial donations from the world's wealthiest countries, including the United States, this amount of funding will dwindle in comparison to the amount PEPFAR countries receive.[52] The gap between focus and nonfocus countries has the potential to increase. However, conquering AIDS requires that both the GFATM and PEPFAR are successful. Declining prevalence rates in focus countries could be reversed with cross-border migration from surrounding countries with high HIV prevalence levels.

This chapter highlights a final theme of the book: institutions matter for building political commitment to AIDS among African leaders and donors themselves. In terms of African officials, neither program requires African states to commit more funding to AIDS or to health. However, the GFATM-required CCM structure creates the potential for African leaders to be accountable to people the disease affects. The GFATM also gives governments resources, something that might increase their stake in AIDS. Because of its centralization and its reliance on US agencies and multinational NGOs, PEPFAR may have a more difficult time fostering this accountability between African leaders and those AIDS affects. African state officials are directly accountable to the GFATM, and the board can cut off funding if states do not show financial transparency. PEPFAR is different, because it provides a limited amount of money directly to African states.

In terms of the political commitment of these two donor institutions, the GFATM, because it lacks a powerful built-in constituency, may have a harder time generating financial support for its endeavors than PEPFAR. PEPFAR's grants to multinational NGOs and US agencies may help to build a constituency for bilateral AIDS spending in the United States. On the other hand, the GFATM's governance structures have sought to incorporate people affected by AIDS, while PEPFAR's centralization has made it more difficult to include these voices. Both programs seek to encourage accountability to their financiers through transparency in reporting. However, PEPFAR's entire structure and its focus on short-term results explicitly highlight its need for accountability to a US Congress (and US people) often skeptical about foreign assistance programs.

These two donor programs present a trade-off in fighting AIDS. Programs like PEPFAR, with its short-term, emergency focus are important. Because of PEPFAR, HIV-positive individuals are receiving ARVs, AIDS orphans are getting food assistance, and HIV-positive pregnant women are getting drugs for PMTCT. These accomplishments should not be discounted. But is there a long-term cost to this efficiency? If, as one AIDS activist asserted, "[some African] leaders are basically . . . acting like AIDS is an issue to get all this money the US is giving away," then the program's attention to results over process may be problematic.[53] On the other hand, the GFATM has been more participatory and inclusive, with its mechanisms for representation and governmental accountability. But it is less efficient, with some groups reporting two-year lags in receiving approved GFATM funds.[54] It is unclear how much this inefficiency may discourage stakeholders in the future.

Both PEPFAR and the GFATM raise questions about how to foster a long-term institutionalized response to AIDS. PEPFAR's emergency, results-oriented approach presents a challenge to building the consensus needed to link AIDS to the long-term problems of development, inequality, and poverty. But, the GFATM's reliance on the whims of Western governments for its funding also may prevent this type of consensus building. In the concluding chapter, I ask what an institutionalized global response to AIDS looks like for individuals in the West and Africa, African leaders, and donor programs such as the GFATM and PEPFAR.

## Notes

1. Some Washington insiders assert the president announced PEPFAR to dispel criticism about the upcoming war with Iraq. Others maintain that the president's religious faith fueled his compassion on the issue. Finally, some say that activist pressure pushed the White House to develop PEPFAR. See Greg Behrman (2004, 302) for a summary of these perspectives.

2. None of the statistics provided include funding for AIDS research. The 2004 funding report uses the Group of Seven (instead of Group of Eight) because it excludes Russia.

3. Directly Observed Treatment Short-Course (DOTS) Therapy is a comprehensive, WHO-endorsed strategy to fight TB that includes five elements: political commitment; access to quality sputum microscopy for diagnosis; uninterrupted supply of quality-assured drugs; standardized short-course chemotherapy to all TB cases under proper case management; and a recording and reporting system enabling outcome assessments for each patient and TB program (WHO 2006a).

4. In comparison to other donors, the United States had one of the lowest

disbursement rates from its approved funds in 2004. Part of the reason for this is that PEPFAR was a new program that only began in 2004 (Kates 2005, 10).

5. Bruce Wilkinson, Chief of Party, Reaching HIV/AIDS Affected People with Integrated Development and Support (RAPIDS) project in Zambia, phone interview with author, April 14, 2005.

6. Given the impact of AIDS on society, particularly in countries with high HIV prevalence rates, the number of citizens affected could be quite large. I use this categorization quite broadly.

7. Individuals from a variety of organizations agreed that evangelical Christians were essential to passage of PEPFAR. Tom Hart, Director of Legislative Relations, Debt, AIDS, Trade and Africa (DATA), interview with author, Washington, DC, February 24, 2005; Jodi Jacobson, Center for Health and Gender Equity (CHANGE), interview with author, Takoma Park, MD, March 11, 2005; Richard Cizik, National Association of Evangelicals, interview with author, Washington, DC, April 11, 2005.

8. Tom Hart, February 24, 2005.

9. Paul Farmer, cofounder of Partners in Health, interview with author, Grand Rapids, MI, January 9, 2006.

10. Anne Peterson, former USAID Assistant Administrator for Global Health, interview with author, Washington, DC, April 15, 2005.

11. Anonymous official at African advocacy organization, interview with author, Washington, DC, March 7, 2005.

12. Interview with author, Washington, DC, March 18, 2005.

13. The legislation authorized the program and set the parameters for spending earmarks. Money for the program, however, must be appropriated each year during the budgetary cycle. Congress appropriated $2.4 billion in fiscal year 2004 and $2.8 billion in fiscal year 2005. President Bush requested $3.2 billion for fiscal year 2006. As of November 2005, the Senate and House had both approved over $3 billion for fiscal year 2006, although the final appropriated amount was not available at the time of printing (Tobias 2005; *Kaiser Daily HIV/AIDS Report*, July 21, 2005; Copson 2005).

14. President Bush announced the Millennium Challenge Account in 2002. The program allows countries that meet governance and market reform criteria to apply for direct funding for country-designed projects. As of June 2005, however, the program had only approved grants to Madagascar, Honduras, Cape Verde, and Nicaragua. It has continually lacked funding from Congress (*New York Times*, June 17, 2005).

15. Poor countries complete these papers roughly every three years for the IMF and World Bank. Written by government, civil society, and donors, the papers outline goals met and challenges that remain in macroeconomic, structural, and social policy and overall poverty reduction.

16. On June 30, 2005, President Bush proposed a new $1.2 billion, five-year malaria initiative to start with $30 million in fiscal year 2006 (*New York Times*, July 1, 2005).

17. Vietnam was added in 2004, after Congress requested an additional country from another geographic region.

18. Anne Peterson, April 15, 2005.

19. Jacqui Patterson, Interchurch Medical Assistance, interview with

author, New Windsor, MD, March 16, 2005. AIDSRelief is a US consortium composed of Catholic Relief Services, Catholic Medical Mission Board, the Futures Group, Interchurch Medical Assistance, and the Institute of Human Virology. It has received a five-year, $335 million grant from PEPFAR to provide ARV treatment in nine countries.

20. The treatment allocation also reflects civil society pressure, the contentious debates over prevention, and the high cost of ARV treatment.

21. On January 20, 2006, Secretary of State Condoleezza Rice nominated Tobias to be the new administrator of USAID as well as the director of foreign assistance at the State Department, a new position to oversee all US foreign aid (*Washington Post*, January 19, 2006, p. A1). It is unclear what this potential restructuring, which Congress must approve, means for OGAC.

22. Josh Ruxin, Director of Access Project in Rwanda, Columbia University, phone interview with author, April 19, 2005.

23. Anil Soni, former Executive Director of Friends of the Global Fight, interview with author, Washington, DC, March 7, 2005.

24. Bruce Wilkinson, April 14, 2005.

25. Anne Peterson, April 15, 2005; Anne Peterson, email correspondence with author, July 7, 2005.

26. Anne Peterson, April 15, 2005; Anne Peterson, July 7, 2005.

27. Jodi Jacobson, March 11, 2005.

28. Jacqui Patterson, March 16, 2005.

29. Bruce Wilkinson, April 14, 2005.

30. Anil Soni, March 7, 2005.

31. The term "sex worker" has gained popularity among public health officials globally because it is less stigmatizing than "prostitute," a word the US legislation uses. I use the terms interchangeably.

32. Richard Cizik, April 11, 2005; Anne Peterson, April 15, 2005.

33. Anne Peterson, April 15, 2005. The same has been true of Glazer Pediatric AIDS Foundation. Anne Peterson (July 7, 2005) writes: "The only reason [staff] turnover wasn't [much] higher is that many see this as a once in a lifetime chance to make a difference in AIDS and [they] work to the detriment of their own health and their families."

34. Anne Peterson, April 15, 2005; Anne Peterson, July 7, 2005.

35. In interviews with numerous secular and faith-based organizations in Washington, DC, between February and May 2005, the vast majority mentioned these groups as among the most powerful in Washington politics.

36. Richard Cizik, April 11, 2005.

37. Jodi Jacobson, March 11, 2005.

38. Ibid.

39. Ibid.

40. There are debates about what Uganda's HIV prevalence rate was in 1990 and how much it declined. See Low-Beer and Stoneburner (2004, 167–170).

41. Alan Goodman, Team leader for HIV/AIDS project, Search for Common Ground, interview with author, Washington, DC, April 27, 2005.

42. This theme also emerged during 2005 congressional hearings on PEPFAR (US House of Representatives Committee on International Relations 2005;

US House of Representatives Appropriations Committee, Subcommittee on Foreign Operations 2005).

43. Jacqui Patterson, March 16, 2005.

44. Josh Ruxin, April 19, 2005.

45. Tom Hart, February 24, 2005; Serge Duss, March 18, 2005.

46. Anonymous official at AIDS advocacy organization, interview with author, Washington, DC, March 21, 2005.

47. Bruce Wilkinson, April 14, 2005.

48. In an apparent response to this concern, Ambassador Tobias said that PEPFAR projects would continue in some form after 2008 (*Boston Globe*, May 31, 2005).

49. The table includes all southern, central, and east African countries, except the Indian Ocean islands, because the pandemic thus far has been concentrated in those regions. It includes all twelve PEPFAR focus countries in Africa and West African states with prevalence levels over 4 percent. Congo is excluded because no data was available on either USAID or GFATM grants to the country in late 2005. Equatorial Guinea and Somalia are excluded because, as of September 2005, UNAIDS provided no HIV prevalence rates for them.

50. Anil Soni, March 7, 2005.

51. Josh Ruxin, April 19, 2005.

52. On the different attitudes toward the GFATM among US officials, see US House of Representatives Appropriations Committee, Subcommittee on Foreign Operations (2005). The fact that the US Congress has approved more for the GFATM for fiscal years 2005 and 2006 than the Bush Administration requested may also illustrate a difference in viewpoints between Congress and the presidency (Copson 2005).

53. Jodi Jacobson, March 11, 2005.

54. Paul Farmer, January 9, 2006.

# 6

---

# Beyond Politics as Usual: Institutionalizing the AIDS Struggle

THE AIDS PANDEMIC provides a window into African politics. This book has demonstrated that politics is crucial for addressing the disease and that our understanding of how AIDS policies and programs are developed and implemented is intricately related to our knowledge about power, representation, and political institutions on the continent. Africa's political challenges are reflected in the slow progress in developing AIDS programs, providing funding, and attracting both domestic and international political attention to the pandemic. There is no one political explanation for why some countries have effectively developed AIDS policies while others have lagged behind. Instead, country context, state characteristics such as neopatrimonialism or power centralization, state-civil society relations, and a country's experience with donors shape the politics of AIDS.

For some African countries such as Zimbabwe and Swaziland, high centralization of power and neopatrimonialism have hampered AIDS efforts. In those countries, it appears likely that state resources have been diverted from public health, and AIDS organizations have been excluded from AIDS decisionmaking. Donors, looking for supportive environments in which to work, have shunned the two countries, despite their high HIV prevalence rates. On the other hand, security concerns contributed to Uganda's proactive AIDS efforts, despite its high state centralization and increasing neopatrimonialism. After Uganda's civil war, local councils sought to mobilize citizens for state reconstruction; in the process, these institutions became crucial for the AIDS fight. While South Africa, a state with low centralization, low neopatrimonialism, and high capacity, has a relatively high API score for its efforts, Thabo Mbeki's centralization of AIDS policymaking in the presidency and his personal views on the disease have prevented the country from doing better. The four case studies in Chapter 2 reveal that while state characteristics shape AIDS efforts, they alone do not explain why some countries have done a better job at fighting the disease than others.

Africa's democratic transitions that began in the 1990s have not been a necessary and sufficient condition for state action on AIDS. The picture among Africa's new democracies is uneven. Although public opinion can constrain policymaking, in many of Africa's democracies the public has not prioritized AIDS. Similarly, elections have not been a means for holding democratic governments accountable for AIDS policies. However, in what may be a hopeful sign, in three countries in which AIDS is salient in public opinion polls and in which HIV prevalence rates are high—Namibia, South Africa, and Botswana—politicians made AIDS an important issue in their 2004 campaigns. While alternation in power in Kenya and Ghana provided opportunities for new leaders to speak openly about AIDS, in post-apartheid South Africa, such openness allowed President Mbeki to question the science of AIDS. Although cross-national research demonstrates that democracies tend to spend more on health because they are accountable to their citizens and civil society, democratic transitions in Africa have yet to have a conclusive impact on these government expenditures. While some increasingly democratic countries such as Mozambique and Benin have spent more on public health, others such as Senegal and South Africa have decreased health spending.

One key component of democratic systems is an active civil society that can hold government accountable for AIDS policies and mobilize citizens for political advocacy. Yet, as the organizations examined in Chapter 4 illustrate, civil society groups face challenges in the AIDS fight. Few have sufficient resources to hire staff, utilize Internet communication, and attend conferences. Their leaders and members often lack political experience, and internal structures may hamper communication and accountability. These obstacles weaken AIDS groups. Additionally, AIDS organizations may lack effectiveness because of the larger political context, their inability to build coalitions with other associations, and their relations with the state. TAC is an exceptional case: it has mobilized large numbers of South Africans, worked effectively through domestic and international coalitions, and used South Africa's new democratic institutions to challenge state AIDS policies. Yet, as Douglas Webb writes (2004, 31): "The high level of international attention received by the Treatment Action Campaign . . . is testament to the fact that genuine and organized activism around AIDS in sub-Saharan Africa is minimal." The AIDS issue provides a prism through which to view the diverse conditions that shape civil society's political influence.

The AIDS pandemic, and particularly the provision of ARVs to the thousands of HIV-positive Africans who need them, necessitates large amounts of external funding. A comparison of the bilateral PEPFAR with the multilateral GFATM, revealed that both donor institutions reflect heightened global interest in the pandemic, and both have made important contributions to AIDS efforts. However, PEPFAR and the GFATM contrast in their potential for shaping political commitment to AIDS among African leaders and donors themselves. The GFATM requires collaboration with civil society and accountability for funds through the CCMs and the representation of PLWHAs on its Governing Board. These structures may make both African leaders and the GFATM itself accountable to people the disease affects. But, because the GFATM lacks a powerful constituency that can advocate for funding, its ability to foster financial commitment to AIDS among Western governments and citizens may be limited. On the other hand, because PEPFAR gives funds primarily to US NGOs and government agencies, these actors have a vested interest in seeing the program continue. However, since PEPFAR seeks to rapidly address the AIDS emergency, its centralized decisionmaking processes may do little to foster accountability among donors or African leaders to those the disease affects.

This book illustrates the complexity of the politics of AIDS. Democratic transitions may provide political space for advocacy, but if civil society groups lack resources or are ravaged by the disease, they may be unable to take advantage of these openings. Political leaders may confuse citizens with mixed messages about AIDS or engage in personal behavior that increases the risk of HIV transmission, while donors or civil society organizations may try to counter these actions. Donors may design AIDS programs to rapidly gain results, limiting the accountability of African leaders to their own citizens.

## Magnitude, Inequality, and Institutions

Three themes of magnitude, inequality, and institutions shape the politics of AIDS. The fact that almost forty million people worldwide are HIV positive galvanized US AIDS groups, FBOs, and development NGOs to push for PEPFAR's passage. The pandemic's magnitude helped civil society organizations mobilize an international treatment coalition that convinced First World policymakers that ARV therapies are feasible in poor countries. The disease's potentially large-scale impact on the Ugandan military urged President Museveni to act on AIDS when he came to power. However, magnitude is not a sufficient condition to cause leaders to address AIDS. Although King Mswati III has bemoaned his country's high HIV prevalence rate, he has not refrained from personal behavior that reinforces society's views about women and contributes to HIV transmission. Zimbabwe's high HIV prevalence rate has not caused President Mugabe to foster better working relations with civil society groups or to end the alleged practice of using the country's AIDS levy for patronage.

Inequality also pervades the politics of AIDS. In countries such as Zimbabwe and Swaziland where power is highly centralized, unequal representation means there are minimal opportunities for PLWHAs or AIDS groups to shape policies. The speculation that ARVs may be used as political patronage in Zimbabwe illustrates that in highly unequal political systems not all citizens have the needed connections to access these medicines. The public good of health care can become a private good used to shore up state elites. Even in Africa's democracies, there is no guarantee that the individuals most vulnerable to HIV—women, children, and migrants—will be represented in policy decisions. While civil society organizations do participate in the CCMs, this representation is uneven across Africa. Moreover, not all AIDS organizations are equal: some, such as TAC, have more resources, clout, experience, and consequently, advocacy successes, than others. Finally, inequality is reflected in the fact that African states must rely heavily on the resources of donors to combat AIDS. This dependence complicates negotiations over program components and may make equal partnership more difficult.

Inequalities embedded in the AIDS pandemic may have intangible consequences. For the vast majority of people who have access to ARV treatment, AIDS has become a manageable health condition. These individuals can continue their jobs; they can get married; they can raise their children; they can plan for the future. In contrast, those without ARV access worry about children who will be left behind, and they use savings that could have been invested in children's education to merely survive (Rugalema 2000). Those with access to ARVs gain some peace of mind; those without AIDS medicines suffer as their very humanity is rejected. This immeasurable inequality not only affects individuals. It also means that the investments in education, business, or industry that are needed for Africa's future are less likely to occur.

Institutions influence political responses to the pandemic. There is no one institutional design that has fostered political commitment to AIDS or led governments to proactively develop AIDS policies. But, any analysis of responses to AIDS cannot be divorced from an examination of the institutions that make those decisions. This book has provided numerous examples. In Uganda, the establishment of resistance councils when the NRM came to power facilitated the country's AIDS efforts. The councils mobilized local groups for AIDS prevention programs and facilitated the education of a diverse group of community members. Swaziland's power centralization in the monarch heightens the king's role in the AIDS fight and calls attention to his actions in the private realm. South Africa's post-apartheid constitution that gives the provincial governments some jurisdiction over health policy enabled some ANC premiers to challenge the national nevirapine policy. GFATM requirements that countries develop grant proposals with the consultation of civil society, government, donor, and business representatives have the potential to foster accountability and consensus building. Institutions matter for the fight against AIDS in Africa.

## Institutionalizing the AIDS Fight

Although AIDS has gained greater global attention since 2000, UNAIDS asserts that much more must be done if the number of AIDS deaths and new HIV infections is to decline by 2025. Its report *AIDS in Africa: Three Scenarios to 2025* outlines future possibilities for the pandemic (UNAIDS 2005a). In the most desolate scenario, governments and donors lose interest in AIDS. Spending levels stagnate, treatment programs and prevention efforts do not expand, and infection rates continue to increase. In the second, more hopeful scenario, African governments emulate the proactive responses of Uganda, Botswana, and Senegal; donors increase financial resources; and AIDS efforts focus on prevention. Even with these efforts, HIV infections do not level off until 2015. The cumulative cost of the second scenario is $100 billion, or roughly $5 billion annually. In the most dramatic scenario, African governments, donors, and civil society actors integrate AIDS efforts into comprehensive plans to foster human rights, women's empowerment, and development. In this scenario, the number of people with AIDS is halved. This path is estimated to cost $200 billion over the next twenty years, or $10 billion annually.

Because power, representation, and decisionmaking institutions shape which of these paths African states will follow, we cannot ignore politics when studying the disease. Yet, some have bemoaned the increasingly political nature of international AIDS debates. For example, the *Los Angeles Times* (July 17, 2004) reported that relatively few

AIDS scientists attended the 2004 International AIDS Conference in Bangkok. A perspective piece in the *New England Journal of Medicine* explained that unlike the early days of the pandemic, when international conferences centered around research findings on the HIV virus, the epidemiology of HIV transmission, and the promises of new treatments, recent conferences had become a political forum for focusing public attention on the pandemic (Steinbrook 2004). Others have argued that the increasingly politicized nature of AIDS research in the United States has driven scientists away from studying the disease (*Washington Post,* October 1, 2002, p. A6). They maintain that politics prevents scientific advancements on vaccines, pediatric ARVs, and microbicides from keeping up with the pandemic.[1] Yet, because AIDS is a public policy problem, how we address the disease is the outcome of political decisionmaking. Politics is about some people convincing others that one policy idea or resource allocation should be accepted over another. Decisions about where money for vaccine research will come from, when drug companies will develop cheap pediatric ARVs, or if granting agencies will prioritize scientific research on microbicides over research on other HIV prevention methods are the outcome of political processes.

Because even the wealthiest societies cannot allocate limitless resources to all social problems, governments must make choices. For Africa, a continent mired in poverty, successfully combating AIDS will require difficult political trade-offs. Yet, there has been very little public discourse about how these political choices will be made (*Boston Globe,* July 16, 2004). On a continent where democratic institutions are in their infancy, and many civil society groups face internal and external challenges, such public policy decisions have often been made haphazardly by presidents and donors. In order to conquer the pandemic, AIDS must become more formally institutionalized into all aspects of African politics. Institutionalization is more than setting up formal AIDS policymaking organizations with state and nonstate participants. It also means that these organizations are linked to society, the members represent constituents with a stake in the outcome, and AIDS is always an issue on the political agenda. It is not that AIDS is merely a pet project of donors or presidents, but an issue all citizens, political parties, civil society groups, media outlets, civil servants, and politicians embrace. Countries with successes in the AIDS struggle demonstrate elements of this institutionalization. In Uganda, not only has President Museveni spoken openly on AIDS, but AIDS programs have been embedded in local communities, and high-level institutions have coordinated AIDS efforts. Moreover, civil society groups like TASO represent stakeholders, and these associations have a real interest in AIDS policies, because of the donor resources that support those policies (Haven 2005). On the other hand, even though Zimbabwe has structures like the AIDS levy and decentralized AIDS committees, these institutions have not been independent from neopatrimonialism and presidential interference. Instead of being avenues through which stakeholders argue over resources, represent their members' interests, and define policy solutions, they sometimes have been used as a political tool.

What does an institutionalized AIDS fight look like for civil society organizations, African governments, donors, and global citizens? For civil society, institutionalization means that these organizations must be strengthened so they can hold government accountable, keep AIDS on the political agenda, and link affected citizens to decisionmaking institutions. To empower these African groups, organizations in industrialized countries must provide funding, technical assistance, staff, and leadership training to Africa's nascent AIDS groups. As TAC illustrates, civil society's strength (and effectiveness) partially rests on the political experience of its leaders. But many civil society leaders in Africa do not have the same social movement experiences that South African civil society leaders gained during the apartheid struggle. Therefore, more ex-government officials must emulate the efforts of former South African President Nelson Mandela and former Zambian President Kenneth Kaunda. These two leaders have used their stature, political knowledge, and personal connections to work with civil society to influence government AIDS policies.

For their long-term legitimacy, civil society groups also must make concerted efforts to be the mouthpiece of society's most politically powerless individuals. Power inequalities that can pervade AIDS (and non-AIDS) groups may hamper these associations' efforts against the disease. Civil society's capacity and unity is crucial if these groups are going to shape political decisions on AIDS, be equal partners with multinational NGOs, and implement successful AIDS programs.[2] TAC has tried to address the impact of race, class, and gender divisions on its organization, partly because its legitimacy rests on the moral nature of its operations.

The state and civil society must find new and creative ways to work together for the AIDS fight to become ingrained in politics. While TAC has been able to both confront and cooperate with the South African state, its resources and leadership probably make it exceptional. Instead, the role of Senegal's Muslim religious leaders (*marabouts*) in HIV education may provide another model for building on prior state-civil society relations to develop AIDS efforts. Ruling elites and the marabouts have worked as political partners since before the country's independence (Coulon 1976; Cruise O'Brien 1970, 160–162; Cruise O'Brien 1971, 163–187). Although the two groups have not always agreed on policies (Villalón 1995, 121; Patterson 1999), their long history of collaboration and dialogue facilitated the cooperation needed to meet the AIDS challenge. When the disease first appeared in the 1980s, state officials and the marabouts designed AIDS education materials and AIDS became a regular topic of Friday sermons at mosques (UNAIDS 1999, 12; *Baltimore Sun*, May 27, 2004; World Bank 2001a). The Senegalese case shows how a foundation of state-civil society collaboration may benefit the AIDS fight.

In terms of the African state, an institutionalized response to AIDS means that all political actors are concerned with the disease, not merely a handful of dynamic African presidents or ministers of health. Opposition parties debate AIDS, presidential candidates make the disease a top campaign issue, and all government ministers prioritize the epidemic in budgetary requests. For this to occur, political actors must have a stake in AIDS. In Africa's democracies, politicians must be concerned that civil society, constituents, and the media will hold them accountable if they do not address the disease. Yet, it appears that African democratic transitions have yet to bring the transparency and accountability needed to institute the AIDS fight. Placing AIDS on the political "front burner" means moving beyond the neopatrimonial logic of state survival that uses AIDS resources as a political tool to reward ruling elites and their supporters. While the neopatrimonial, centralized state of Uganda has committed to the AIDS fight, it may be exceptional because President Museveni linked AIDS to security concerns. It is uncertain that other neopatrimonial, centralized states will sustain a similar, long-run interest in AIDS without increased political accountability and transparency.

To institutionalize AIDS, government bureaucracies must have enough well-trained, experienced personnel to lobby for resources for the disease. Therefore, state capacity matters not only for addressing AIDS, but also for the continent's ability to infuse the AIDS issue into all government activities. State officials must be independent enough from presidential control to defend their AIDS budgets if the executive threatens cuts, and they must be able to build ties to a wide variety of civil society groups, which can advocate for needed AIDS programs. It is doubtful that any sub-Saharan African state has this capacity; even relatively well-developed South Africa shows that this is problematic.

While South Africa has resources, because AIDS policymaking has been centralized in the presidency, there is a lack of bureaucratic independence needed to develop policies. Thus, institutionalizing the AIDS fight relies on building a stronger, independent civil service throughout the continent.

Donor programs like PEPFAR and the World Bank MAP initiative may not help the bureaucracy play this independent role, because they tend to give local and multinational NGOs, not state officials, the funds to fight AIDS. Without controlling the finances, African state officials have little incentive to engage in the AIDS fight. These structures may depoliticize AIDS by "stripping away the state's resources and entrusting nonstate actors with the responsibility and accountability for programmes" (Haven 2005, 36). Ultimately, nonstate actors are accountable to group members or to the donors that provide their funding, but they do not have to respond to the broad citizenry like elected democratic leaders or even traditional rulers do. Part of institutionalizing the AIDS fight requires that state officials become more accountable in the AIDS fight; to be accountable, though, they must control the public good of AIDS resources.

Institutionalizing AIDS in politics means that the disease has to become a topic that African leaders willingly discuss, without resorting to symbolic platitudes or racial imagery. King Mswati's plea, "My people are dying," is emotionally moving, but not enough. In a country where women are the majority of HIV-positive people, the king must also talk about the hard issues of gender equality, domestic violence, polygamy, and rape. Similarly, when President Mbeki says that discussing HIV as a sexually transmitted disease drums up racist images of black, promiscuous Africans, he detracts from the real issues of personal and public responsibility that surround the pandemic. His rhetoric stigmatizes the disease, further driving citizens to view it as a personal, private issue, not a public policy problem that the state must address. Instead of empowering and mobilizing all South Africans to fight the disease, Mbeki cuts off the AIDS debate. A more affirming rhetoric comes from TAC's message that we are all HIV positive. When Nelson Mandela wears the "HIV positive" t-shirt, he does so in solidarity with the millions of people worldwide with the disease; the shirt implies that, because of its negative economic, social, and political effects, AIDS harms us all.

Although the word "institutionalization" implies rigidity, AIDS decisionmaking processes should not be inflexible. Rooting the AIDS struggle in society and government means there is space for state officials and civil society organizations to be innovative in their policy responses. Botswana provides a positive example. In 2004, Botswana President Festus Mogae introduced a policy of routine HIV testing. In routine testing, an HIV test is offered to anyone seen in the health care system, not just those patients presenting AIDS symptoms or requesting the test. Mogae's goal was to channel those who are HIV positive into the country's free treatment programs before they became extremely sick. The policy recognized the inappropriateness of the Western practice of VCT, in which an individual voluntarily and confidentially agrees to the test after receiving counseling about the implications of a possible positive result. The VCT model scared patients away from the test and was not aggressive enough in a country where HIV is rampant. Although some Western human rights organizations criticized the new policy, routine testing has quadrupled the number of citizens tested and has led to greater enrollment in Botswana's ARV programs.[3] By treating the HIV test like any other medical test, the practice also makes AIDS less of an "exceptional" disease and challenges the AIDS stigma (*Washington Times*, May 10, 2004; *New York Times*, June 14, 2004, p. A1).

The Botswana example illustrates that political space for developing innovative AIDS policies can yield positive results. But it also provides a lesson for donors, who have tended to encourage a common model of AIDS policymaking that may inhibit such creativity. In return for loans, the World Bank MAP initiative requires recipient countries to set up national AIDS commissions to allocate money to ministries, NGOs, and community groups. This approach has been emulated in roughly thirty African countries that have received MAP loans since 2000 (World Bank 2005a). Although MAP seeks to give high-level state and nonstate actors a stake in AIDS policymaking by requiring that commission members be senior government officials, civil society representatives, and international donors, creating the same institution across the continent has meant that some effective AIDS programs in ministries of health have been abandoned (Eboko 2005, 51; Putzel 2004). PEPFAR also has copied this "one-size-fits-all" model through its centralization of decisionmaking in Washington and US embassies. With their underlying distrust of African state institutions and their emphasis on nonstate actors, both MAP and PEPFAR do not recognize that African states differ in their transparency and state capacity. The cookie-cutter approach to AIDS institutions treats Botswana, Swaziland, South Africa, Zimbabwe, Uganda, Malawi, Ghana, and Senegal similarly, even though, as this volume has shown, there are various political factors such as democratic transitions, civil society activities, state centralization, and neopatrimonialism that shape different AIDS efforts in each. In contrast, the GFATM provides opportunities for making the state and civil society work together to develop creative AIDS programs. The possibilities for consensus building, accountability, and civil society participation that the GFATM presents may help to institutionalize AIDS throughout African political life. However, it is too soon to tell if this will be the case. And it will not happen if the GFATM does not have continuous financial support from Western governments, citizens, and foundations.

Institutionalizing the AIDS struggle means that donors model the same type of participation and accountability that they demand from their partners. The quotations in Chapter 5 from people working in the field attest to the long-term importance of this partnership for appropriate, legitimate AIDS policies. Donors should strive to more formally incorporate women, migrants, PLWHAs, and the poor into decisionmaking structures. CCM requirements for civil society participation and PEPFAR mandates that multinational NGOs work with local partners are positive steps in this direction. Yet, donors can do more. They can hire qualified women to reinforce the point that women's empowerment is crucial for the AIDS fight; they can encourage the input of migrants, the poor, and children in AIDS project development (Patterson 2003a; Siplon 2005). Donors also must strive to be more transparent. They should make all reports and grant applications available to the public through their organizations' websites. While the GFATM strives for this transparency, OGAC's efforts have been much slower.

For donors to change how they do business, they must embrace a model of partnership with Africa, in which each side listens to and learns from the other. Josh Ruxin of Columbia University's Access Project in Rwanda explains that this type of learning may be occurring with PEPFAR: "With some experience under its belt, PEPFAR's leaders have changed course and made impressive improvements."[4] But because of domestic policy considerations, some of PEPFAR's unique aspects— its approach to generic ARVs, its antiprostitution pledge, and its ABC prevention policy—have the potential to hinder partnership. Because of global inequality, African states desperately need donor resources to fight AIDS. This makes challenging PEPFAR's unique elements more difficult. In response to such obstacles and in order to harmonize efforts, the World Bank, GFATM, and OGAC set up the Three Ones program in 2003. It calls for a single coordinating AIDS authority modeled on the national commissions, a single national framework of AIDS objectives, and a single monitoring and evaluation system for results for each country with donor programs (UNAIDS 2005d). But few African states have used the potential power of this "common basket" approach to insist donors actually coordinate their efforts. One exception is Rwanda, which demanded that all donors—World Bank, GFATM, and PEP-FAR—work under its national AIDS strategy and use generic ARVs. This common approach has decreased drug prices and costs for training health care personnel. The common policy also may create a foundation for the long-run institutionalization of the AIDS fight, because communication and trust have increased among donors and between donors and the government (Kerry 2005).

The partnership that may be starting to develop in Rwanda challenges the inequalities found in the global system. It also requires that donors move beyond framing AIDS as a short-term emergency. While the emergency rhetoric mobilized the US Congress to quickly pass PEP-FAR, it may become problematic when the AIDS emergency is not easily solved and Western lawmakers and citizens lose hope. In reality, the pandemic reflects Africa's political and economic underdevelopment, the continent's gender inequalities, and the limited protection of human rights for Africans. This broader framework necessitates that AIDS efforts be embedded in long-term development, human rights protection, and gender empowerment programs. Such a paradigm shift has implications for civil society, the state, and donors. It means all civil society groups must incorporate AIDS into their work, and African state leaders must include AIDS program components in all government sectors. For donor programs like PEPFAR, it means there must be more "wrap around" programming; for example, PMTCT must be one component of family planning and maternal health programs (OGAC 2005b, 59–64).

One way to encourage donors to have a long-run approach to AIDS is for government agencies beyond traditional development ministries to be given a programmatic and budgetary stake in the pandemic. PEPFAR is innovative in this regard; by providing $10 billion in new funding, it has generated interest in AIDS among many US agencies and NGOs. No doubt, when the annual US budget is debated, these political actors will advocate for continued AIDS money. In the long term, PEPFAR may help to institutionalize global AIDS programs in many US departments. This is an advantage the multilateral GFATM does not have.

On the other hand, the history of bilateral and multilateral AIDS efforts over the last twenty-five years demonstrates that donor interest and funding have waxed and waned (Behrman 2004). Even programs that have been entrenched in bureaucratic agencies can be cut if Western legislators do not continue to see their value. (The decline in funding for environmental programs in the US foreign aid budget after 2000 illustrates the tenuous nature of donor funding for development issues; see CRS 2004.) Both PEPFAR and the GFATM rely on the annual budgetary appropriations of Western governments, but institutionalizing the AIDS fight requires a more consistent income source. Additionally, legislative funding allocations make the stake that Western citizens have in AIDS quite distant, since these appropriations are often buried in the budgetary process. A possible idea for a direct means of funding the AIDS fight emerged at the World Economic Forum in Davos, Switzerland, in January 2005. French President Jacques Chirac called for a tax on international airline tickets to raise money to fight pandemics such as AIDS, TB, and malaria in Africa. He suggested that a tax of $1 per ticket could raise roughly $10 billion annually. Algeria, Germany, Spain, Brazil, and Chile support the idea, while the United States, Japan, and the international business community do not (*Financial Times London*, May 16, 2005; *Agence France Presse*, March 28, 2005). Despite the lack of global consensus, the French parliament passed the tax on flights departing from French airports in late 2005 (*New York Times*, December 23, 2005). The tax uses one tool of globalization—airline travel—to give predominantly Western citizens a financial stake in the AIDS pandemic.

Institutionalization of the AIDS fight requires a global movement of citizens in both the First and Third Worlds.[5] The potential power of such activism is evident in the successes of the global treatment coalition. While First World publics have become more aware of the pandemic because of the efforts of AIDS groups, FBOs, and celebrities, these citizens are notoriously fickle in their support of foreign assistance programs (Lancaster 2000, 53–54). Yet, because of inequality in the global structure, these people's long-run concern and knowledge about the pandemic is essential to institutionalize the AIDS fight. The agents of globalization such as international travel, the Internet, and twenty-four-hour media outlets can be tools to fuel this awareness and concern. I have been struck every time that I present my research on AIDS to students, churches, or community groups that at least one member of the audience has a connection to Africa and the pandemic. Invariably, someone approaches me afterward to tell me about his cousin who works with an FBO in Uganda, his pastor who traveled with World Vision to Kenyan AIDS clinics, her sister who has studied abroad in Tanzania, the email messages she gets from an NGO working on AIDS in Mozambique, or the article she read in her denomination's newsletter about AIDS in Ghana. While these individuals' efforts may be proverbial drops in the bucket in fighting the pandemic, their real value lies in the connections they forge between First World citizens and Africans. As these anecdotes show, globalization has made AIDS an issue that an increasing number of citizens in wealthy countries have encountered. These individuals will be crucial for demanding that AIDS remain on the global political agenda.

Such political participation requires new understandings of citizenship in Africa and the West. Africans must be empowered to participate as individuals and through civil society organizations to demand their officials respond to society's health needs. TAC's successes demonstrate the possibilities for civil society, and increased health spending in some African democracies may reflect government responsiveness to citizens. Because citizen activism is crucial for the long-run AIDS fight, AIDS programs should not be divorced from advocacy training or citizenship education efforts. For people in Western countries, notions of citizenship must be broadened from an individual rights perspective to a perspective that recognizes how all people have citizenship responsibilities in today's world. First World citizens must believe that if AIDS decimates African individuals, families, economies, and nations, *everyone's* political and moral community is diminished (Nattrass 2004, 179). The mobilization of thousands of members of FBOs and human rights groups to push for PEPFAR's passage shows that this view of citizenship is possible. Whether it will be sustained, however, is a more difficult question.

A final crucial step needed to institutionalize the AIDS response is achieving progress in the AIDS fight itself. Because the pandemic has seemed invincible, the fear of failure may have paralyzed politicians, civil society groups, and donors (Caldwell 2000, 121). Paralysis causes political actors to use the rhetoric of sustainability and costs as an excuse to not develop AIDS initiatives. But, as TAC shows, successful treatment programs can bring hope to HIV-positive Africans. Healthy, HIV-positive people can participate in civil society, tackle the AIDS stigma, and become powerful voices for HIV prevention. AIDS itself is an obstacle to civil society organizations having the strength to influence AIDS policies. Moreover, progress in conquering AIDS will make politicians more likely to devote resources and attention to the disease. As seen in Uganda and Rwanda (Table 5.1), donors may reward progress or, more generally, genuine state efforts, with financial support. And, as PEPFAR and the GFATM illustrate, successes are necessary to continue funding from Western publics and governments. Strong AIDS efforts create momentum that helps to entrench the issue into political life.

Without these aspects of institutionalization, the politics of AIDS will remain "politics as usual." AIDS politics will continue to reflect the lack of state capacity, uneven democratization, dependence on donors, short-term donor interests, and state centralization found to various degrees throughout the continent. AIDS requires new thinking about political leadership, First World-Third World relations, citizenship, and state-civil society consultation. It challenges leaders in Africa and the West to revamp decisionmaking institutions, to change their political calculations, and to listen to new voices. Because the disease threatens an entire continent, AIDS cannot be tackled through the haphazard responses of African rulers or through donors' inconsistent attention to Africa's problems. For the sake of millions of Africans with the disease, let us hope for a new political paradigm to fight AIDS.

## Notes

1. Microbicides include a range of products such as gels, creams, suppositories, films, or sponges that can prevent the sexual transmission of HIV and STIs when applied topically. While scientists are currently testing microbicides, as of 2005 none were available to the public for use (Global Campaign for Microbicides 2005).

2. Josh Ruxin, Director of Access Project in Rwanda, Columbia University, phone interview with author, April 19, 2005.

3. Some human rights organizations were concerned that routine testing could become mandatory testing. During the first year of the testing policy's implementation, this did not occur. Other human rights activists, however, argued that there is a right to health care, and this right cannot be met if people do not know their serostatus (*Washington Times*, May 10, 2004).

4. Josh Ruxin, April 19, 2005.

5. Paul Farmer, cofounder of Partners in Health, speech to the January Series at Calvin College, Grand Rapids, MI, January 9, 2006.

# Acronyms

| | |
|---|---|
| AB (Policy) | Abstinence, Be Faithful |
| ABC (Policy) | Abstinence, Be Faithful, Use a Condom |
| ACT UP | AIDS Coalition to Unleash Power |
| AIDS | Acquired Immunodeficiency Syndrome |
| ALP | AIDS Law Project (South Africa) |
| ANC | African National Congress (South Africa) |
| API (Score) | AIDS Program Effort Index |
| ARV | Antiretroviral |
| AZT | Zidovudine (brand name Retrovir; also referred to as ZDV) |
| BDP | Botswana Democratic Party |
| CCM | Country Coordinating Mechanism |
| CDC | Centers for Disease Control and Prevention (United States) |
| CHANGE | Center for Health and Gender Equity |
| CIA | Central Intelligence Agency (United States) |
| CIDA | Canadian International Development Agency |
| COSATU | Congress of South African Trade Unions |
| CRS | Congressional Research Service (United States) |
| DATA | Debt, AIDS, Trade, Africa |
| DFID | Department for International Development (United Kingdom) |
| DOD | Department of Defense (United States) |
| DOE | Department of Energy (United States) |
| DOL | Department of Labor (United States) |
| DOTS | Directly Observed Treatment Short-Course Therapy |
| DRC | Democratic Republic of Congo |

| | |
|---|---|
| FBO | Faith-Based Organization |
| FDA | Food and Drug Administration (United States) |
| GAC | Ghana AIDS Commission |
| GAO | Government Accounting Office (United States) |
| GARFUND | Ghana AIDS Response Fund |
| GATAG | Ghana AIDS Treatment Access Group |
| GDP | Gross Domestic Product |
| GFATM | Global Fund to Fight AIDS, Tuberculosis and Malaria |
| GHANET | Ghana HIV/AIDS Network |
| GNI | Gross National Income |
| GNP+ | Global Network of People Living with HIV/AIDS |
| GPA | Global Program on AIDS |
| HDI | Human Development Index |
| Health GAP | Health Global Access Project |
| HHS | Health and Human Services (United States) |
| HIV | Human Immunodeficiency Virus |
| ICASA | International Conference on AIDS and STDs in Africa |
| IMF | International Monetary Fund |
| KZN | Kwazulu-Natal Province (South Africa) |
| LRA | Lord's Resistance Army (Uganda) |
| MAP | Multi-Country AIDS Program (World Bank) |
| MDC | Movement for Democratic Change (Zimbabwe) |
| MSF | Médecins sans Frontières (Doctors Without Borders) |
| NAPWA | National Association of People with AIDS |
| NEPAD | New Partnership for Africa's Development |
| NERCHA | National Emergency Response Committee on HIV/AIDS (Swaziland) |
| NGO | Nongovernmental Organization |
| NPP | National Patriotic Party (Ghana) |
| NRA | National Resistance Army (Uganda) |
| NRM | National Resistance Movement (Uganda) |
| NUDO | National Unity Democratic Organization (Namibia) |
| OGAC | Office of the US Global AIDS Coordinator |
| PATAM | Pan-African Treatment Access Movement |
| PEPFAR | President's Emergency Plan for AIDS Relief (United States) |
| PLWHA | People Living with HIV/AIDS |
| PMA | Pharmaceutical Manufacturers' Association |
| PMTCT | Prevention of Mother-to-Child Transmission |
| RAPIDS | Reaching HIV/AIDS Affected People with Integrated Development and Support (Zambia) |

| | |
|---|---|
| SACP | South African Communist Party |
| SANAC | South Africa National AIDS Council |
| SAP | Structural Adjustment Program |
| STI | Sexually Transmitted Infection |
| SWAPO | South West Africa People's Organization (Namibia) |
| TAC | Treatment Action Campaign (South Africa) |
| TASO | The AIDS Support Organisation (Uganda) |
| TB | Tuberculosis |
| TRIPS | Trade Related Intellectual Property Rights (Agreement) |
| UN | United Nations |
| UNAIDS | Joint United Nations Program on HIV/AIDS |
| UNDP | United Nations Development Program |
| UNICEF | United Nations Children's Fund |
| UNLA | Uganda National Liberation Army |
| USAID | United States Agency for International Development |
| VCT | Voluntary Counseling and Testing |
| WHO | World Health Organization |
| WTO | World Trade Organization |
| ZANU-PF | Zimbabwe African National Union-Patriotic Front |
| ZNAC | Zimbabwe National AIDS Committee |
| ZNNP+ | Zimbabwe National Network for People Living with HIV/AIDS |

# Bibliography

Abraham, Priya. 2003. The ABCs of AIDS. *World Magazine on the Web.* http://www.worldmag.com/world/issue/05-10-03/opening_3.asp.

Adelman, Carol. 2003. The Privatization of Foreign Aid: Reassessing National Largesse. *Foreign Affairs* 82 (6): 9–14.

Adelzadeh, Asghar. 2003. *South Africa Human Development Report 2003.* Cape Town: Oxford University Press Southern Africa. http://www.undp.org.za/NHDR2003/NHDRSumFull.pdf.

Africa: Learning to Survive. 2004. *AfricaFocus Bulletin*, April 27. http://www.africafocus.org/docs04/educ0404.php.

African National Congress. 2004. President Mbeki's Inauguration Address. http://www.anc.org.za/ancdocs.

Afrobarometer. 2003. *Trends in Political Party Support in South Africa.* Briefing Paper 6. http://www.afrobarometer.org/papers/AfrobriefNo6.pdf.

———. 2004. *Public Opinion and HIV/AIDS: Facing Up to the Future?* Briefing Paper 12. http://www.afrobarometer.org/AfrobriefNo12.pdf.

AIDS Budget Unit. 2004. New Allocations for ARV Treatment: An Analysis of 2004/5 National Budget from an HIV/AIDS Perspective. http://www.idasact.org.za.

AIDS Law Project. 2004. Background Information. http://www.alp.org.za.

ALP. *See* AIDS Law Project.

Anderson, Brian. 2004. Secular Europe, Religious America. *Public Interest* 155 (Spring): 143–158.

Azarya, Victor. 1988. Reordering State-Society Relations: Incorporation and Disengagement. In *The Precarious Balance: State and Society in Africa*, ed. Donald Rothchild and Naomi Chazan, 3–21. Boulder, CO: Westview Press.

Bardes, Barbara, and Robert W. Oldendick. 2000. *Public Opinion: Measuring the American Mind.* Stamford, CT: Wadsworth Thompson.

Barnett, Tony, and Alan Whiteside. 2002. *AIDS in the Twenty-First Century: Disease and Globalisation.* New York: Palgrave Macmillan.

Bass, Emily. 2005. The Two Sides of PEPFAR in Uganda. *Lancet* 365 (9477): 2077–2078.

Bass, Loretta. 2004. *Child Labor in Sub-Saharan Africa*. Boulder, CO: Lynne Rienner Publishers.

Batsell, Jake. 2005. AIDS, Politics and NGOs in Zimbabwe. In *The African State and the AIDS Crisis*, ed. Amy S. Patterson, 59–78. Aldershot, UK: Ashgate Publishing.

Bauer, Gretchen, and Scott Taylor. 2005. *Politics in Southern Africa: State and Society in Transition*. Boulder, CO: Lynne Rienner Publishers.

Baylies, Carolyn. 1999. International Partnership in the Fight Against AIDS: Addressing Need and Redressing Injustice? *Review of African Political Economy* 26 (81): 387–414.

———. 2002. HIV/AIDS and Older Women in Zambia: Concern for Self, Worry Over Daughters, Towers of Strength. *Third World Quarterly* 23 (2): 351–375.

Bearman, Peter, and Hannah Brueckner. 2001. Promising the Future: Virginity Pledges and First Intercourse. *American Journal of Sociology* 106 (4): 859-912.

———. 2005. After the Promise: The STD Consequences of Adolescent Virginity Pledges. *Journal of Adolescent Health* 36 (4): 271–278.

Beck, Linda. 2003. Democratization and the "Hidden Public": The Impact of Patronage Politics on Senegalese Women. *Comparative Politics* 35 (2): 147–171.

Behrman, Greg. 2004. *The Invisible People: How the U.S. Has Slept Through the Global AIDS Pandemic, the Greatest Humanitarian Catastrophe of Our Time*. New York: Free Press.

Benatar, Solomon. 2001. South Africa's Transition in a Globalizing World: HIV/AIDS As a Window and a Mirror. *International Affairs* 77 (2): 247–275.

Berry, Sara. 1993. *No Condition Is Permanent: The Social Dynamics of Agrarian Change in Sub-Saharan Africa*. Madison: University of Wisconsin Press.

Black, Amy, Douglas Koopman, and David Ryden. 2004. *Of Little Faith: The Politics of George W. Bush's Faith-Based Initiatives*. Washington, DC: Georgetown University Press.

Boafo-Arthur, Kwame. 1999. Structural Adjustment, Democratization, and the Politics of Continuity in Ghana. *African Studies Review* 42 (2): 41–72.

Boone, Catherine, and Jake Batsell. 2001. Politics and AIDS in Africa: Research Agendas in Political Science and International Relations. *Africa Today* 48 (2): 3–33.

Booth, Karen. 2004. *Local Women, Global Science: Fighting AIDS in Kenya*. Bloomington: Indiana University Press.

Bratton, Michael. 1999. Second Elections in Africa: The Rebirth of African Liberalism. In *Democratization in Africa*, ed. Larry Diamond and Marc Plattner, 18–33. Baltimore: Johns Hopkins University Press.

———. 2005. Building Democracy in Africa's Weak States. *Democracy at Large* 1 (3): 12–15.

Bratton, Michael, and Gina Lambright. 2001. Uganda's Referendum 2000: The Silent Boycott. *African Affairs* 100 (400): 429–452.

Bratton, Michael, Peter Lewis, and Emmanuel Gyimah-Boadi. 2001. Constituencies for Reform in Ghana. *Journal of Modern African Studies* 39 (2): 231–259.

Bratton, Michael, and Nicolas van de Walle. 1992. Toward Governance in Africa: Popular Demands and State Responses. In *Governance and Politics in Africa*, ed. Michael Bratton and Goran Hyden, 27–55. Boulder, CO: Lynne Rienner Publishers.

———. 1997. *Democratic Experiments in Africa: Regime Transitions in Comparative Perspective*. New York: Cambridge University Press.

Bryant, Elizabeth. 2004. Lessons for Living. *Ford Foundation Report*. Spring: 8–15.

Bureau of Democracy, Human Rights, and Labor. 2004. *Zimbabwe: Country Reports on Human Rights Practices 2004*. Report for US Department of State. http://www.state.gov/g/drl/rls/hrrpt/2004/41634.htm.

Burnside, Craig, and David Dollar. 2000. Aid, Policies, and Growth. *American Economic Review* 90 (4): 847–868.

Bush, George W. 2003. State of the Union Address. http://www.whitehouse.gov/news/releases/2003/01/print/20030128-19.html.

Butler, Anthony. 2002. South Africa's Political Future: The Positive and Negative Implications of One-Party Dominance. Paper presented for the Electoral Institute of Southern Africa seminar series, University of Cape Town, August 7. http://www.eisa.org.za.

———. 2005. South Africa's HIV/AIDS Policy, 1994–2004: How Can It Be Explained? *African Affairs* 104 (417): 591–614.

Caldwell, John. 2000. Rethinking the African AIDS Epidemic. *Population and Development Review* 26 (1): 117–135.

Cameron, Edwin. 2005. *Witness to AIDS*. New York: I. B. Tauris and Co.

Campbell, Catherine. 2003. *"Letting Them Die": Why HIV/AIDS Prevention Programmes Fail*. Bloomington: Indiana University Press.

Canadian International Development Agency. 2005. Swaziland. Report for Canadian Department of Foreign Affairs and Trade, April 8. http://www.dfait-maeci.gc.ca/africa/pdf/Swaziland-en.pdf.

Center for Health and Gender Equity. 2004. *Debunking the Myths in the U.S. Global AIDS Strategy: An Evidence-Based Analysis*. Report for Center for Health and Gender Equity. http://www.genderhealth.org/pubs/AIDS5-YearStratAnalysisMar-04.pdf.

Central Intelligence Agency. 1987. Sub-Saharan Africa: Implications of the AIDS Pandemic. Report for the National Foreign Intelligence Board. Washington, DC: CIA.

———. 2004. *World Factbook*. http://www.cia.gov/cia/publications.

Chabal, Patrick, and Jean-Pascal Daloz. 1999. *Africa Works: Disorder As Political Instrument*. Bloomington: Indiana University Press.

CHANGE. *See* Center for Health and Gender Equity.

Cheek, Randy. 2001. Playing God with HIV: Rationing HIV Treatment in Southern Africa. *African Security Review* 10 (4): 19–28.

Chirambo, Kondwani, and Mary Caesar. 2004. *AIDS and Governance in Southern Africa: Emerging Theories and Perspectives*. Cape Town: Institute for Democracy in South Africa.

Chirwa, Wiseman Chijere. 1998. Aliens and AIDS in Southern Africa: The Malawi-South Africa Debate. *African Affairs* 97 (386): 53–79.

Christodoulides, Nikos. 2005. Do Democracies Have the Same Values? The Transatlantic Case. *Whitehead Journal of Diplomacy and International Relations* 6 (3): 167–175.

CIA. *See* Central Intelligence Agency.

CIDA. *See* Canadian International Development Agency.

Clark, John. 1990. *Democratizing Development: The Role of Voluntary Organizations.* West Hartford, CT: Kumarian Press.

Cnaan, Ram. 1999. *The Newer Deal: Social Work and Religion in Partnership.* New York: Columbia University Press.

Collier, Paul, and David Dollar. 2002. Aid Allocation and Poverty Reduction. *European Economic Review* 45 (1): 1–26.

Congress of South African Trade Unions. 2002. Report and Resolutions of the COSATU/TAC National HIV/AIDS Treatment Congress. http://www.tac. org.za/Documents/TreatmentPlan/CongressReportVersionTabledAtNedlac. doc.

Congressional Research Service. 2004. *Foreign Aid: An Introductory Overview of U.S. Programs and Policy.* Report for Congress. Washington, DC: The Library of Congress.

Cooke, Jennifer. 2004. *Battling HIV/AIDS in Ethiopia: U.S. Approach Needs Nuance, Flexibility.* A Report of the CSIS HIV/AIDS Delegation to Ethiopia, May 23–28, 2004. http://www.csis.org/hivaids/0411_Ethiopia. pdf.

Copson, Raymond. 2005. The Global Fund and PEPFAR in U.S. International AIDS Policy: Implications for Africa. Paper presented for the annual meeting of the African Studies Association, Washington, DC, November 17.

COSATU. *See* Congress of South African Trade Unions.

Coulon, Christian. 1976. Prophètes de Dieu ou prophètes anti-colonialism: quelques reflexions à partir d'exemples Sénégalais. *African Perspectives* 2: 45–60.

Creevey, Lucy. 1991. The Impact of Islam on Women in Senegal. *Journal of Developing Areas* 25 (3): 347–368.

CRS. *See* Congressional Research Service.

Cruise O'Brien, Donal B. 1970. The Saint and the Squire: Personalities and Social Forces in the Development of a Religious Brotherhood. In *African Perspectives: Papers in the History, Politics, and Economics of Africa Presented to Thomas Hodgkin,* ed. Christopher Allen and Richard William Johnson, 157–169. New York: Cambridge University Press.

———. 1971. *The Mourides of Senegal.* Oxford: Clarendon Press.

D'Adesky, Anne-Christine. 2004. *Moving Mountains: The Race to Treat Global AIDS.* New York: Verso.

Daly, John. 2003. Human Security and Psychosocial Losses for Southern Africa's AIDS Orphans. Paper presented at the African Studies Association meeting, Boston, MA, October 29–31.

de Waal, Alex. 2003a. A Disaster with No Name: The HIV/AIDS Pandemic and the Limits of Governance. In *Learning from HIV and AIDS,* ed. George Ellison, Melissa Parker, and Catherine Campbell, 238–267. New York: Cambridge University Press.

————. 2003b. How Will HIV/AIDS Transform African Governance? *African Affairs* 102 (206): 1–23.

————. 2004. British Government Policy on AIDS: Analysis for African Civil Society. *GAIN Briefing Note*, October 15.

Deegan, Heather. 2001. *The Politics of the New South Africa: Apartheid and After*. New York: Pearson Longman.

della Porta, Donatella, and Sidney Tarrow. 2005. *Transnational Protest and Global Activism*. Lanham, MD: Rowman & Littlefield.

DFID. *See* United Kingdom Department for International Development.

DOE. *See* United States Department of Energy.

Dowden, Richard. 2002. Swaziland's Conquering Heroines. *New Statesman* 131 (August): 10–11.

Easterly, William. 2002. The Cartel of Good Intentions. *Foreign Policy* 131 (July/August): 40–49.

Eaton, David. 2004. Understanding AIDS in Public Lives. In *HIV & AIDS in Africa: Beyond Epidemiology*, ed. Ezekiel Kalipeni, Susan Craddock, Joseph Oppong, and Jayati Ghosh, 279–290. Malden, MA: Blackwell Publishers.

Eboko, Fred. 2005. Patterns of Mobilization: Political Culture in the Fight Against AIDS. In *The African State and the AIDS Crisis*, ed. Amy S. Patterson, 37–58. Aldershot, UK: Ashgate Publishers.

Edet, T. 1997. *Cultural Politics, HIV/AIDS and Higher Education in Nigeria: Research and Policy Implications*. MA thesis, School of Development Studies. Norwich, UK: University of East Anglia.

Elections in Malawi. 2004. *Report for Election World*. http://www.election-world.org/malawi.htm.

Englebert, Pierre. 2002. *State Legitimacy and Development in Africa*. Boulder, CO: Lynne Rienner Publishers.

Ernberg, Gunilla, Margorie Opuni, Bernhard Schwartlander, Neff Walker, Daniel Tarantola, and Mary Pat Kieffer. 1999. *Level and Flow of National and International Resources for the Response to HIV/AIDS, 1996–1997*. http://www.unaids.org/html/pub/publications/irc-pub01/jc213-level-flow_en_pdf.pdf.

Esman, Milton, and Norman Uphoff. 1984. *Local Organizations: Intermediaries in Rural Development*. Ithaca, NY: Cornell University Press.

Ewert, Lowell. 2004. Human Rights, the Foundation for Civil Society. In *Local Ownership and Global Change: Can Civil Society Save the World?* ed. Roland Hoksbergen and Lowell Ewert, 96–114. Monrovia, CA: World Vision Publishers.

Farmer, Paul. 2003. AIDS: A Biosocial Problem with Social Solutions. *Anthropology News* 44 (6): 6–7.

————. 2005. *Pathologies of Power: Health, Human Rights, and the New War on the Poor*. Berkeley: University of California Press.

Fatton, Robert. 1988. Bringing the Ruling Class Back In: Class, State, and Hegemony in Africa. *Comparative Politics* 2 (3): 253–264.

————. 1995. Africa in the Age of Democratization: The Civic Limitations of Civil Society. *African Studies Review* 38 (2): 67–110.

Fenio, Kenly Greer. 2005. Bush's Funding of Religion in Ethiopia Through

PEPFAR: HIV/AIDS, the Ethiopian Orthodox Church, and Community Beliefs. Paper presented at the African Health and Illness Conference, University of Texas-Austin, March 25–27.

Fleischman, Janet. 2005. *Strengthening HIV/AIDS Programs for Women: Lessons from U.S. Policy from Zambia and Kenya.* Report for Center for Strategic and International Studies. http://www.csis.org/hivaids/0505_strengthening.pdf.

Fortin, Alfred. 1987. The Politics of AIDS in Kenya. *Third World Quarterly* 9 (3): 906–919.

Fowler, Alan. 1997. *Striking a Balance: A Guide to Enhancing the Effectiveness of Non-Governmental Organizations in International Development.* London: Earthscan.

Freedom House. 1981. Freedom in the World 1980. http://www.freedomhouse.org/ratings/index.htm.

———. 1991. Freedom in the World 1990. http://www.freedomhouse.org/ratings/index.htm.

———. 2004. Zimbabwe Report. http://www.freedomhouse.org/research/freeworld/2004/countryratings/zimbabwe.htm.

———. 2005a. Combined Average Ratings—Independent Countries. http://www.freedomhouse.org/research/freeworld/2005/combined2005.pdf.

———. 2005b. Freedom in the World 2004. http://www.freedomhouse.org/research/survey2005.htm.

Friedman, Steven. 2004. South Africa: Building Democracy After Apartheid. In *Democratic Reform in Africa: The Quality of Progress*, ed. Emmanuel Gyimah-Boadi, 235–262. Boulder, CO: Lynne Rienner Publishers.

Friedman, Steven, and Ivor Chipkin. 2001. *A Poor Voice?: The Politics of Inequality in South Africa.* Social Policy Series Report 87. Johannesburg: Centre for Policy Studies.

Friedman, Steven, and Shauna Mottiar. 2004. A Moral to the Tale: The Treatment Action Campaign and the Politics of HIV/AIDS. Paper for the Centre for Policy Studies. Durban: University of KwaZulu-Natal.

Furlong, Patrick, and Karen Ball. 2005. The More Things Change: AIDS and the State in South Africa, 1987–2003. In *The African State and the AIDS Crisis*, ed. Amy S. Patterson, 127–155. Aldershot, UK: Ashgate Publishers.

GAO. *See* Government Accounting Office.

Garbus, Lisa. 2003. *HIV/AIDS in Malawi.* Report for the AIDS Policy Research Center, University of California-San Francisco.

Garbus, Lisa, and Elliot Marseille. 2003. *HIV/AIDS in Uganda.* San Francisco: AIDS Policy Research Center, University of California-San Francisco.

GATAG. *See* Ghana AIDS Treatment Access Group.

GFATM. *See* Global Fund to Fight AIDS, Tuberculosis and Malaria.

Ghana AIDS Commission. 2003. *Annual Report.* http://www.ghanaids.gov.gh.

Ghana AIDS Treatment Access Group. 2005. About GATAG. http://www.gatag.org.

Ghana HIV/AIDS Network. 2005. About Us. http://www.ghanet.org/members.htm.

Ghana Ministry of Health. 2001. *HIV/AIDS in Ghana: Background, Projections, Impacts, Interventions, and Policy.* Accra: Government of Ghana.

Ghana National AIDS/STDs Control Programme. 2000. *Draft for National HIV/AIDS and STI Policy.* Accra: Government of Ghana.

GHANET. *See* Ghana HIV/AIDS Network.

Ghobarah, Hazem, Paul Huth, and Bruce Russett. 2004. Comparative Public Health: The Political Economy of Human Misery and Well-Being. *International Studies Quarterly* 48 (1): 73–94.

Gibson, James, and Amanda Gouws. 2003. *Overcoming Intolerance in South Africa.* New York: Cambridge University Press.

Giliomee, Hermann. 1999. South Africa's Emerging Dominant-Party Regime. In *Democratization in Africa,* ed. Larry Diamond and Marc Plattner, 140–153. Baltimore: Johns Hopkins University Press.

Global Campaign for Microbicides. 2005. About Microbicides. http://www.global-campaign.org/about_microbicides.htm.

Global Fund to Fight AIDS, Tuberculosis and Malaria. 2005a. CCM Breakdown for Round Four. http://www.theglobalfund.org/en/about/structures/ccm_analysis/#4.

———. 2005b. CCM Member Lists. http://www.theglobalfund.org.

———. 2005c. Country Proposals. http://www.theglobalfund.org.

———. 2005d. Global Fund Closes Funding Gap. Press Release. http://www.theglobalfund.org/en/media_center/press/pr_051216.asp.

———. 2005e. HIV/AIDS, Tuberculosis and Malaria: The Status and Impact of the Three Diseases. http://www.theglobalfund.org/en/file/about/replenishment/disease_report_malaria_en.pdf.

———. 2005f. How the Fund Works. http://www.theglobalfund.org/en/about/how/.

———. 2006a. Global Fund Grants—Progress Details. Progress Reports: Funds Committed and Dispersed. http://www.theglobalfund.org/en.

———. 2006b. Voting Board Members. http://www.theglobalfund.org/en/about/board/members.

Global Network of People Living with HIV/AIDS. 2004. *A Multi-Country Study of the Involvement of People Living with HIV/AIDS (PLWHA) in the Country Coordinating Mechanisms (CCM).* Report for GNP+. http://www.gnpplus.net.

GNP+. *See* Global Network of People Living with HIV/AIDS.

Government Accounting Office. 2004. *U.S. AIDS Coordinator Addressing Some Key Challenges to Expanding Treatment, But Others Remain.* Report to the Chairman, Subcommittee on Foreign Operations, Export Financing, and Related Programs, Committee on Appropriations, House of Representatives. http://www.gao.gov/cgi-bin/getrpt?GAO-04-784.

———. 2005. *Selection of Antiretroviral Medications Provided Under U.S. Emergency Plan Is Limited.* Report for Congress. http://www.gao.gov/new.items/d05133.pdf.

Green, Edward. 2003a. *Faith-Based Organizations: Contributions to HIV Prevention.* Report for the US Agency for International Development. Washington, DC: USAID.

———. 2003b. *Rethinking AIDS Prevention: Learning from Successes in Developing Countries.* Westport, CT: Praeger.

Green, Edward, Vinand Nantulya, Rand Stoneburner, and John Stover. 2002.

*What Happened in Uganda? Declining HIV Prevalence, Behavior Change and the National Response.* Report for USAID and the Synergy Project. Washington, DC: TVT Associates, September. http://www.usaid.gov/our_work/global_health/aids/countries/africa/uganda_report.pdf.

Guay, L.A., P. Musoke, T. Fleming, M. Allen, C. Nakabiito, J. Sherman, P. Bakaki, C. Ducar, M. Deseyve, L. Emel, M. Mirochnick, M.G. Fowler, L. Mofenson, P. Miotti, K. Dransfield, D. Bray, F. Mmiro, and J.B. Jackson. 1999. Intrapartum and Neonatal Single-Dose Nevirapine Compared with Zidovudine for Prevention of Mother-To-Child Transmission of HIV-1 in Kampala, Uganda: HIVNET 012 Randomised Trial. *Lancet* 354 (9181): 795–802.

Guest, Emma. 2001. *Children of AIDS: Africa's Orphan Crisis.* London: Pluto Press.

Guth, James, Lyman Kellstedt, John Green, and Corwin Smidt. 2001. America Fifty/Fifty. *First Things* 116 (October): 19–26.

Gyimah-Boadi, Emmanuel. 1999. The Rebirth of African Liberalism. In *Democratization in Africa,* ed. Larry Diamond and Marc Plattner, 34–47. Baltimore: Johns Hopkins University Press.

———. 2001. A Peaceful Turnover in Ghana. *Journal of Democracy* 12 (2): 103–117.

———. 2004a. Africa: The Quality of Political Reform. In *Democratic Reform in Africa: The Quality of Progress,* ed. Emmanuel Gyimah-Boadi, 5–27. Boulder, CO: Lynne Rienner Publishers.

———. 2004b. Civil Society and Democratic Development. In *Democratic Reform in Africa: The Quality of Progress,* ed. Emmanuel Gyimah-Boadi, 99–119. Boulder, CO: Lynne Rienner Publishers.

Gyimah-Boadi, Emmanuel, and Kwabena Amoah Awuah Mensah. 2003. *The Growth of Democracy in Ghana Despite Economic Dissatisfaction: A Power Alternation Bonus?* Afrobarometer Paper 28. http://www.afrobarometer.org/papers/AfropaperNo28.pdf.

Halbert, Debora, and Christopher May. 2005. AIDS, Pharmaceutical Patents, and the African State. In *The African State and the AIDS Crisis,* ed. Amy S. Patterson, 195–218. Aldershot, UK: Ashgate Publishers.

Halperin, Daniel, Markus Steiner, Michael Cassell, Edward Green, Norman Hearst, Douglas Kirby, Helene Gayle, and Willard Cates. 2004. The Time Has Come for Common Ground on Preventing Sexual Transmission of HIV. *Lancet* 364 (9449): 1913–1915.

Harbeson, John, Donald Rothchild, and Naomi Chazan, ed. 1994. *Civil Society and the State in Africa.* Boulder, CO: Lynne Rienner Publishers.

Harvard School of Public Health. 2004. South Africa PEPFAR Program Overview. http://www.globalhealth.harvard.edu/ Files/South%20Africa% 20Description.pdf.

Hatendi, Felicity, Edward Makondo, and Mary Caesar-Katsenga. 2005. *Understanding the Institutional Dynamics of Zimbabwe's Response to the HIV/AIDS Pandemic.* Report for Institute for Democracy in South Africa. http://www.idasa.org.za.

Hauser, Ellen. 1999. Ugandan Relations with Western Donors in the 1990s: What Impact on Democratisation? *Journal of Modern African Studies* 37 (4): 621–641.

Haven, Bernard. 2003. Politics, Patronage, and Poverty: Local HIV/AIDS NGOs in Ghana. Paper completed for political science independent study, Calvin College, Grand Rapids, MI.

———. 2005. Is Aid for AIDS "Exceptional"? Risk, Dependence and the Good Governance Paradigm. MS thesis, London School of Economics.

Hechter, Michael. 1987. *Principles of Group Solidarity.* Berkeley: University of California Press.

Hertzke, Allen. 2004. *Freeing God's Children: The Unlikely Alliance for Global Human Rights.* Lanham, MD: Rowman & Littlefield.

Heywood, Mark. 2004. The Price of Denial. *Development Update* 5 (3): 95–96.

Hickey, Alison, Nhlanhla Ndlovu, and Teresa Guthrie. 2004. South Africa. In *Funding the Fight: Budgeting for HIV/AIDS in Developing Countries,* ed. Teresa Guthrie and Alison Hickey, 98–177. Cape Town: Institute for Democracy in South Africa.

Hill, Kent. 2005. A Helping Hand and Clear Witness: The Christian Response to Global Suffering. *Brandywine Review of Faith and International Affairs* 2 (3): 43–49.

HIV/AIDS: The Faith Community Responds. 2003. Report from Faith-Based Initiatives and the President's Emergency Plan for AIDS Relief Conference, Georgetown University, Washington, DC, November.

Hoksbergen, Roland. 2003. Partnering for Development: Why It's So Important, Why It's So Hard, How to Go About It. *REC Focus* 3 (4): 3–21.

Hudson, C.P., Jagidesa Moodley, and A.N. Smith. 2002. Stage of the Epidemic and Viral Phenotype Should Influence Recommendations Regarding Mother-To-Child Transmission of HIV-1. *Lancet Infectious Diseases* 2 (2): 115–119.

Human Rights Watch. 2001. *In the Shadow of Death: HIV/AIDS and Children's Rights in Kenya.* Report for Human Rights Watch. http://www.hrw.org/reports/2001/kenya.

———. 2002. *Zimbabwe: Fast Track Land Reform in Zimbabwe.* Report for Human Rights Watch. http://www.hrw.org/reports/2002/zimbabwe.

———. 2003a. *Congressional Testimony on HIV/AIDS and Women's Property Rights Violations in Sub-Saharan Africa.* Congressional Human Rights Caucus Briefing, April 10. http://hrw.org/press/2003/04/us041003-test.htm.

———. 2003b. *Policy Paralysis: A Call for Action on HIV/AIDS-Related Human Rights Abuses Against Women and Girls in Africa.* Report for Human Rights Watch. http://www.hrw.org/reports/2003/africa1203/.

———. 2004. *Deadly Delay: South Africa's Efforts to Prevent HIV in Survivors of Sexual Violence.* Summary of Human Rights Watch Report. http://hrw.org/reports/2004/southafrica0304/.

———. 2005a. *The Less They Know, the Better: Abstinence-Only HIV/AIDS Programs in Uganda.* Report for Human Rights Watch. http://hrw.org/reports/2005/uganda0305.

———. 2005b. *Uganda.* Human Rights Watch Report. http://hrw.org/english/docs/2006/01/18/uganda12284.htm.

———. 2005c. U.S.: Restrictive Policies Undermine Anti-AIDS Efforts. See http://www.hrw.org/english/docs/2005/05/18/usdom10978.htm. Letter to President Bush Opposing Mandatory "Anti-Prostitution Pledge," Which

Threatens Lives of Sex Workers and Trafficking Victims, May 18. http://hrw.org/campaigns/hivaids/hiv-aids-letter/.

Human Sciences Research Council. 2002. *Nelson Mandela Foundation/HSRC Study of HIV/AIDS*. http://www.nelsonmandela.org.

Hunter, Susan. 2003. *Black Death: AIDS in Africa*. New York: Palgrave Macmillan.

Hunter, Susan, and John Williamson. 2000. *Children on the Brink: Executive Summary*. Report for US Agency for International Development. Washington, DC: USAID.

Hyde, Henry. 2005. Opening Remarks of Chairman Henry J. Hyde Before the Full Committee. "US Response to the Global AIDS Crisis: A Two-Year Review." House Committee on International Relations, Rayburn Office Building, Washington, DC, April 13.

Hyman, Jennifer. 2003. Health and Human Rights: Double-edged Sword for Mann Award Winner. *Global AIDS Link* 80 (July): 16–18. http://www.globalhealth.org/assets/publication/AL80.pdf.

International Crisis Group. 2001. HIV/AIDS as a Security Issue. http://www.crisisgroup.org/library/documents/report/archives/A400321_19062001.pdf.

Inter-Parliamentary Union. 2005. Women in National Parliaments. http://www.ipu.org/wmn-e/classif.htm.

Irwin, Alexander, Joyce Millen, and Dorothy Fallows. 2003. *Global AIDS: Myths and Facts*. Cambridge: South End Press.

James, Wilmot, and Daria Caliguire.1999. The New South Africa: Renewing Civil Society. In *Democratization in Africa*, ed. Larry Diamond and Marc Plattner, 83–93. Baltimore: Johns Hopkins University Press.

Johnson, Krista. 2004. The Politics of AIDS Policy Development and Implementation in Postapartheid South Africa. *Africa Today* 51 (2): 107–128.

Johnson, Krista A., and Robert Rector. 2005. Adolescent Virginity Pledges and Risky Sexual Behaviors. Research Welfare Paper for the Heritage Foundation. http://www.heritage.org/Research/Welfare/whitepaper061420051.cfm.

Joint United Nations Program on HIV/AIDS. 1999. Acting Early to Prevent AIDS: The Case of Senegal. Geneva: UNAIDS.

———. 2002a. *Ghana: Epidemiological Fact Sheets*. Geneva: UNAIDS.

———. 2002b. *Sex Work and HIV/AIDS: UNAIDS Technical Update*. Geneva: UNAIDS.

———. 2002c. *South Africa: Epidemiological Fact Sheets*. Geneva: UNAIDS.

———. 2003. *AIDS Epidemic Update: December 2003*. Geneva: UNAIDS.

———. 2004a. *AIDS Epidemic Update: December 2004*. http://www.unaids.org/wad2004/report.htm.

———. 2004b. *Report on the Global AIDS Epidemic*. http://www.unaids.org/bangkok2004/report_pdf.html.

———. 2004c. *Zimbabwe 2004 Update*. Epidemiological Fact Sheets on HIV/AIDS and Sexually Transmitted Infections. http://www.unaids.org/html/pub/publications/fact-sheets01/zimbabwe_en_pdf.pdf.

———. 2005a. *AIDS in Africa: Three Scenarios to 2025*. http://www.unaids.org/en/AIDS+in+Africa_Three+scenarios+to+2025.asp.

———. 2005b. Evidence for HIV Decline in Zimbabwe: A Comprehensive Review of the Epidemiological Data. http://data.unaids.org/Publications/IRC-pub06/Zimbabwe_Epi?report_Nov05_en.pdf?preview= true.

———. 2005c. Resource Needs for an Expanded Response to AIDS in Low- and Middle-Income Countries. Report for UNAIDS. http://www.unaids. org/NetTools/Misc/DocInfo.aspx?LANG=en&href=http://gva-doc-owl/WEBcontent/Documents/pub/Publications/IRC-pub06/Resource NeedsReport_en.pdf.

———. 2005d. *The "Three Ones" in Action: Where We Are and Where We Go from Here.* Geneva: UNAIDS.

———. 2005e. *UNAIDS/WHO AIDS Epidemic Update: December 2005.* http://www.unaids.org/Epi2005/doc/report_pdf.html.

———. 2005f. Zimbabwe Country Situation Analysis. http://www.unaids. org/en/geographical+area/by+country/zimbabwe.asp.

Joseph, Richard. 1999. Africa, 1990–1997: From *Abertura* to Closure. In *Democratization in Africa,* ed. Larry Diamond and Marc Plattner, 3–17. Baltimore: Johns Hopkins University Press.

Kaiser Family Foundation. 2004a. HIV/AIDS Policy Fact Sheet. http://www.kff.org.

———. 2004b. Survey of Americans on HIV/AIDS. Part One—Global HIV/AIDS. Summary and Chart Pack. http://www.kff.org/hivaids/7093. cfm.

Karim, Quarraisha Abdool. 2004. Address to International AIDS Conference, Bangkok, July 17.

Kates, Jennifer. 2005. *Financing the Response to HIV/AIDS in Low and Middle Income Countries: Funding for HIV/AIDS from the G7 and the European Commission.* Report for the Kaiser Family Foundation. http://www.kff.org/hivaids/hiv072105pkg.cfm.

Kates, Jennifer, and Phillip Nieburg. 2005. *Prevention Indicators for the President's Emergency Plan for AIDS Relief.* Report for Center for Strategic and International Studies. http://www.csis.org/hivaids/preven-tionindicators.pdf.

Kenya Government. 2003. Cabinet Approves HIV/AIDS Prevention and Control Bill. http://www.statehousekenya.go.ke.

Kerry, Vanessa. 2005. Synchronizing Donor Aid with National Policy for the Coordination of International Efforts to Scale-Up Treatment for HIV/AIDS: A Case Study of Rwanda and Its Policy for Coordinated Procurement for ARVs. Unpublished paper submitted to Harvard Medical School. Boston, September.

Kiirya, Stephen. 1998. *HIV/AIDS in Uganda: A Comprehensive Analysis of the Epidemic and the Response.* Report for Uganda AIDS Commission. http://www.aidsuganda.org/pdf/Status_report_1998.pdf.

Kingdon, John. 1984. *Agendas, Alternatives and Public Policies.* Glenview, IL: Scott, Foresman and Company.

Knight, Jack. 1992. *Institutions and Social Conflict.* New York: Cambridge University Press.

Kolbe, Jim. 2003. Lessons and New Directions for Foreign Assistance. *Washington Quarterly* 26 (2): 189–198.

Kriger, Norma. 2003. Robert Mugabe, Another Too-Long-Serving African Ruler: A Review Essay. *Political Science Quarterly* 118 (2): 307–313.

Lancaster, Carol. 2000. *Transforming Foreign Aid*. Washington, DC: Institute for International Economics.

Legum, Colin. 2001. Robert Mugabe: Once Hailed As a New African Hero and a Non-Racist, His Behaviour Is Now That of a Paranoidal Personality. *New Statesman* 130 (August): 18–19.

Lentfer, Jennifer. 2002. Principles of Programming for OVCs: Operationalization of the Rights-Based Approach. Paper presented at the HIV/AIDS and the African Child Conference, Ohio University, Athens, OH, April 11–13.

Lewis, Stephen. 2004. Report Back on Swaziland: Notes for Press Briefing, United Nations. http://www.sarpn.org.za/documents/d0000774/P879-Swaziland_Lewis_31032004.pdf.

Lodge, Tom. 2003. *Politics in South Africa: From Mandela to Mbeki*. Bloomington: Indiana University Press.

Low-Beer, Daniel, and Rand Stoneburner. 2004. Uganda and the Challenge of AIDS. In *The Political Economy of AIDS*, ed. Nana Poku and Alan Whiteside, 165–190. Aldershot, UK: Ashgate Publishers.

Lurie, Peter, Percy Hintzen, and Robert Lowe. 2004. Socioeconomic Obstacles to HIV Prevention and Treatment in Developing Countries: The Roles of the International Monetary Fund and the World Bank. In *HIV & AIDS in Africa: Beyond Epidemiology*, ed. Ezekiel Kalipeni, Susan Craddock, Joseph Oppong, and Jayati Ghosh, 204–212. Malden, MA: Blackwell Publishers.

Maclean, Sandra. 2002. Mugabe at War: The Political Economy of Conflict in Zimbabwe. *Third World Quarterly* 23 (3): 513–528.

Malawi. 2002. Final Draft: Malawi Poverty Reduction Strategy Paper. http://poverty2.forumone.com/files/Malawi_PRSP.pdf.

Mamdani, Mahmood. 1996. *Citizen and Subject: Contemporary Africa and the Legacy of Colonialism*. Princeton, NJ: Princeton University Press.

Mameli, Peter Angelo. 1998. *Sparks and Embers: The HIV/AIDS Pandemic, Public Administration and International Relations in the Twenty-First Century*. Ph.D. diss., Syracuse, NY: Syracuse University.

Manning, Ryann. 2002. *The Impact of HIV/AIDS on Civil Society*. Report for the Health Economics and HIV/AIDS Research Division, University of Natal, Durban. http://www.ukzn.ac.za/heard/research/ResearchReports/2002/NGO%20Report%20%20Toolkit.pdf.

March, James, and Johan Olsen. 1989. *Rediscovering Institutions: The Organizational Basis of Politics*. New York: The Free Press.

Maré, Gerhard. 1999. The Inkatha Freedom Party. In *Election '99 South Africa: From Mandela to Mbeki*, ed. Andrew Reynolds, 101–113. New York: St. Martin's Press.

Martin, H. Gayle. 2003. *A Comparative Analysis of the Financing of HIV/AIDS Programmes*. Report prepared for the Human Sciences Research Council. http://www.hsrcpublishers.co.za.

Matshiqi, Aubrey. 2005. In the Movement. In *Trajectories for South Africa: Reflections on the ANC's 2nd National General Council's Discussion*

*Documents*, ed. Omano Edigheji, 51–53. Johannesburg: Centre for Policy Studies.

Mattes, Robert, Christiaan Keulder, Annie Chikwana, Cherrel Africa, and Yul Derek Davids. 2003. *Democratic Governance in South Africa: The People's View*. Afrobarometer Paper 24. http://www.afrobarometer.org.

Mbali, Mandisa. 2004. The Treatment Action Campaign and the History of Rights-Based, Patient-Driven HIV/AIDS Activism in South Africa. *Research Report* 29. Durban: University of Kwazulu-Natal, Centre for Civil Society.

———. 2005. The Treatment Action Campaign's Strategies to Influence Government AIDS Policy in South Africa. Paper commissioned by the German Overseas Institute. http://www.duei.de/ghg/pdf/ProjectMbali4.pdf.

Mbeki, Thabo. 1997. Speech of Deputy President Thabo Mbeki, at the National Assembly, during the Debate on Budget Vote No. 2, June 10. http://www.anc.org.za/ancdocs/history/mbeki/1997/sp970610.01.

———. 2000. Untitled Letter to World Leaders. *New African* 397: 18–20.

Media Monitoring Project Zimbabwe. 2003. Weekly Media Update 40, October 6. http://www.mmpz.org.zw/archives/2003/week2003/week40_2003.html.

Messer, Donald. 2004. *Breaking the Conspiracy of Silence: Christian Churches and the Global AIDS Crisis*. Minneapolis: Fortress Press.

Michael, Sarah. 2004. *Undermining Development: The Absence of Power Among Local NGOs in Africa*. Bloomington: Indiana University Press.

Migdal, Joel. 1988. *Strong Societies and Weak States: State-Society Relations and State Capabilities in the Third World*. Princeton, NJ: Princeton University Press.

Moe, Terry. 1990. Political Institutions: The Neglected Side of the Story. *Journal of Law, Economics, and Organization*. Special edition: 213–253.

Molutsi, Patrick. 2004. Botswana: The Path to Democracy and Development. In *Democratic Reform in Africa: The Quality of Progress*, ed. Emmanuel Gyimah-Boadi, 159–181. Boulder, CO: Lynne Rienner Publishers.

Morrison, Stephen, and Heather Hurlburt. 2004. *Botswana's Strategy to Combat HIV/AIDS: Lessons for Africa and President Bush's Emergency Plan for AIDS Relief*. A Conference Report for the CSIS Task Force on HIV/AIDS. http://www.csis.org/africa/0401_BotswanaHIV.pdf.

Mugisha, Anne. 2004. Museveni's Machinations. *Journal of Democracy* 15 (2): 140–144.

Mwenda, Andrew, and Roger Tangri. 2005. Patronage Politics, Donor Reforms, and Regime Consolidation in Uganda. *African Affairs* 104 (416): 449–467.

NAPWA. *See* National Association of People with AIDS.

Nation Master. 2005. Encyclopedia: Demographics of South Africa. http://www.nationmaster.com/encyclopedia/Demographics-of-South-Africa.

National Association of People with AIDS. 2003. About NAPWA. http://www.napwa.org.za.

National Emergency Response Council on HIV/AIDS. 2004. *Annual Report for the Year Ended 31st March 2004*. http://www.nercha.org.sz/AR2004.pdf.

Nattrass, Nicoli. 2004. *The Moral Economy of AIDS in South Africa*. New York: Cambridge University Press.

Ndegwa, Stephen. 1996. *The Two Faces of Civil Society: NGOs and Politics in Africa*. West Hartford, CT: Kumarian Press.

NERCHA. *See* National Emergency Response Council on HIV/AIDS.

NGO Network Alliance. 2005. Zimbabwe National Network for People Living with HIV/AIDS. http://www.kubatana.net.

Nieburg, Phillip, Jennifer Kates, and J. Stephen Morrison. 2004. *Enhancing the Rapid Response Capacity of the U.S. Global AIDS Coordinator*. Report of the CSIS HIV/AIDS Task Force. http://www.csis.org/africa/0406_EmergencyResponse.pdf.

Nnoko, Soori, Betty Chidou, Flora Wilson, Wences Msuya, and Gabriel Mwaluko. 2000. Tanzania: AIDS Care—Learning from Experience. *Review of African Political Economy* 28 (86): 547–557.

Norman, Andrew. 2004. *Robert Mugabe and the Betrayal of Zimbabwe*. Jefferson, NC: McFarland & Company.

North, Douglass. 1990. *Institutions, Institutional Change and Economic Performance*. New York: Cambridge University Press.

Nugent, Paul. 2001. Winners, Losers and Also Rans: Money, Moral Authority and Voting Patterns in the Ghana 2000 Election. *African Affairs* 100 (400): 405–428.

Office of Global AIDS Coordinator. 2004a. Emergency Plan for AIDS Relief Fiscal Year 2005 Operational Plan. http://www.state.gov/s/gac/rl/or/44535.htm.

———. 2004b. The President's Emergency Plan for AIDS Relief: U.S. Five Year Global HIV/AIDS Strategy. http://www.state.gov/s/gac/r1/or/c11652.htm.

———. 2005a. Compassionate Action Provides Hope Through Treatment Success. Fact Sheet on President Bush's Emergency Plan for AIDS Relief. http://www.state.gov/documents/organization/47903.pdf.

———. 2005b. *Engendering Bold Leadership: The President's Emergency Plan for AIDS Relief*. First Annual Report to Congress. http://www.state.gov/documents/organization/43885.pdf.

———. 2005c. Partners in the Focus Countries: Fiscal Year 2004. http://www.state.gov/s/gac/rl/46144.htm.

OGAC. *See* Office of Global AIDS Coordinator.

Oloka-Onyango, Joseph. 2004. "New-Breed" Leadership, Conflict, and Reconstruction in the Great Lakes Region of Africa: A Sociopolitical Biography of Uganda's Yoweri Kaguta Museveni. *Africa Today* 50 (3): 29–52.

Oppong, Joseph, and Samuel Agyei-Mensah. 2004. HIV/AIDS in West Africa: The Case of Senegal, Ghana, and Nigeria. In *HIV & AIDS in Africa: Beyond Epidemiology*, ed. Ezekiel Kalipeni, Susan Craddock, Joseph Oppong, and Jayati Ghosh, 70–82. Malden, MA: Blackwell Publishers.

Ostergard, Robert. 2002. Politics in the Hot Zone: AIDS and National Security in Africa. *Third World Quarterly* 23 (2): 333–350.

Ostergard, Robert, and Crystal Barcelo. 2005. Personalist Regimes and the Insecurity Dilemma: Prioritizing AIDS as a National Security Threat in Uganda. In *The African State and the AIDS Crisis*, ed. Amy S. Patterson, 155–170. Aldershot, UK: Ashgate Publishers.

Ostrom, Elinor. 1990. *Governing the Commons: The Evolution of Institutions for Collective Action.* New York: Cambridge University Press.

Ottaway, Marina. 1999. *Africa's New Leaders: Democracy or State Reconstruction?* Washington, DC: Carnegie Endowment for International Peace.

Page, Benjamin, and Robert Shapiro. 1983. Effects of Public Opinion on Policy. *American Political Science Review* 77 (1): 175–190.

Pan-African Treatment Access Movement. 2004. About PATAM. http://www.patam.org.

PATAM. *See* Pan-African Treatment Access Movement.

Patterson, Amy S. 1998. A Reappraisal of Democracy in Civil Society: Evidence from Rural Senegal. *Journal of Modern African Studies* 36 (3): 423–441.

———. 1999. The Dynamic Nature of Citizenship and Participation: Lessons from Three Rural Senegalese Cases. *Africa Today* 46 (1): 3–28.

———. 2002. The Impact of Senegal's Decentralization on Women in Local Governance. *Canadian Journal of African Studies* 36 (3): 490–529.

———. 2003a. AIDS, Orphans, and the Future of Democracy in Africa. In *The Children of Africa Confront AIDS: From Vulnerability to Possibility*, ed. Arvind Singhal and Stephen Howard, 13–39. Athens: Ohio University Press.

———. 2003b. Power Inequalities and the Institutions of Senegalese Development Organizations. *African Studies Review* 46 (3): 35–54.

Patterson, Amy S., and Dave Cieminis. 2005. Weak and Ineffective? African States and Recent International AIDS Policies. In *The African State and the AIDS Crisis*, ed. Amy S. Patterson, 171–193. Aldershot, UK: Ashgate Publishers.

Patterson, Amy S., and Bernard Haven. 2003. AIDS Policy Making in Africa: A Comparison of Ghana and South Africa. Paper presented to the annual meeting of the Midwest Political Science Association, Chicago, IL, April 10–12.

———. 2005. AIDS, Democracy and International Donors in Ghana. In *The African State and the AIDS Crisis*, ed. Amy Patterson, 79–97. Aldershot, UK: Ashgate Publishers.

———. n.d. AIDS Policy in Ghana: A Disconnect Between Government and NGOs. Unpublished manuscript.

Peterson, Anne. 2003. Testimony of Dr. Anne Peterson, USAID Assistant Administrator for Global Health. Subcommittee on African Affairs, Committee on Foreign Relations, US Senate, May 19. http://www.usaid.gov/press/speeches/2003/ty030519.html.

Pharoah, Robyn, ed. 2004. *A Generation at Risk? HIV/AIDS, Vulnerable Children and Security in Southern Africa.* Institute for Security Studies Monograph 109. http://www.iss.co.za/pubs/Monographs/No109/Contents. htm.

Piot, Peter. 2001. UNAIDS Head Speaks on AIDS and Global Security. http://usinfo.state.gov/regional/af/a1100301.htm.

Poku, Nana, and Alan Whiteside. 2004. *The Political Economy of AIDS in Africa.* Aldershot, UK: Ashgate Publishers.

Pottie, David. 1999. The First Five Years of Provincial Government. In *Election '99 South Africa: From Mandela to Mbeki*, ed. Andrew Reynolds, 16–36. New York: St. Martin's Press.

Power, Samantha. 2003a. The AIDS Rebel. *New Yorker* 79 (May 19): 54–67.

———. 2003b. How to Kill a Country. *Atlantic Monthly* 292 (5): 86–100.

Prempeh, H. Kwasi. 2001. A New Jurisprudence for Africa. In *The Global Divergence of Democracies*, ed. Larry Diamond and Marc Plattner, 260–274. Baltimore: Johns Hopkins University Press.

Price-Smith, Andrew. 2002. *The Health of Nations: Infectious Disease, Environmental Change, and Their Effects on National Security and Development*. Cambridge: MIT Press.

Price-Smith, Andrew, Steven Tauber, and Anand Bhat. 2004. Preliminary Empirical Evidence of a Positive Association Between State Capacity and HIV Incidence Reduction. *University of South Florida Occasional Papers on Globalization* 1 (2): 1–8.

Privacy International. 2003. Silenced—Zimbabwe, September 21. http://www.privacyinternational.org/article.shtml?cmd[347]=x-347-103795.

Przeworski, Adam, Jose Antonio Cheibub, and Fernando Limongi. 2000. *Democracy and Development: Political Institutions and Well-Being in the World, 1950–1990*. New York: Cambridge University Press.

Putnam, Robert. 1993. *Making Democracy Work: Civic Traditions in Modern Italy*. Princeton, NJ: Princeton University Press.

Putzel, James. 2004. The Global Fight Against AIDS: How Adequate Are the National Commissions? *Journal of International Development* 16 (8): 1129–1140.

Ranger, Terence. 2002. Cultural Revolution. *World Today* 58 (2): 23–25.

Reynolds, Andrew, ed. 1999. *Election '99 South Africa: From Mandela to Mbeki*. New York: St. Martin's Press.

Ribot, Jesse. 1995. From Exclusion to Participation: Turning Senegal's Forestry Policy Around. *World Development* 23 (9): 1587–1600.

———. 1999. Decentralization, Participation and Accountability in Sahelian Forestry: Legal Instruments of Political-Administrative Control. *Africa* 69 (1): 23–66.

Roll Back Malaria. 2005. Malaria in Africa. http://www.rbm.who.int/cmc_upload/0/000/015/370/RMBInfosheet_3.htm.

Rosberg, Carl, and Robert Jackson. 1982a. *Personal Rule in Black Africa*. Berkeley: University of California Press.

———. 1982b. Why Africa's Weak States Persist: The Empirical and the Juridical in Statehood. *World Politics* 35 (1): 1–24.

Rugalema, Gabriel. 2000. Coping or Struggling? A Journey into the Impact of HIV/AIDS in Southern Africa. *Review of African Political Economy* 27 (86): 537–545.

Rupiya, Martin. 2002. A Political and Military Review of Zimbabwe's Involvement in the Second Congo War. In *The African Stakes of the Congo War*, ed. John Clark, 93–105. New York: Palgrave Macmillan.

Russell, Alec. 2000. *Big Men, Little People: The Leaders Who Defined Africa*. New York: New York University Press.

SANGONet. 2006. Directory of NGOs. http://www.prodder.org.za.

Scheckels, Theodore. 2004. The Rhetoric of Thabo Mbeki on HIV/AIDS: Strategic Scapegoating? *Howard Journal of Communications* 15 (20): 69–82.

Schneider, Helen. 2002. On the Fault-Line: The Politics of AIDS Policy in Contemporary South Africa. *African Studies* 61 (1): 145–167.

Schoepf, Brooke Grundfest. 2003. Uganda: Lessons for AIDS Control in Africa. *Review of African Political Economy* 30 (98): 553–572.

Sen, Amartya. 2001. Democracy as a Universal Value. In *The Global Divergence of Democracies*, ed. Larry Diamond and Marc Plattner, 3–17. Baltimore: Johns Hopkins University Press.

Shaffer, Martin. 2000. Coalition Work Among Environmental Groups: Who Participates? In *Research in Social Movements, Conflicts and Change*, ed. Patrick Coy, 111–126. Greenwich, CT: JAI Press.

Siplon, Patricia. 2002. *AIDS and the Policy Struggle in the United States.* Washington, DC: Georgetown University Press.

———. 2005. AIDS and Patriarchy: Ideological Obstacles to Effective Policy Making. In *The African State and the AIDS Crisis*, ed. Amy S. Patterson, 17–36. Aldershot, UK: Ashgate Publishers.

Skillen, Jim. 2004. *Pursuit of Justice: Christian-Democratic Explorations.* Lanham, MD: Rowman & Littlefield.

Skocpol, Theda. 1985. Bringing the State Back In: Strategies of Analysis in Current Research. In *Bringing the State Back In*, ed. Peter Evans, Dietrich Rueschemeyer, and Theda Skocpol, 3–37. New York: Cambridge University Press.

Smith, Jackie, and Joe Bandy. 2005. Introduction: Cooperation and Conflict in Transnational Protest. In *Coalitions Across Borders: Transnational Protest and the Neoliberal Order*, ed. Joe Bandy and Jackie Smith, 1–20. Lanham, MD: Rowman & Littlefield.

Smith, Raymond. 2001. *Encyclopedia of AIDS: A Social, Political, Cultural, and Scientific Record of the HIV Epidemic.* New York: Penguin Books.

———. 2002. Bridging the Gap: The Emergence of a US Activist Movement to Confront AIDS in the Developing World. Paper presented at the annual meeting of the American Political Science Association, Boston, MA, August 30–September 2.

Söderholm, Peter. 1997. *Global Governance of AIDS: Partnerships with Civil Society.* Lund, Sweden: Lund University Press.

South Africa Government. 2000. *HIV/AIDS/STD Strategic Plan for South Africa 2000–2005.* http://www.gov.za/documents/2000/aidsplan2000.pdf.

———. 2002. *Summary Report: National HIV and Syphilis Antenatal Sero-Prevalence Survey in South Africa 2002.* Department of Health, Pretoria. http://www.doh.gov.za/aids.

Ssempa, Martin. 2005. Testimony Before the Full Committee on "US Response to the Global AIDS Crisis: A Two-Year Review." US House Committee on International Relations, Rayburn Office Building, Washington, DC, April 13.

Staggenborg, Suzanne. 1986. Coalition Work in the Pro-Choice Movement: Organizational and Environmental Opportunities and Obstacles. *Social Problems* 33 (5): 374–389.

Staley, Krista-Ann. 2005. Swaziland Adopts New Constitution. *Jurist: Legal News and Research.* http://jurist.law.pitt.edu/paperchase/2005/06/swaziland-adopts-new-constitution.php.

Steinbrook, Robert. 2004. After Bangkok—Expanding the Global Response to AIDS. *New England Journal of Medicine* 351 (8): 738–742.

Steytler, Nico. 2003. Federal Homogeneity from the Bottom Up: Provincial Shaping of National HIV/AIDS Policy in South Africa. *Publius: The Journal of Federalism* 33 (1): 59–74.

Stover, John, Neff Walker, Geoff P. Garnett, Joshua A. Salomon, Karen A. Stanecki, Peter D. Ghys, Nicholas C. Grassly, Roy M. Anderson, and Berhnard Schwartländer. 2002. Can We Reverse the HIV/AIDS Pandemic with an Expanded Response? *Lancet* 360 (9326): 73–77.

Swidler, Ann. 2001. *Talk of Love: How Culture Matters.* Chicago: University of Chicago Press.

TAC. *See* Treatment Action Campaign.

Tangri, Roger, and Andrew Mwenda. 2001. Corruption and Cronyism in Uganda's Privatization in the 1990s. *African Affairs* 100 (398): 117–133.

TASO. *See* The AIDS Service Organisation.

The AIDS Service Organisation. 2005. Background Information. http://www.tasouganda.org.

Tobias, Randall. 2005. Testimony for Hearing on HIV/AIDS Budget Request. United States House of Representatives Appropriations Committee, Subcommittee on Foreign Operations, Export Financing, and Related Programs. Rayburn Office Building, Washington, DC, March 2.

Treatment Action Campaign. 2003. Report of the Joint Health and Treasury Task Team Charged with Examining Options to Supplement Comprehensive HIV/AIDS Care in the Public Health Sector. http://www.tac.org.za/Documents/TreatmentPlan/slideshowongovernmentcostingstudy.pdf.

———. 2004a. Condemn the Threats by NAPWA Against AIDS Activists. Report on TAC News Service, March 30. http://www.tac.org.za/newsletter/2004/ns30_03_2004.htm.

———. 2004b. Facts About Nevirapine Are Simple—But Unnecessary Confusion Endangers Lives. Report on TAC News Service, July 15. http://www.tac.org.za/newsletter/news_2004.htm.

———. 2004c. Prince Nelisuzulu Buthelezi Dies of AIDS-Related Illnesses—TAC Extends Condolences. Report on TAC News Service, May 2. http://www.tac.org.za/newsletter/news_2004.htm.

———. 2004d. TAC Statement on Auditor-General's Qualified Audit Opinion of the Department of Health. Report on TAC News Service, October 18. http://www.tac.org.za/newsletter/TACStatementonAuditor.htm.

———. 2004e. Why the TAC Is Going to Court Tomorrow and Holding Country-Wide Demonstrations. Report on TAC News Service, November 3. http://www.tac.org.za/Documents/AccessToInfoCourtCase/WhyTACGoingtoCourt4Nov2004.htm.

———. 2005. TAC Audit for Year Ending February 2004. http://www.tac.org.za/Documents/FinancialDocs.htm.

———. 2006a. About TAC. http://www.tac.org.za.

———. 2006b. TAC Electronic Newsletter, January 17. http://www.tac.org.za.

Treatment Action Campaign, and AIDS Law Project. 2004. Our People Are Suffering, We Need Treatment. Report on the Operational Plan for

Comprehensive HIV and AIDS Care, Management and Treatment for South Africa. http://www.tac.org.za/Documents/ARVRollout/FinalFirstARV RolloutReport.pdf.

Tripp, Aili Mari. 2001. The Politics of Autonomy and Cooptation in Africa: The Case of the Ugandan Women's Movement. *Journal of Modern African Studies* 39 (1): 101–128.

TroCaire. 2004. The Zimbabwean Struggle: Obstacles to Democracy. http://www.trocaire.org/newsandinformation/zimbabwe/Obstacles%20to% 20Democracy.pdf.

UNAIDS. *See* Joint United Nations Program on HIV/AIDS.

UNDP. *See* United Nations Development Program.

UNICEF. *See* United Nations Children's Fund.

United Kingdom Department for International Development. 2004. *Statistics on International Development 2004.* http://www.dfid.gov.uk/pubs/files/ sid2004/sid2004-table7-1.pdf.

United Nations. 2001. *Declaration of Commitment on HIV/AIDS.* http://www.un.org/ga/aids/docs/aress262.pdf.

———. 2005. *Progress Made in the Implementation of the Declaration of Commitment on HIV/AIDS.* Report of the Secretary-General. http://www. unaids.org/en/events/un+special+session+on+hiv_aids/2005+general+ assembly+high+level+meeting+on+hiv_aids.asp.

United Nations Children's Fund. 2004. Information on Convention on the Rights of the Child. http://www.unicef.org/crc/crc.htm.

———. 2005a. At a Glance: Swaziland. http://www.unicef.org/infobycountry/ swaziland.html.

———. 2005b. UNICEF Goodwill Ambassador Femi Kuti Speaks Out Against the Suffering of Zimbabwean Children. News Notes. http://www.unicef. org/media/media_26326.html.

United Nations Development Program. 1990. *Human Development Report.* New York: Oxford University Press.

———. 2002. *Gender Focused Responses to HIV/AIDS in Swaziland: The Needs of Women Infected and Affected by HIV/AIDS.* Mbabane: UNDP.

———. 2003a. *Human Development Report 2003.* New York: Oxford University Press.

———. 2003b. *Zimbabwe Human Development Report 2003: Redirecting Our Responses to HIV and AIDS.* Harare: Institute of Development Studies, University of Zimbabwe.

———. 2004. *Human Development Report 2004: Cultural Liberty in Today's Diverse World.* New York: Oxford University Press. http://hdr.undp.org/ reports/global/2004/pdf/hdr04_HDI.pdf.

———. 2005. *Human Development Report 2005: International Cooperation at a Crossroads.* New York: Oxford University Press.

United States Agency for International Development. 2004. Directory of Associations of People Living with HIV/AIDS. http://www.usaid.gov/our_ work/global_health/aids/Publications/docs/hivaidsdirectory.pdf.

———. 2005a. Acquisition & Assistance Policy Directive. AAPD 05-04. June 9. http://www.usaid.gov/business/business_opportunities/cib/pdf/aapd05_ 04.pdf.

———. 2005b. 2006 Congressional Budget Justification. http://www.usaid. gov/policy/budget/cbj2006/afr/ao.html.

———. 2005c. USAID's Strategy in Zimbabwe. http://www.usaid.gov/locations/sub-saharan_africa/countries/zimbabwe.

United States Agency for International Development, Joint United Nations Program on HIV/AIDS, World Health Organization, and the POLICY Project. 2003. *The Level of Effort in the National Response to HIV/AIDS: The AIDS Program Effort Index (API) 2003 Round.* http://www.policyproject.com/pubs/monographs/API2003.pdf.

United States Committee for Refugees and Immigrants. 2004. Zimbabwe. *World Refugee Survey: Country Report.* http://www.refugees.org/countryreports.aspx?id=191.

United States Department of Energy. 2005. Crude Oil and Total Petroleum Imports, Top 15 Countries. http://www.eia.doe.gov/pub/oil_gas/petroleum/data_publications/company_level_imports.

United States Embassy in Mbabane, Swaziland. 2005. News from Washington: The US Government's Response to Swaziland's HIV & AIDS Epidemic 2005. http://mbabane.usembassy.gov/hiv_aids_issues.html.

United States House of Representatives Appropriations Committee, Subcommittee on Foreign Operations, Export Financing, and Related Programs. 2005. Hearing on HIV/AIDS Budget Request. Rayburn Office Building, Washington, DC, March 2.

United States House of Representatives Committee on International Relations. 2005. Hearing on "U.S. Response to the Global AIDS Crisis: A Two-Year Review." Rayburn Office Building, Washington, DC, April 13.

USAID. *See* United States Agency for International Development.

van de Walle, Nicolas. 2001. *African Economies and the Politics of Permanent Crisis, 1979–1999.* New York: Cambridge University Press.

Vavi, Zwelinzima. 2005. Speech to TAC Congress. http://www.sarpn.org.za/documents/d0001620/ZV_TAC-congress_Sept2005.pdf.

Velyvis, Kristen. 2002. Nets That Catch Migrant Women: The Social Networks of Migrant Women in Dakar and Implications for the Spread of HIV. Paper presented at the African Studies Association Conference, Washington, DC, December 3–5.

Villalón, Leonardo. 1995. *Islamic Society and State Power in Senegal.* New York: Cambridge University Press.

Walgate, Robert. 2004. Bush's AIDS Plan Criticised for Emphasizing Abstinence and Forbidding Condoms. *British Medical Journal* 329 (July): 192.

Walker, Liz, Graeme Reid, and Morna Cornell. 2004. *Waiting to Happen: HIV/AIDS in South Africa (The Bigger Picture).* Boulder, CO: Lynne Rienner Publishers.

Wanyeki, L. Muthoni. 2003. *Women and Land in Africa: Culture, Religion and Realizing Women's Rights.* London: Zed Books.

*Washington Post,* Kaiser Family Foundation, and Harvard University. 2004. *South Africa: Ten Years of Democracy.* http://www.washingtonpost.com.

Wawer, Maria, Ronald Gray, David Serwadda, Zikulah Namukwaya, Fred Makumbi, Nelson Sewankambo, Xianbin Li, Tom Lutalo, Fred Nalugoda, Thomas Quinn. 2005. Declines in HIV Prevalence in Uganda: Not as Simple as ABC. Oral abstract 27LB, Session 8. Paper presented at the 12th Annual Conference on Retroviruses and Opportunistic Infections, Boston, MA, February 22–25.

Webb, Douglas. 2004. Legitimate Actors? The Future Role for NGOs Against HIV/AIDS in Sub-Saharan Africa. In *The Political Economy of AIDS*, ed. Nana Poku and Alan Whiteside, 19–32. Aldershot, UK: Ashgate Publishers.

Weissberg, Robert. 1976. *Public Opinion and Popular Government*. Englewood Cliffs, NJ: Prentice-Hall.

Whiteside, Alan. 2002. Poverty and HIV/AIDS in Africa. *Third World Quarterly* 23 (2): 313–332.

———. 2005. The Economic, Social, and Political Drivers of the AIDS Epidemic in Swaziland: A Case Study. In *The African State and the AIDS Crisis*, ed. Amy S. Patterson, 97–126. Aldershot, UK: Ashgate Publishers.

Whiteside, Alan, Robert Mattes, Samantha Willan, and Ryann Manning. 2002. *Examining HIV/AIDS in South Africa Through the Eyes of Ordinary Southern Africans*. Afrobarometer Paper 21. http://www.afrobarometer.org/papers/AfropaperNo21.pdf.

WHO. *See* World Health Organization.

Will, Kurt Dieter. 1991. The Global Politics of AIDS: The World Health Organization and the International Regime for AIDS. Ph.D. diss., University of South Carolina.

World Bank. 1993. *World Development Report 1993: Investing in Health*. New York: Oxford University Press.

———. 2001a. Indigenous Knowledge and HIV/AIDS: Ghana and Zambia. *IK Notes* 30, newsletter, World Bank.

———. 2001b. *World Development Report 2000/2001: Attacking Poverty*. New York: Oxford University Press.

———. 2002. *World Development Indicators*. Washington, DC: World Bank.

———. 2005a. About the Multi-Country HIV/AIDS Program (MAP). http://www.worldbank.org/afr/aids/map.htm.

———. 2005b. Governance Indicators, 1996–2004. http://www.worldbank.org/wbi/governance/govdata.

———. 2005c. Key Development Data and Statistics by Country. http://www.worldbank.org.

———. 2005d. *World Development Indicators*. http://www.worldbank.org/data/wdi2005/index.htm.

World Health Organization. 2002. *World Health Report 2002: Reducing Risks, Promoting Healthy Life*. http://www.who.int/whr/2002/en/whr2002_annex5.pdf.

———. 2004. Epidemiological Fact Sheets on HIV/AIDS and Sexually Transmitted Infections, 2004 Update. *HIV/AIDS Publications 2004*. http://www.who.int/hiv/pub/epidemiology/pubfacts/en/index.html.

———. 2005. *World Health Report 2005: Make Every Mother and Every Child Count*. http://www.who.int/whr/2005/annex/annexe5_en.pdf.

———. 2006a. DOTS. http://www.who.int/tb/dots/whatisdots/en/print.html.

———. 2006b. Joint HIV/Tuberculosis Interventions. http://www.who.int/hiv/topics/tb/tuberculosis/en/print.html.

Zimbabwe Human Rights NGO Forum. 2002. *Human Rights and Zimbabwe's Presidential Election, March 2002*. A Special Report by the Research Unit. http://www.hrforumzim.com/special_hrru/Special_Report_4_2002%20Election/SR_07.htm.

Zweifel, Thomas, and Patricio Navia. 2000. Democracy, Dictatorship and Infant Mortality. *Journal of Democracy* 11 (2): 99–114.

# Index

Achmat, Zackie, 103, 107, 119, 122
Africa: borrowing history, 14; civil society in, 95–128; declining demands for export commodities, 14; democratic institutions in, 72–82; donor funding in, 131–169; effect of inequality on pandemic, 8–15; health care spending in, 82, 84–90; increase in democratization in, 84, 85; legislative role in, 78–79; levels of debt in, 14; loss of women in, 9; magnitude of pandemic in, 4–8, 175–177; political institutions in, 15–17; politics of AIDS in, 1–18; role of democracy in fight against HIV/AIDS, 59–92; role of state in AIDS fight, 21–57; socioeconomic development in, 8; structural adjustment programs in, 14; subnational institutions in, 79–81; unequal impact of HIV/AIDS, 8–15; weak judiciaries in, 12, 81–82; weakness in global negotiations, 14. *See also* individual countries
African National Congress (ANC), 35, 39, 43, 67, 70, 103, 119
African Summit on HIV/AIDS and Other Related Infectious Diseases, 90
AIDS Coalition to Unleash Power (ACT UP), 120
AIDS commitment: among donors, 162–164; among state leaders, 158–162
AIDS pandemic: African state and, 21–57; diversity in, 6, 7; donor politi-

cal stake in, 1; inequality and, 8–15; magnitude of, 4–8, 175–177; orphans and, 6, 7; political institutions and, 15–17; resources for, 8; uneven attention paid to, 2, 4
AIDS policy and decisionmaking: centralization of power and, 22, 23, 23*tab*; civil society and; democracy and, 1, 59–92; donor influence on, 1; political analysis of, 4; role of the state in, 1
AIDS Support Organisation (TASO), 31; membership, 31–32
AIDS Treatment Data Network, 121
American Jewish World Service, 100
Amin, Idi, 29, 30
Anglican Communion, 136
Angola: Global Fund to Fight AIDS, Tuberculosis and Malaria in, 166*tab*; health care spending in, 83*tab*; prevalence rate in, 5*tab,* 166*tab*; representation on Country Coordinating Mechanism in, 74*tab*
Annan, Kofi, 135, 136
Anyimadu-Amaning, Sam, 107
Ark Foundation, 100
Asamoah, Israel, 102
Asmal, Kader, 39, 58*n9,* 70
Atlantic Philanthropies, 100

Banda, Hastings, 64
Benin: AIDS coverage in election campaigns, 68; democratization in, 84; donor dependence in, 89; health care

214